American

Joe R. and Teresa Lozano Long Series
in Latin American and Latino Art and Culture

Americans All

Good Neighbor Cultural Diplomacy in World War II

Darlene J. Sadlier

UNIVERSITY OF TEXAS PRESS ⌄ AUSTIN

The publication of this book was supported in part
by Ambassador and Mrs. Keith L. Brown.

Permissions
University of Texas Press
P.O. Box 7819
Austin, TX 78713-7819
utpress.utexas.edu/index.php/rp-form

Library of Congress Cataloging-in-Publication Data
Sadlier, Darlene J. (Darlene Joy)
  Americans all : good neighbor cultural diplomacy in World War II /
by Darlene J. Sadlier. — 1st ed.
      p.   cm.— (Joe R. and Teresa Lozano Long Series in Latin
American and Latino Art and Culture)
  Includes bibliographical references and index.
  ISBN 978-0-292-75685-4
  1. United States—Relations—Latin America. 2. Latin America—
Relations—United States. 3. World War, 1939–1945—Diplomatic
history. 4. United States—Cultural policy. 5. United States—
Foreign relations—1933–1945. 6. United States—Intellectual life—
20th century. 7. Cultural industries—Political aspects—United
States—History—20th century. 8. Popular culture—Political
aspects—United States—History—20th century. I. Title.
  F1418.S16   2012
  327.730809' 04—dc23   2012020602

For JAMES NAREMORE
and
in memory of ROBERT W. SADLIER

Contents

Abbreviations

ACLS	American Council of Learned Societies
ALA	American Library Association
BBF	Biblioteca Benjamín Franklin, Mexico City
CIAA	Office of the Coordinator of Inter-American Affairs
COI	Committee on Information
CPDOC/ FGV	Centro de Pesquisa e Documentação de História Contemporânea do Brasil/Fundação Getúlio Vargas, Brazil
CPI	Committee on Public Information
DIP	Departamento de Imprensa e Propaganda, Brazil
EMH, II	Early Museum History: Administrative Records II. The Museum of Modern Art Archives, New York
FDRL	Franklin D. Roosevelt Library, Hyde Park, New York
LL	Lilly Library, Bloomington, Indiana
LOC	Library of Congress
MHL	Margaret Herrick Library, Los Angeles
MoMA	Museum of Modern Art, New York
MPSA	Motion Picture Society for the Americas
NARAII, RG229	National Archives and Records Administration II, Record Group 229
NYPL	New York Public Library
OCD	Office of Civilian Defense
OFF	Office of Facts and Figures
OSS	Office of Strategic Services
OWI	Office of War Information
RAC	Rockefeller Archive Center, Tarrytown, New York
RdH	René d'Harnoncourt Papers. The Museum of Modern Art Archives, New York
SFMoMAt	San Francisco Museum of Modern Art
WB	William Benton Papers, University of Chicago Archives

Acknowledgments

Productive archival research depends greatly upon the knowledge and helpfulness of library specialists, who not only train us in the art of using collections but also frequently point us to little-known treasure troves of information. Research for this book took me to more than a dozen archives beginning several years ago with a visit to the Margaret Herrick Library in Los Angeles and ending with a second visit to the National Archives II in College Park, Maryland. Stops between those places included collections at the University of Louisiana; the University of Texas at Austin; the University of Chicago; the University of California Los Angeles; the Library of Congress; the Franklin D. Roosevelt Library in Hyde Park, New York; the Museum of Modern Art; the New York Public Library; the Rockefeller Archive Center in Tarrytown, New York; and the Fundação Getúlio Vargas in Rio de Janeiro. I also greatly benefited from holdings at Indiana University's Lilly Library and Presidential Archive of Herman B. Wells. Special thanks go to Latin American specialist Becky Cape at the Lilly Library, Katherine D. McCann and Jan Grenci at the Library of Congress, Jean Kiesel at the University of Louisiana, Martha Harsanyi at Indiana University, Carol Radovich at the Rockefeller Archive Center, and Barbara Hall at the Margaret Herrick Library.

I was fortunate to receive a number of grants to support my research, including fellowships from Indiana University's College of Arts and Humanities Institute, Office of the Vice Provost for Research–New Frontiers in Arts and Humanities, Center for Latin American and Caribbean Studies, and Office of the Vice President for International Affairs. A Rockefeller Archive Center Fellowship supported my research there. Along with grants, I want to single out the support and friendship of Gisela Cramer and Ursula Prutsch, whose work on the National Archive II files on the Office of the Coordinator of Inter-American Affairs (CIAA) was invaluable.

Anthony N. Doob at the University of Toronto was extremely generous in providing me with the personal papers of his father, Leonard W. Doob, who was Nelson Rockefeller's public opinion adviser in the first years of the CIAA. Sam Bryan was always graciously attentive to my queries about his father, Julien Bryan, who made close to two dozen 16 mm educational films for the CIAA. I was also pleased to correspond with Ted Thomas, whose father, Frank Thomas, was one of Walt Disney's most talented artists. Ted's documentary *Walt and El Grupo* (2009) provides important additional evidence of the CIAA's promotion of the "Good Neighbor." Brazilianist and World War II historian Frank D. McCann provided me with generous detailed feedback on early chapters of the book. I also benefited greatly from suggestions by Nicholas J. Cull, whose writings on U.S. public diplomacy were inspirational. Julie Maguire of the Brett Weston Archives and Barbara Rominski of the San Francisco Museum of Modern Art allowed me to include Weston's 1940 photograph of Grace McCann Morley, who worked closely with the CIAA on traveling art exhibits. Lauren Post, great-granddaughter of U.S. cartoonist Rollin Kirby, gave me permission to include his "Good Neighbor" cartoon. At the University of Texas Press, I am especially grateful to Theresa May, who initially encouraged this project, and to Jim Burr, who has been a wonderful editor.

Although the Franklin D. Roosevelt administration is not part of my personal history, the 1930s and especially the 1940s hold a special interest for me. This period was one of the few times in U.S. history when culture's importance in domestic and world affairs was recognized and discussed alongside issues of finance and commerce. Having a loving and highly knowledgeable companion who has written extensively about the 1940s and who contributed to the chapters in this volume made the book all the more exciting and enjoyable to write. The book is dedicated to him and to the memory of my father, who was a U.S. infantry soldier in North Africa and Europe during World War II.

INTRODUCTION

Cultural diplomacy, including what Joseph S. Nye in 1990 described in slightly broader terms as "soft power," has never been completely absent from U.S. foreign policy, though it has rarely been given major emphasis.[1] During the period of the cold war, for example, there were occasional, well-publicized cultural encounters between West and East, among them Jacqueline Kennedy's appearance at social events during the 1961 Vienna Summit (*Life* magazine's photo of a laughing Jackie seated next to an obviously charmed Nikita Khrushchev was captioned "Our Loveliest Diplomat")[2] and the much-discussed "ping pong diplomacy" of 1971, which helped begin a thaw in U.S.-Chinese enmity and led to President Richard M. Nixon's visit to China in 1972. These, however, were exceptions to the rule. Summing up this period and others in *Foreign Affairs* in 2003, senior U.S. Public Affairs Officer Helena K. Finn wrote: "Cultural diplomacy is one of the most potent weapons in the United States' armory, yet its importance has been consistently downplayed in favor of dramatic displays of military might. It should never be an optional extra, a nice thing to do if there's time but hardly a national priority."[3]

Fortunately, if the recent surge in publications, national and international conferences, and websites on the topic is any measure and if the nation's move at the time of this writing toward greater dialogue and face-to-face negotiation is symptomatic of things to come, cultural diplomacy is likely to show signs of renewal and health. There continues to be debate about the means and ends of such diplomacy, questioning the idea that it automatically leads to better international relations; nevertheless, the evidence suggests that the U.S. image both regionally and worldwide has rarely been more positive than when cultural or "public" diplomacy at its best is part of the foreign policy mix.[4] It is, one might say, the brainy aspect of "smart power," or what Nye has described as "a dynamic of hard and soft power diplomacy."[5]

The present study moves back in time to the most fully developed and intensive use of soft power in U.S. history: Nelson A. Rockefeller's Office of the Coordinator of Inter-American Affairs (CIAA, 1940–1945), one of the first U.S. government agencies specifically created to enact a large-scale cultural diplomacy initiative.[6] The primary objective of the CIAA was to influence governments and individuals throughout Latin America as well as the public at home about the vital importance of hemispheric solidarity and defense in combating Axis infiltration and domination. These were the "Good Neighbor" years, a period unique in U.S. relations with Latin America and perhaps the only time in U.S. history when the terms "Americas" and "Americans" were regularly employed to convey an image of a North-South family of twenty-one united republics. Great emphasis was placed on inter-American cultural values alongside economic and political policies beneficial to hemispheric well-being, or what public diplomacy scholars term "mutuality."[7] In what follows, I offer the first in-depth study of the CIAA's wide-ranging, ambitious plan to persuade "all Americans" of their common wartime cause.

A brief history of key terms may be of use at the outset. The word "culture" has had a number of meanings and originally signified religious worship, together with cultivation of crops and farm animals and "artificial development of microscopic organisms." The sixteenth century saw an anthropocentric shift in usage to denote the "development of the mind, faculties, and manners." By the nineteenth century, "culture" was synonymous with "civilization" and connoted a "particular form of intellectual development."[8] In the second half of the twentieth century, Raymond Williams divested the term of romantic, lofty implications and argued that it should be used to describe not simply high culture but also "a particular way of life" (*Keywords*, 80), including all the practices of a given society, "from language through the arts and philosophy to journalism, fashion and advertising" as well as "the practice of consumption" (*Culture*, 13). In the wake of this development, the cultural studies and postcolonial movements in academia have increasingly focused on culture in the broadest sense as both a democratic phenomenon and an arm in the imperialist arsenal—or, in John Tomlinson's words, as "a discourse caught up in ironies that flow from its position of discursive power" (2). In my examination of the CIAA, we shall encounter some of these ironies.

Derived from the word "diploma," which originally meant a folded piece of paper used as a credential, the term "diplomacy" seems to have found a firm footing in the eighteenth century, referring to a "business" and an "art" of international relations negotiation and management—a meaning it more or less retains today.[9] At the height of Victorian-era British Empire, Lord Salisbury, the prime minister who served as his own foreign secretary, described the activities of diplomacy as more or less clandestine dealings among elite representatives. The victory of diplomacy, he claimed, was activated by a "series of microscopic advantages; a judicious suggestion here, an opportune civility there, a wise concession at one moment and a farsighted persistence at another; of sleepless tact, immovable, calmness and patience that no folly, no provocation, no blunder can shake" (in Tuchman, 35).

When we speak of "cultural diplomacy," however, the relations between nations tend to become entangled with such terms as "belief," "ideology," and "propaganda." For many in the United States, the last of these words means little more than the lies and deceptions of officialdom; but we should remember that in many historical and ideological contexts, ranging from the Catholic Church to Soviet communism, "propaganda" has had benign implications. Consider the case of Pope Gregory XV, who, in his effort to disseminate Catholic doctrine during the Thirty Years' War against Protestants (1618–1648), required followers of Catholicism to profess their faith according to "creeds," a word derived from the Latin *credo* ("I believe"); this term soon acquired a religious connotation, suggesting a faith that is to be propagated, from the Latin verb *propagare*.

To a certain extent the various definitions and connotations of culture, diplomacy, and propaganda—negative and positive, religious and scientific, involving art, media, consumption and power politics—were in play in the CIAA, which, as a both a commercial and cultural mission, bore characteristics not only of government but also of both a business and an art. Its creation at the threshold of the U.S. entry into the war was accompanied by an escalating sense of urgency about hemispheric solidarity in the face of the Axis occupation of Europe. The CIAA had no domestic model to emulate, although a World War I congressional group headed by George Creel, the Committee on Public Information, was founded in quasireligious terms to carry "the gospel of Americanism to every corner of the globe."[10] Beginning with William McKinley, who recognized the power of film at its inception, various presidents used the media successfully to push their agendas and shape public opinion.[11] But mounting an entire agency during an international crisis with the hope, if not the expectation, of immediate domestic and foreign returns was a far more challenging endeavor requiring a rapid conceptual formulation, the creation of multiple divisions and departments, and the recruiting of an astonishingly large number of talented artists and intellectuals.

The process of establishing the agency often led to missteps and confusion that resulted in conflicts between the CIAA and other government agencies as well as many internal disagreements and departures.[12] One of the major problems, indeed the central one, as we shall see, was deciding on what in fact the U.S. "way of life" might be and how it corresponded with life in the various Latin American nations, which were different from one another not only in language and political organization but also in their particular mixtures of races and their degrees of separation between rich and poor. From an assemblage of selected cultural interests, values, and traits, the CIAA tried to shape a Good Neighbor U.S. imaginary that would seem familiar and/or appeal to Latin Americans while offering U.S. audiences equally familiar and/or attractive images of Good Neighbors to the south. Ultimately, the "way of life" promoted abroad was sharply focused on modernity and prosperity, emphasizing the growth of an industrial economy and proffering utopian visions of a rising middle class. Where and whenever possible, the CIAA touted these values in its information on and image-making of the other Americas. The agency also offered financial and other assistance and incentives so that countries of strategic importance to U.S. wartime commerce might achieve a way of life akin to capitalist democracy in the United States. Most of the south-of-the-border leaders negotiated successfully for U.S. investments in industry, agriculture, public health reform, and cultural projects in return for development of U.S. air bases, vital wartime supplies, policy support, and continued goodwill. At the same time, Latin American governments themselves had a role to play in the CIAA's propagandistic messages. If there was ever a concerted effort by the United States toward inter-American dialogue and cultural exchange, it was this one. Modernity and prosperity were also major concerns for Latin American leaders, some of whom could be quite firm and selective about the CIAA's portrayal of their nations and sensitive to anything that made them seem "underdeveloped."

It bears mentioning here that U.S. concern for the unity of the hemisphere sometimes caused diplomats to overlook political differences in the countries of Latin America, some of which were not democracies. Attention focused on big, strategically positioned, and resource-rich nations, particularly Brazil and Argentina, where substantial Italian and German immigrant populations lived. (Brazil also had the largest Japanese-speaking community outside Japan.) These two South American countries had long-standing friendly relations with Germany and Italy. In 1940 Argentina commanded the strongest military force in Latin America, and its succession of right-wing military leaders, like the pro-Nazi administration in Chile, refused to declare war on the Axis powers in the months and years following Pearl Harbor. Chile in early 1943 and Argentina in 1944 broke relations with Germany and Japan, but official declarations of war were delayed until 1945. Brazil's Estado Novo (New State) regime under Getúlio Vargas allowed U.S. air bases to be built in Natal in 1940 that would prove crucial to the Allied war effort. Following the torpedoing of Brazilian ships by German submarines in February and August 1942, Brazil declared war. Its air force, navy, and ground troops would bring distinction to the nation—the only Latin Americans to serve on the European front.[13]

Years of prewar tension had strained relations between the United States and Mexico, culminating in the 1939 nationalization of the oil industry by the liberal administration of President Lázaro Cárdenas. But like Brazil, Mexico was actively cultivated by the United States, in this case to ensure unity in the North American continent. In 1942 Germany attacked Mexican ships bearing petroleum to the United States; Mexico responded by declaring war on the Axis powers in May of that year and later sent a fighter squadron to support Allied efforts in the Philippines.

There is a general tendency among scholars to discuss U.S.–Latin American cultural diplomacy past and present in highly specific or broad, even abstract terms. Although numerous studies in the areas of diplomatic history, film, music education, public health, library science, literature, and art comment on the Rockefeller agency, the full story of its cultural activities has yet to be told.[14] My own aim is to provide an in-depth, fine-grained study of how a government office was conceived and organized and an analysis of the various strategies and techniques, some dubious and some progressive, it developed to promote hemispheric defense and bolster inter-American cultural ties through the use of film, radio, and the press as well as through various educational and high-art activities. I intend to show that the agency was a rare and not ignoble instance of U.S. government investment in culture as a way of reaching out to other nations and to people at home. The home-front side of the program—selective, occasionally patronizing toward Latin America, and filled with stereotypical representations—was, despite all its deficiencies, a benchmark for what came to be known as "reverse mandate" diplomacy, whose goal is to inform the United States about the rest of the world. If we regard widespread popular appeal and support as the ideal achievement of diplomacy, then the CIAA may serve as one of its more successful applications. The agency was far from free of ideological self-interest, and it suffered many external and internal tensions, but it raised a broad public awareness in the United States of the importance of good neighbor relations and achieved an unparalleled awareness throughout Latin America of the country's recognition of that importance.

Throughout my study I criticize some aspects of the CIAA while also recognizing its positive achievements. In my view, one of the chief reasons for its successes and its failures was that it took place at a historical moment when the nation was engaged in what mythmakers have dubbed "the good war." At the time, U.S. citizens of most political persuasions tended to think of World War II as a morally justified crusade; even the normally alienated or critical artistic community was committed to it, in large part because of the coalition of liberal and socialist writers, painters, musicians, and filmmakers that had formed in the New Deal era and made up what Michael Denning has called the U.S. "cultural front." These artists and intellectuals believed that the death of fascist ideology might change the entire world for the better. Their attitudes temporarily masked or muted tensions between the political left and right that were to emerge with stark clarity immediately after the war, when U.S. foreign policy began to undergo a sea change. In a sense the tensions were always there, as will become apparent in the chapters that follow; but for several years they were secondary to cultural achievements that are worth remembering and that this study aims to record.

THE CULTURE INDUSTRY GOES TO WAR

The attempt to persuade [Latin Americans] not by facts, but by works, not by propaganda but by submission of the documents—the books, the poetry, the music and the painting—is neither hypocritical nor self-righteous. It is, on the contrary, an exceedingly frank and forthright undertaking. It is also an undertaking as difficult as it may be dangerous.

Archibald MacLeish, "The Art of the Good Neighbor," 1940

When the United States entered World War II in December 1941, most of Europe and Asia were under control of the Axis powers, and the U.S. military was small and out of date. Latin America appeared marginal to the battles being waged in Britain, North Africa, and the Pacific, but U.S. planning had focused on the nations south of the border since at least 1938, and some of those nations were now led by protofascist dictators whose peoples were increasingly subject to modern forms of propaganda. Hence as the United States began arming for war overseas, it also mounted a major cultural offensive aimed at the south, administered by a coalition of government officials and business and industrial leaders, some of whom had direct financial interests in Latin America. A huge bureaucracy with centers on the east and west coasts and in Washington, D.C., was created, recruiting and guiding the work of artists, social scientists, statisticians, and diplomats. The major production centers of U.S. culture—located mostly in Hollywood and New York—were brought to bear on a single ideological mission, outlined by the government and disseminated throughout the Western Hemisphere.

This was a period in which the most powerful nations in Europe and the United States achieved all the technological, political, and economic conditions necessary for the emergence of a true mass culture, controlled by what theoreticians Max Horkheimer and Theodor Adorno famously called "the culture industry." In the penultimate chapter of *Dialectic of Enlightenment*, a savage critique of modernity written during World War II but not published until 1947, Horkheimer and Adorno defined the culture industry as a nexus of film, radio, and print media working in harmony with big government and big business. "Film, radio, and magazines form a system," Horkheimer and Adorno wrote, operating by "the same inflexible rhythm" and "infecting everything with sameness" (94). All aspects of cultural production, they argued, were now answerable to the same network of industrial and economic forces—radio to the electrical companies, film to the banks, and so forth—with the result that everything was "intertwined" (96). The metropolitan production centers were creating a variety of standardized, mechanically reproduced cultural products that were distributed to widely dispersed points of reception. Under these conditions, social relations were completely reified, mapped by statisticians and sociologists: "[O]n the charts of research organizations, indistinguishable from those of political propaganda, consumers are divided up as statistical material into red, green, and blue areas according to income group . . . Something is provided for everyone so that no one can escape" (97).

It should perhaps be noted here that *Dialectic of Enlightenment* was aimed at modern mass culture as a whole, not at the Good Neighbor policy and the activities of the CIAA, which were never mentioned in the book. As Fredric Jameson has observed (xviii), Horkheimer and Adorno thought of modernity in general in "Weberian" terms, as an iron cage constructed by a "tendential web of bureaucratic control" and "the interpenetration of government and big business." Whatever one thinks of their dark analysis (in my own view it is insufficiently dialectical), the U.S. Good Neighbor policy was undoubtedly symptomatic of what they identified as "the culture industry" and was organized along the very lines they described. As we shall see, however, artists had minds of their own, and it was difficult, if not impossible, to impose cultural "sameness" on neighbors to the south or even on neighbors at home.

Historically speaking, the U.S. government was relatively slow to recognize the persuasive power of mass culture as propaganda, although an early effort along such lines took place under Woodrow Wilson, who convened the short-term Committee on Public Information (CPI) from April 1917 to August 1919 to boost U.S. public support for World War I. Headed by investigative journalist George Creel and popularly known as the Creel Committee, the CPI launched initiatives in film and print media that focused on audiences both domestically and abroad.[1] As a result, Hollywood became involved in the war propaganda effort in selective ways. D. W. Griffith's *Hearts of the World* (1915) was filmed on location in Britain and France in an attempt to sway U.S. public opinion toward the British; Charles Chaplin, Douglas Fairbanks, and Mary Pickford appeared at huge war-bond rallies; and the Warner brothers had their first box-office success with *My Four Years in Germany* (1918), based on the book of the same title by James W. Gerard, former U.S. ambassador to Germany. But prior to a 1935 speech on hemispheric relations by Under Secretary of State Sumner Welles, most efforts in this area were largely the domain of philanthropic and professional organizations.

The Carnegie Endowment, the Rockefeller Foundation, and the American Council of Learned Societies offered grants for international study and travel, while the American Library Association supported the publication of literary translations.[2] Welles's speech "The Roosevelt Administration and Its Dealings with the Republics of the Western Hemisphere"—delivered at the annual convention of the Association of American Colleges in Atlanta on January 17, 1935—focused on the importance of cultural relations as a diplomatic means to remedy lack of interest, misunderstandings, and misconceptions between the United States and Latin America:

> In Latin America there is a frank skepticism as to the existence of interest here in the things of the mind and of the spirit. There is admiration of our capacity for organization and achievements in industry and business, but open incredulity of our interest in literature, music, art, and philosophy. On the other hand, in the United States, knowledge of Latin American civilization, social institutions, and economic moves is pathetically limited. (10)

Welles especially emphasized the need for more college courses on Latin American literature: "Next to personal contact, the method by which one people learns to know and understand another is by reading its literature" (12).

In his study of diplomacy during World War II, Frank A. Ninkovich describes the State Department's Division of Cultural Relations, created by Franklin D. Roosevelt in 1938, as ancillary to the private sector's activities (*Diplomacy of Ideas*, 33). He quotes Laurence Duggan, head of the State Department's Division of American Republics at the time, who argued against cultural diplomacy initiatives predicated exclusively on Axis rhetoric: "'The important thing seems, with respect to our cultural activities, not to act on a competitive counterproposal basis but rather to proceed to develop *real* cultural relations that cannot be accused of propaganda'" (ibid., 26; my emphasis).[3] Duggan's reference to "real" was synonymous with "truthful," a word used liberally in the late 1930s and throughout the war to describe the forthrightness of inter-American cultural activities, in contrast to the "false" German propaganda being disseminated throughout Latin America.[4] Sumner Welles emphasized this attribute in his 1939 speech titled "Practical Pan-Americanism": "'Underlying all of the complex pattern of international relationships is the basic need for a *real* understanding among peoples'" (ibid., 29; my emphasis).

These debates are background to our story proper, which begins when, on August 16, 1940, President Franklin D. Roosevelt appointed Nelson A. Rockefeller to lead the Office for the Coordination of Commercial and Cultural Relations between the American Republics, a new civilian agency that would report directly to the president. Established by order of the Council of National Defense, the agency's mission was to promote inter-American cooperation through commercial and cultural initiatives. A year later, on July 30, 1941, FDR expanded the office's activities in cultural relations and renamed it the Office of the Coordinator of Inter-American Affairs. Despite the name change and greater responsibilities, the agency's primary mission remained the same: to build strong U.S. commercial and cultural ties with Latin America and ensure hemispheric solidarity in the face of a growing Axis presence. As the United States moved closer to declaring war, the agency's early emphasis on economic and psychological defense measures shifted to that of economic and psychological warfare.

Rockefeller seemed an unusual candidate to head the office, and there were some who criticized his appointment.[5] A rakish, rather boisterous thirty-two-year-old, he had no political experience in Washington and no record of public service. ("Hi ya, fella!" was his customary greeting to the people he encountered; after the war, Orson Welles would give that line to one of the villains in *The Lady from Shanghai* [1947], which can be viewed as an allegory of Welles's unhappy experience with both Hollywood and the CIAA.) Somewhat liberal-minded, Rockefeller was a registered Republican from a stolid, enormously wealthy family of capitalist plutocrats; despite his youth and lack of political credentials, he was a seasoned business executive who founded his own company outside the Rockefeller empire and had an interest in art and aesthetics. He sat on the Metropolitan Museum of Art's board of trustees and the Westchester County Board of Health and was actively involved in a family project, the Rockefeller Center. In 1939 he was named president of the Museum of Modern Art (MoMA).

Rockefeller had important business interests in Latin American oil and a passion for Latin American art.[6] Like his mother, Abby, an art patron and the driving force behind MoMA, he greatly admired the muralist Diego Rivera, but his liberalism had its limits. In 1932 he contracted Rivera to paint a large mu-

THE WEEKLY NEWSMAGAZINE

NELSON ROCKEFELLER

Peter A. Nyholm

Nelson A. Rockefeller on the May 22, 1939, cover of *Time*.

ral for the Rockefeller Center lobby. Although Rivera's "Man at the Crossroads" mural depicted a Soviet May Day celebration, Rockefeller remained enthusiastic about the project—even as Rivera's representations of "progress" grew to include such things as gas masks and death rays. Then Lenin's face suddenly appeared in the mural. Unable to convince Rivera to remove or substitute Lenin's face for someone else's and unwilling to agree to Rivera's offer to counterbalance the Lenin figure with one of Abraham Lincoln, Rockefeller stopped work on the project. Rivera was paid his commission and the mural was covered to prevent further public viewing and bad press. Sometime later it was pick-axed and quietly removed in pieces from the building.

The mural fiasco was a major public embarrassment for the up-and-coming art patron, but Rockefeller's interest in Latin America was far from diminished by the incident. The following year he traveled to Mexico, where he began collecting pre-Columbian and folk art. Returning to New York, he joined a small group of prominent government officials and business heads who met informally but regularly to talk about Latin America; and in 1937, he toured the South American continent. After seeing up close the poverty of Venezuelan workers employed by his family's Standard Oil affiliate, he concluded that a more socially conscious approach to capitalist enterprise, including the construction of schools, hospitals, and decent housing for workers and their families, was essential to ensuring "good neighbor" relations and future capitalist development.[7] Moving quickly from the planning to the construction phase, his "missionary capitalist" initiative, as studied in depth by historian Darlene S. Rivas, was both shrewd and timely, particularly in the face of Nazi Germany's increasing presence in Latin America and Mexico's decision to nationalize its oil reserves.

Cary Reich, author of *The Life of Nelson A. Rockefeller*, examines in precise and vivid detail Rockefeller's maneuverings to become a political player in Washington. After various interventions on his behalf by government insiders, he was invited to meet with FDR adviser Harry Hopkins on June 14, 1940, to whom he pitched a plan for bolstering U.S.–Latin American relations that called for, among other things, "increasing the U.S. diplomatic presence through a 'vigorous program' of cultural, educational and scientific exchange" (178).[8] By the time of that meeting, FDR's Good Neighbor policy was already seven years old. No one was more aware of the need for hemispheric solidarity than the president, particularly when, on June 14, 1940, German troops marched into Paris. Rockefeller's plan also tapped into FDR's firm belief in the central role of cultural relations in U.S. foreign diplomacy—a belief that led the president in 1938 to create the Division of Cultural Relations, which, as already noted, was the first government program to focus on U.S. international cultural cooperation as an arm of domestic and foreign policy.[9] Shortly after Rockefeller's meeting with Hopkins, Roosevelt expanded the division's mission to include more diverse communications efforts in radio, the press, and Hollywood. At the same moment, an agency for inter-American affairs was firmly launched.

Prior to Pearl Harbor and at the behest of Britain's Ministry of Information, a number of British writers with popular followings in the United States, such as Somerset Maugham and J. B. Priestly, used their book tours and speaking engagements to convince U.S. audiences to join the war effort.[10] Maugham, for example, told the California audience in 1940: "'If by any chance we [British] are beaten, then your danger will be great. It isn't a ruined Europe that Hitler wants, it isn't an unproductive Africa; it's those great undeveloped territories of South America, with their inexhaustible stores of raw material that he hankers after.'"[11] While celebrity author visits and lecture tours were common British propaganda initiatives, they were relatively new to U.S. domestic and foreign policy. To plan for these and many other cultural activities, Rockefeller invited his good friend Robert G. Caldwell, a former minister to Portugal and Bolivia and Massachusetts Institute of Technology professor, to chair a CIAA policy committee that would advise him on projects under consideration.[12]

In addition to committee comments on projects as diverse as a Portuguese-English dictionary, a South American guidebook, a textbook for teaching English in Latin America, and a magazine on defense, Caldwell submitted a brief working definition of "cultural relations" for Rockefeller's consideration. He wrote: "Cultural influences are those that affect life and thought among large numbers of people. For our program, preference should be given to efforts that will yield quick results in the two Americas, especially Latin America."[13]

Rockefeller quoted Caldwell's definition in a November 29, 1940, letter to his friend Robert M. Hutchins, the celebrated University of Chicago president. Rockefeller asked Hutchins to convene a committee of University of Chicago scholars from various areas who would write up their own views on cultural relations and suggest projects for the CIAA initiative. Rockefeller emphasized that the government had already allocated substantial funding for cultural relations and that support was readily available for jump-start and short-term proposals.[14] University of Chicago sociologist and international law professor Quincy Wright, co-founder of the first graduate program of international relations in the United States, wrote to University of Chicago vice president and Rockefeller adviser William Benton on December 7, 1940, offering advice on how to tie together Caldwell's definition tailored specifically for the CIAA and a broader view of the concept. He suggested the following:

> The term "cultural relations" includes all interactions of distinctive cultures upon one another. As used in this office [CIAA] it includes only those contacts which increase sympathetic understanding and friendship among the peoples of different nations. Such understanding among the American Republics is stimulated by the dissemination of knowledge of each other's history, language and social organization. It is further stimulated by the development of appreciation of each other's characteristic beliefs, habits, ways of thought, work and creative efforts—especially in their best expression. A positive program of cultural relations, such as this office is sponsoring, seeks above all to foster those cultural objectives and ideas held in common among the peoples of the Western Hemisphere. Preference is given to projects that promise quick results with large numbers of people, particularly in South America.[15]

Wright's colleague and Latin American historian J. Fred Rippy filed a five-page memorandum identifying more specific sociopolitical strategies to win over Latin Americans, the most important of which was the need to "ascertain the pattern of values of the ruling groups of the various states and of those likely to get their hands on the controls in any immediate future. In other words, it is necessary to ascertain their ideals with respect to what a civilization or culture should be."[16] Understanding that pattern, he wrote, required "examining concepts, attitudes, and emotions clustering about the following institutions: (1) Government, its functions, limitations, and those who should participate; (2) Property; (3) Religion; (4) Family; (5) Educational agencies; (6) Social classes; (7) Art; and (8) Etiquette."[17]

The next step, according to Rippy, was to determine a "pattern of values" in the United States, then to identify common values in Latin American and the United States, and finally to use persuasion in crucial areas of difference. As one possible example, Rippy mentions that heroic figures in U.S. movies and literature might be made to appeal to Latin Americans. Equally important, he states, is U.S. understanding and admiration for Latin American values. In this regard Rippy emphasizes the importance of education and the need for college and university courses on the literature, history, and geography of the Americas. He encourages study of Latin American newspapers, magazines, textbooks, literary works, and cultural exchange programs as ways to comprehend their patterns of values. He adds:

> Travel must be encouraged in every way; so likewise educational interchange. . . . The countries with few exceptions, are ruled politically, socially and economically

by an aristocracy who must be met on a fairly high cultural level. . . . We might find that a number of them to be [sic] graduates of our universities. We should see to it that more of them enroll in our institutions of learning, and with this growing alumni we should never lose our contacts. Almost every Rhodes scholar is likely in the United States to be pro-English. We can profit by this suggestion.[18]

The optimum result, Rippy argues, would be the forging of a "consciousness of unity" among the Americas based on a shared heritage as European colonies and newly independent nations; this would promote a hemisphere united for a more secure future.[19] Rippy's argument, it must be noted, is aimed almost entirely at ruling classes and cultural elites. He expresses doubt about targeting the "masses" and counsels careful study of the issue.[20] In formulating his various suggestions, he calls attention to a basic concern about the ability of anyone to articulate what the U.S. pattern of values might be: "Many allege that we are confused. Perhaps we are. If so, we must clarify. Our enemies [Axis leaders] do not seem to suffer from confusion and doubt."[21]

Harold Lasswell, a University of Chicago political scientist and communications expert, sidestepped this particular concern in a twelve-page, four-point report titled "Some Basic Problems of the Cultural Relations Program."[22] His report proposed primary goals of the program, key symbols to promote hemispheric unity, clear principles for coordinating the program with other government units, and measures for determining success or failure. Perhaps a result of his own special interest in Nazi propaganda, Lasswell's communiqué seems less concerned with who U.S. citizens were and what cultural attributes the nation wanted to convey than with a need to form anti-Axis propaganda strategies.[23]

Bizarrely, Laswell suggested an insignia for, among other things, postage stamps, buttons, banners, armbands, and logos for films about South America: "Possibly the best insignia would be a round circle with a double A to signify the two American continents of the Western Hemisphere." He posed but then rejected a special salute and was more enthusiastic about a hemispheric anthem that might be determined through an open competition. He suggested the use of an all-American broadcast signature as well as a map symbol other than Mercator's, which "grossly exaggerated the size of Canada and minimized the relative importance of South America." Unity, friendship, and national defense were all themes in his report, but he wondered about alternative kinds of unions, such as a United States of Free Nations; a United States of North and South America; a United States of South America; and, even more disconcertingly, "an enlarged United States." He ultimately rejected number three because of national security, in the belief that South American nations were more easily controlled when separate as opposed to united, and number four as "thinkable only under conditions of the utmost extremity." His report is one of the more obvious examples of how a Good Neighbor policy might become a naked form of imperialism.

Lasswell recognized that a cultural relations initiative requires major scientific and humanistic study and endeavor, but the only specific project mentioned in his report is a diplomatic history. He discussed the importance of examining U.S. and Latin American newspapers, magazines, broadcasts, and films to assess past and future trends in shaping and controlling public opinion—not a new idea, but one that would be fully embraced by the CIAA. More significantly, he argued for small-business investments in Latin America to increase industrial production and create a desirable, healthy middle class to "support democratic institutions" and "mediate between the Indians and the ruling class."[24] Ultimately, modernization, the middle class, and what Lasswell termed "competent 'Middletowns' of South America" would emerge as key themes in the CIAA's propaganda efforts to influence and win over good neighbors to the south. What follows is an account of how those themes and others, sometimes contradictory, were articulated in practice.

In practical terms, the CIAA needed to recognize difference and develop sophisticated methods of persuasion. Among Rockefeller's many acquaintances tapped for positions in the agency was his former Dartmouth classmate Leonard W. Doob, a Harvard Ph.D. in psychology who was on the faculty at Yale University. In 1935 Doob published *Propaganda: Its Psychology and Technique*, which was based on his research conducted in Germany. In an October 10, 1941, memo to Rockefeller and CIAA division heads, Doob responded to a CIAA directive to create a program of "hemisphere enlightenment" for combating the initiatives of Germany's Ministry for Public Enlightenment and Propaganda, created by Hitler in 1933 and administered by Joseph Goebbels.[25]

Doob's twelve-page report is important for several reasons. He disagreed with Duggan and others who felt that the United States should not respond to Axis propaganda; Doob argued that the Nazis were highly skilled propagandists who used every conceivable means of communication to reach their public. To reinforce his argument, he described how their strategies targeted not only the mass media but also schools and social organizations at home and abroad, especially in countries with large German immigrant populations.[26] Doob identified local and international companies sympathetic to the Axis cause, such as the Transocean Agency, which distributed German news

throughout Latin America. (His investigation resulted in an official U.S. blacklist of 1,800 companies in Latin America that aided Germany or Italy.)[27] His report described the effectiveness of Rome and Berlin radio programs transmitted to Latin America and noted in particular the popularity of Juan Iversen, the
Mexican-born German broadcaster known as "Don Juan."[28] Doob's memo was
reassuring to the extent that he believed the Axis "love us–hate them" approach
often failed to win over Latin American audiences. He contended that while
German propaganda and its agents were everywhere in Latin America, they did
not deserve their "awesome reputation . . . Germans, in spite of their ingenuity
and thoroughness, cannot accomplish miracles. . . . They are not supermen;
frequently they are just very cunning in the ways of human behavior."[29]

The CIAA's response to Doob's profile and analysis of Axis communications
is perhaps best reflected in a 1942 report titled "Philosophy and Organization
of the Office of the Coordinator of Inter-American Affairs," which includes a
section for a proposed Department of Propaganda and three "credos" to be established for U.S. citizens toward Latin America and vice versa.[30] Described as
"founded on truth," these credos were cast in opposition to the "Axis Credo,"
which was "founded on falsehood" and "not in the best interest of Latin Americans."[31] Although the document describes all three credos in detail, the "U.S.
Credo for the Individual Latin American Citizen" is by far the longest, its four
main points beginning with the following phrases: 1) "I believe that my best interests are linked with the U.S. because . . ."; 2) "I believe that my best interests
will be harmed by the Axis because . . ."; 3) "I believe that the U.S. is going to win
the war, although it will be a difficult struggle, because . . ."; and 4) "Therefore
I am supporting the U.S. and stand ready to cooperate with the Americas and
to make additional personal sacrifices along with the American people so that
I can help the U.S. win the war and establish a better world." Each of the four
parts contains subsections that outline specific reasons for the belief and support. For example, point one, or the rationale for best-served interests, begins:
"I like the U.S. way of life—especially I like its social, political, and economic
institutions; its art, literature, drama, and motion pictures; its sports and other forms of recreation; its science and medicine; and its general philosophy."
Another rationale assumed the status of a CIAA mantra: "My own country has
much in common with the U.S."

Although designing wartime credos for citizens of the United States and other countries seems a naïve and even dangerous way to try and "win minds and
hearts,"[32] the CIAA was, as I have already suggested, following an old, proven
tradition of spreading, or "propagating," faith and ideology. The 1942 report

"Europe is getting hot! We've got to move to the Western Hemisphere. . . ." Cartoon by Arthur Szyk, 1944. Courtesy of the Library of Congress, Prints and Photographs Division.

was at bottom not much different from the aims of Catholic propaganda in the seventeenth century or Soviet propaganda in the early twentieth century; like them, it was designed to construct beliefs through an efficient and widespread information program. The report's language on Latin Americans' adoption of the credos is clearly influenced by Doob's analysis of the psychology of propaganda and its (desired) reception:

> In order to have Latin Americans believe this Credo, the CIAA must carry on propaganda and must accomplish certain deeds.... The Credo represents the responses which Latin Americans must make if they are to support the United States in military and economic ways. Through the use of certain media of communication they are presented with certain stimuli which seek to promote the desired responses. Propaganda consists of stimuli; and the entire process of employing media to convey the stimuli in order to bring about the desired responses is what is known as psychological warfare.[33]

In a book published shortly after the war, Doob wrote about the CIAA's uneasiness with the word "propaganda," whose associations with Soviet and German totalitarianism were anathema to proponents of Western liberalism.[34] Thus, the CIAA preferred the term "information"—as if it were more honest, truthful, and devoid of value judgments. This attitude was not unique to the CIAA; on the contrary, it was implied or even explicit in the titles given to wartime propaganda agencies such as the Office of War Information (OWI) and the Office of Facts and Figures (OFF).[35] Thus, toward the end of the war, in a 1945 hearing before a Senate committee, coordinator Rockefeller praised the accomplishments of the CIAA and reinforced the truth-in-information approach to achieve mutual understanding based on shared beliefs and values among the Americas. He emphasized the idea that despite their differences, everyone in the hemisphere was fundamentally alike, open to appeal on the basis of commonality, or "sameness" (the very quality that Horkheimer and Adorno regarded as the sinister goal of the culture industry in general):

> We consider [the CIAA] an information program [with the objective of preserving] freedom and the way of life which we have believed in as a nation from the beginning. We attempt to bring to [Latin Americans] an understanding of this country, honestly portraying life in the United States. We try to picture for them our appreciation of spiritual and cultural values, so that they might understand us better and recognize that—in common with them—we have similar aspirations, share the same sense of decency and the same desire to create opportunities for all to better themselves through their own efforts. We believe that only people who know, trust, and understand each other can effectively work together for their future best self-

Public opinion expert Leonard W. Doob.
Photograph by Nick Doob. Courtesy of
Anthony N. Doob.

interests. That has been the basis of our information activities and will continue to
be the basis as long as it is carried on. (In Rowland, 42n7)

Rockefeller's statement is accurate insofar as the aims of the agency were
concerned, but it paints a rosy picture and makes the United States seem a superior model. In *Our Good Neighbor Hurdle* (1943), foreign correspondent John
W. White presented a quite different view, pointing out sharp differences between the United States and its neighbors to the south, some of which indicated that Latin America had a more sophisticated culture:

> Our southern neighbors are better read than North Americans of corresponding
> social and economic position. They are much more tolerant than we toward the
> idea of others. They are more loyal than we in their personal friendships, and they
> have made the family a much stronger social institution than we have. The people
> of even the smaller towns are infinitely better informed on world affairs than are
> the residents of our largest cities. There is no newspaper in the United States that
> gives such a thorough day by day picture of what is going on in the world as do sev-
> eral Argentine papers and as did the leading papers of Brazil before they were put
> under State control. Their news editors have international minds; ours have pro-
> vincial minds. (10)

Too few of the major players in the CIAA were aware of the Latin American cultural sophistication identified by White, and much of the agency's propaganda was aimed at naïve audiences. I shall have more to say about such matters, but before examining how they manifested themselves in specific local instances, it is important to understand the structural organization of the CIAA at the peak of its operation. By the time the CIAA's 1942 "Philosophy and Organization" report appeared, Rockefeller had created separate information divisions, including Motion Picture, Radio, and what ultimately became Press and Publication, alongside commercial divisions for economic development and transportation.[36] The agency as a whole was shaped in what might be described as modernist rather than postmodernist fashion, with separate units devoted to specific media, each charged with disseminating a vision of "Americans all." Here I offer a brief account of the major divisions and the people behind them.

Films West and East

A memo highlighting nearly one hundred CIAA topics for press release between October 4, 1940, and April 23, 1942, lists dozens of Rockefeller appointments to the agency's cultural arm.[37] Among the first to be named was multimillionaire John Hay (Jock) Whitney, who was vice president of MoMA, president of its Film Library, and on the board of trustees with Rockefeller. Having established himself in Hollywood by financing both the Technicolor Company and David O. Selnick's production studio, which made *Gone with the Wind* (1939), he was well connected in elite East Coast society and Rockefeller's choice to direct the CIAA's Motion Picture Division in Los Angeles. Although Whitney's tenure was relatively short (he joined the Air Force in 1942 and was replaced in the CIAA by his assistant, Francis Alstock), he was a pivotal figure in the early days of the Motion Picture Society for the Americas (MPSA), a nonprofit corporation created by the Hollywood industry in March 1941 and partially funded by the CIAA.[38] Its mission was to bolster inter-American relations by producing 35mm features and shorts on Latin American topics, which, unlike many Hollywood films about Latin America, would portray the region and people in a positive light. From the CIAA's perspective, it was equally imperative for Hollywood to cease Latin American distribution of films that gave a bad impression of the United States—in particular, movies about juvenile delinquents, gangsters, and corrupt officials who framed and jailed innocent people (Rowland, 71).[39]

The stature and weight of the Hollywood MPSA is perhaps best suggested by its initial board of directors, whose membership included Y. Frank Freeman, Frank Capra, Louis B. Mayer, George Schaefer, Walter Wanger, David O. Selznick, Darryl Zanuck, Samuel Goldwyn, and Harry M. Warner. In a speech on June 18, 1941, actor and board member Edward Arnold assured a Rotary International audience that it was about to see "another side of Hollywood" in its hemispheric efforts.[40] Just one year later, the MPSA had a staff of thirty-two salaried members and a budget of more than $2 million (Roberts, 160). Among those who served as president of the association was Joseph I. Breen, chief enforcer of the Motion Picture Production Code. In a July 21, 1943, memo

Left to right: Merian Cooper, John Hay (Jock) Whitney, and David O. Selznick in Hollywood. Harry Ransom Humanities Center, University of Texas at Austin.

to Francis Alstock, Breen reaffirmed the MPSA's commitment "to render assistance and to report on all picture projects in California affecting in any way the program of the Coordinator."[41]

Two wartime projects were especially high-profile and have become well known in film history generally. During his brief CIAA tenure Jock Whitney negotiated a deal with Walt Disney in 1941 for a series of animated shorts on hemispheric relations—a deal made at a critical time for Disney, whose company was experiencing serious labor problems and an artists' strike. In order to become familiar with the region, Disney and a small number of artists went on a CIAA-funded tour, which became the basis of his 16mm *South of the Border with Disney* (1943). This was an early "making of" documentary about Disney's feature film *Saludos amigos* (1942), a box-office hit that had its world premiere in Rio de Janeiro. Then, in February 1942, Rockefeller personally invited Orson Welles, who was broadcasting his CBS Mercury Theater radio show from New York, to travel to Latin America as a Good Neighbor ambassador and to make a documentary with RKO based on his experiences there.[42] Brazilian propaganda minister Lourival Fontes, a *Citizen Kane* enthusiast, apparently posed the idea to Rockefeller (Rowland, 79), who signed a government-sponsored deal with Welles that, like the CIAA Disney contract, indemnified RKO (in which Rockefeller had major holdings) for losses up to $300,000.[43]

Both Disney and Welles were highly successful as goodwill ambassadors. Disney attended barbecues and banquets, joined in Latin American folk dances, and produced on-the-spot caricature sketches for his hosts, many of whom were major dignitaries. In September 1941, foreign affairs minister Oswaldo Aranha presented Disney with Brazil's prestigious Order of the Southern Cross. Welles traveled widely and lectured on U.S. topics, broadcasting two U.S. radio shows that featured Brazilian samba from Rio's famous Urca Casino. But Welles's unorthodox quasidocumentary, ironically titled *It's All True*, was never completed. Aranha liked Welles, who was very popular in Brazil as a moviemaker and personality, and penned him a warm farewell when a discouraged Welles left Brazil in August 1942. He wrote: "[Your] non-diplomatic ways, gestures and lifestyle caused such a spontaneously sympathetic impression [in Brazil]—perhaps in part as a reaction to embassy 'stiff shirts' who convince few, bore many and irritate the rest."[44] Aranha's expectations that Welles's Latin American film would be unique in representing Brazil's people, lands, and customs were never fulfilled. The tragic history of the incomplete film has been discussed by several writers—most completely by Catherine L. Benamou in her book on *It's All True*—and I do not plan to describe it in detail here. It should be noted, however, that one of the chief reasons RKO and the CIAA lost faith in the project was that Welles was filming the black and dispossessed in Brazil. The Vargas government strongly objected to such imagery; together with Hollywood and the CIAA, it made sure that the picture would not be seen.

In addition to the West Coast operation, in April 1941 the CIAA contracted the MoMA Film Library to oversee an East Coast branch that would purchase available 16mm shorts or stock footage on U.S. subjects for Latin American distribution. The museum was also responsible for contracting independent filmmakers and companies to produce documentary shorts about Latin America and the United States. It hired speakers of Spanish and Portuguese to dub and subtitle films sent abroad while it oversaw 16mm film distribution throughout the hemisphere. Among those involved early on in the MoMA operation was Luis Buñuel, who was employed briefly as editor in chief for anti-Axis propaganda dubbing and distribution.[45] Julien Bryan, Herbert Knapp, and Willard Van Dyke, who had recently returned from Venezuela, were among the independent directors hired by MoMA to make 35mm and 16mm nontheatrical shorts. Bryan was by far the most prolific, with twenty-three documentaries on topics for both Latin American and U.S. consumption.

Disillusioned with the CIAA's initial slowness to fund documentaries, Van Dyke, whose documentaries on the poor and working-class are a valuable source for the New Deal years, moved to the OWI in 1943. In an interview conducted by the Oral History Research Office at Columbia University in 1981, Van Dyke remarked:

> I had just come back from Latin America, I knew something about it so I went to work for them [CIAA]. . . . I went there with the idea that we'd make films, and I started to work in August [1942], and by the first of January it was clear that these guys didn't know what they were doing, and they had no program, they were improvising as they went, they certainly were not going to make films if they could avoid it, although they had a whole apparatus for it, and I quit, and went to work for the Office of War Information.

But because any films dealing with Latin America were under CIAA control, all OWI films that featured the Americas were made in collaboration with Rockefeller's agency. This was also the case of Office of Strategic Services films, which included those shot by the John Ford Mission stationed in Rio de Janeiro.

As Leonard Doob's analysis firmly established, information on public reception was important to the success of any propaganda venture. Because of its strategic importance, commercial value, and close ties that had been estab-

Orson Welles on the beachfront in Rio de Janeiro. Courtesy of the Lilly Library, Bloomington, Indiana.

lished by its former ambassador to the United States Oswaldo Aranha, Brazil was considered the optimal site for a special division in the CIAA that would report to Whitney and Alstock about movie audiences' reactions.[46] On June 23, 1942, the division sent Alstock a report listing audience preferences for film genres in the following order: costume, war, society, cowboy, music, opera, small town, juvenile, slapstick, and gangster. It was also concluded that 29.5 percent of the audiences in Rio went to movies because of the appeal of the stars and 71.5 percent because of interest in the subjects.[47]

The report's reference to the popularity of war films in Rio de Janeiro is quite different from a later, December 23, 1942, report from the Bureau of Latin American Research in Washington, D.C., concerning São Paulo audiences' dissatisfaction with war films, with two exceptions:

> "The Mortal Storm" and above all "Mrs. Miniver" [because it] stirred the public. The others were too hastily prepared, coarse and, what is worse, sometimes had an altogether contrary effect. . . . Fifth column, espionage, and sabotage were the most often used themes, but [they] were badly used, giving the idea that the unchallenged dominators of English and American life were the Nazis and the Nazis alone. . . . The Brazilian public was invariably drawn unwillingly to back the few (Nazis) against the many (anti-Nazis).[48]

This final comment reinforced MacLeish's 1940 observation about the dangerous business of persuasion as well as Doob's cautionary note about how blatant or facile forms of propaganda can backfire.

The division's report went on to applaud *Mrs. Miniver* because it was then the only war film that represented the "masses." It commended the work of Charlie Chaplin although *The Great Dictator* "arrived in Brazil too late, when the tragedy of war had overshadowed the pathos of the occurrences of before the war."[49] But the document advised that fewer political and war films be sent to Brazil because "even though the Brazilian public is neither refined nor very mature politically, it rebels when it sees this tragic war and its driving forces represented with the technique and style of Western films." According to this strange logic, the supposedly refined and mature audience in North America did not mind when Hollywood portrayed the war in the style of a western shoot-'em-up. The bureau report gives special praise to Disney's forthcoming *Saludos amigos*, wherein "paternalism is substituted by *camaradagem* (camaraderie)," and concludes with another, albeit less explicit, critique of Brazilian viewers by way of a cautionary comment about Welles and his *It's All True* project: "If the director does not show an extraordinarily light touch . . . , it will prove to be a great disappointment." As history has shown in the case of *It's All True*, the disappointment was far greater for Welles than for any individual, studio, or group. RKO withdrew funding, and the unfinished film was believed lost for decades. On the other hand, with the artists' strike resolved during his South American tour, with the widespread success of *Saludos amigos*, and with additional government contracts for propaganda and educational films in hand, Disney was well on his way to creating the empire that we know today.[50]

Broadcasting

Although there was some concern in Washington about the advisability of direct U.S. response to Axis rhetoric in Latin America, there was unanimous consensus that the twelve U.S. shortwave radio stations transmitting programs to Latin America in 1940 (Rowland, 57) were woefully insufficient for the war effort. It is important to remember that radio was the most popular form of mass communication during the war, reaching into many areas where films were nonexistent. Rockefeller himself was highly cognizant of radio's potential. He estimated that in comparison to the forty million Latin Americans who saw movies on a weekly basis or the forty to sixty million who read some form of print material on a monthly basis, fifteen to twenty million tuned in to radio on a daily basis (Maxwell, 75).

Germany was in the vanguard of international radio and by the early 1930s was broadcasting shortwave programs with news and music to its immigrant populations around the world. Many of those immigrants lived in Latin America, especially in Argentina, Chile, and southern Brazil, where their families arrived in the late nineteenth century and where the German language and customs were preserved. According to media historian Fred Fejes, by 1936 Berlin radio was broadcasting weekly forty-two hours of music, conversation, and news directed specifically to Central and South American listeners. To ensure as large an audience as possible, programs were transmitted in several languages (80).

Under the direction of Don Francisco, president of the Lloyd and Thomas advertising firm, the CIAA Radio Division had at least three early objectives: increasing the number and kilowatt power of radio stations transmitting to Latin America; analyzing Axis radio propaganda for its content and reception; and creating Good Neighbor programming that would appeal to U.S. and Latin American listeners. The last objective was perhaps the most difficult and complicated because Latin America was more different and differentiated than the CIAA mission statements recognized. As Francisco astutely noted in a 1942 memorandum to Rockefeller, "We are dealing, not with one area, but with twenty different nations, each varying according to political and psychological background. Programs suitable for the U.S. may not be suitable for any part of Latin America, and programs suitable for Mexico may not be appropriate for Argentina. Likewise, the question of Brazil, where programs must be written in Portuguese, is a problem in itself."[51]

In his 1941 CIAA report "Principles of Nazi Propaganda," Leonard Doob outlined the major strengths of Axis radio transmission to Latin America, noting that Axis radio programs were broadcast simultaneously throughout the American republics in Spanish, Portuguese, German, and sometimes even Italian. Doob speculated that Axis radio contained coded messages that enabled German and Italian agents in Latin America to keep abreast of homeland news that they could pass on at informal gatherings. Finally, he observed that because Axis shortwave transmitters were more powerful than those of the United States, the messages were frequently picked up and retransmitted on conventional longwave stations to larger audiences.[52]

Although the CIAA focused more of its energies on populations south of the border, it also used radio to indoctrinate U.S. audiences about Latin America and the Good Neighbor policy, working with network broadcasters, marketing agencies, and 850 local stations throughout the United States in advancing the project of inter-American friendship and understanding.[53] By July 1, 1942, there were approximately 1,500 network programs on Latin America broadcast weekly in the United States, one-third of which were feature programs about the other Americas. These included single episodes of Blue Network's *Ripley's Believe It or Not* and *The Breakfast Club* and CBS's equally popular *School of the Air*. Latin-themed shows included Red Network's *Down Mexico Way* and NBC's highly successful *Inter-American University of the Air*. Latin American material also became a regular feature on commercial celebrity programs, such as the shows of Eddie Cantor, Jack Benny, Xavier Cugat, George Burns and Gracie Allen, Bob Hope, and Fibber McGee and Molly.

The Radio Division prepared hundreds of scripts for local broadcasts. *Salute to the Twenty Republics*, *Visiting Our Americas*, *The South American Way*, and *Pan American Power* were among the weekly offerings. Successful dramatic programs in the United States, such as NBC's *This Is War!*, *Cavalcade of the Americas*, and *March of Time*, were rebroadcast on NBC affiliates simultaneously so audiences throughout the Americas could listen. The CIAA negotiated for air time and ads with companies that transmitted radio programs to Latin America. A May 20, 1942, report describes negotiations with manufacturing giant Sterling Products that resulted in the placement of the CIAA slogan "Las

U.S. schoolchildren learning about Latin America. Courtesy of the Library of Congress, Prints and Photographs Division.

Radio broadcast of a program about Latin America, with U.S. schoolchildren. Courtesy of the Library of Congress, Prints and Photographs Division.

Américas Unidas—Unidas Vencerán" (The Americas United—United They Will Win) in all Sterling radio shows as well as its newspaper and magazine ads in Latin America. The agency created an inter-American anthem based on the "Las Americas Unidas—Unidas Vencerán" slogan for Sterling's musical radio programs.[54]

Besides "listeners' reports," the CIAA conducted telephone, door-to-door, and mail surveys on CIAA radio programs to gauge audience reaction in the United States and Latin America. It was suggested that a "V" pin might be offered as a premium for those who completed direct-mail surveys or newspaper questionnaires. The guidelines for telephone and door-to-door surveys were detailed and explicit. At least one hundred completed interviews were required to assess the popularity of any program, and it was estimated that between 350 and 400 calls would be necessary in order to reach that number. The CIAA tried to poll not only male heads of households but also women, for whom 6:15 a.m. programs such as *Diálogos femeninos* on Sundays and *La página femenina* on Wednesdays were specially designed.[55] Special forms were prepared for telephone surveys that asked about station preferences and favorite and least favorite programs. Instructions called for solicitor courtesy but firmness in calls: "The investigator should try to get past the servant, if possible, to talk with the head of the household or his wife," referred to earlier in the instructions as "the señor or señora." Another form was drawn up for house-to-house or business-office interviews that asked for personal information such as occupation, economic status, and place of birth alongside program preferences.

The September 1945 Radio Division report by CIAA adviser William Benton outlined how shortwave programming had been dictated by war trends. In 1942, programs electrically transcribed for shipment to Latin American radio stations included *U.S. and Industry at War*, about the U.S. industrial conversion from peace to wartime production; *Programs of Freedom*, a musical program with anti-Axis and pro-Allies commentary; and *Songs of America*, which featured readings of Whitman's poems on freedom and democracy. By 1943, programming trends shifted to focus increasingly on the Axis powers with programs such as *The Real Enemy* and *The Mysterious One*, dramas about Nazi brutality and infiltration. At the same time, musical programs grew in number to include *Music in the United States*, *The Lovers of Music*, and *¡Saludos, amigos!*, a variety program that featured U.S. Spanish-speaking entertainers. By 1945, dramatizations and narrative programs were discontinued, leaving a schedule almost exclusively of music. Shows such as *Metropolitan Opera*, *From Hollywood at War*, *The NBC Symphony Orchestra*, and *Music of the New World* were supplemented with other, equally cost-effective musical programming. Network radio reported high percentages of CIAA material being used daily in Portuguese and Spanish news broadcasts, although by this time Washington was turning increasingly to postwar efforts in Europe and Japan.

Print Media

A February 12, 1942, confidential report addressed to Rockefeller and compiled by American Social Surveys on "Opinion in the United States Concerning Latin America" showed that the CIAA had an uphill task in creating a more informed and favorable opinion of Latin Americans in the United States.[56] The questions asked of Latin Americans were formulated by public-opinion analysts Hadley Cantril and Fredric Swift, both of whom had been recommended to Rockefeller by George Gallup. (Cantril, a Princeton psychologist, was well known as the author of *Invasion from Mars* [1940], an analysis of the social psychology behind public reaction to Orson Welles's famous 1938 "War of the Worlds" radio broadcast.) Their findings were not encouraging:

> The stereotype which emerged shows Latin Americans to be dark-skinned, religious, lazy, suspicious, quick tempered, emotional, proud, friendly and backward. (The adjectives which were rejected were efficient, intelligent, progressive, shrewd, dirty, brave, generous, honest, imaginative, and ignorant.) It is interesting to observe that this stereotype is held by significantly more of the college educated group than of the rest of the population.[57]

When asked about sources for information on Latin America, respondents overall listed newspapers and magazines first, followed by radio, books, movies, and conversation.[58] Among the printed materials most frequently mentioned were *Reader's Digest*, *National Geographic*, *Time*, and *Life*, followed by *Collier's*, *Saturday Evening Post*, and *Newsweek*. The only book mentioned with any regularity was best-selling author John Gunther's *Inside Latin America* (1941), part of his popular *Inside* series about his travel experiences and interviews abroad.

While Cantril and Swift were constructing their report, Leonard Doob was carrying out a survey on the number of stories with a Latin American dateline that had appeared in U.S. newspapers from October 1941 to July 1942.[59] The results were equally dispiriting. Doob summarized his findings with three points: 1) despite the importance of Latin America to the war, less than one story per day appeared during the weeks surveyed; 2) the stories were quite variable in their attitudes and values; and 3) only the large metropolitan newspapers printed stories from Latin America.[60] Doob calculated that the ten-month average for newspapers nationwide was only six stories per month.

United Press's Harry Frantz, CIAA Press Division director prior to the creation of the Press and Publication Division under Pulitzer Prize–winning journalist Francis A. Jamieson, was displeased with Doob's survey and responded three days later with a memo to complain that datelined materials constituted only a portion of the newspaper stories on Latin America.[61] Frantz recommended the discontinuance of Doob's dateline survey, arguing that the division's priority since the U.S. entry into the war had shifted to developing CIAA materials for U.S. as well as Latin American newspapers, magazines, and radio.[62] More than a month later, on October 20, 1941, he wrote to both Rockefeller and Jamieson about the growing interest in inter-American journalistic relations and forecast an increase in hemispheric picture-news dissemination for 1942. In a third, undated, and lengthier report, he outlined the division's overall mission, placing emphasis on topics for Good Neighbor materials that would "hammer home, through the cumulative effect of all our media, the message which the [CIAA] seeks to convey."[63]

During its first year the CIAA operated fairly independently of the State Department, despite overlapping Latin American interests. That relative independence came to an abrupt halt when it was discovered that Rockefeller had approved an expensive advertising campaign in Latin American newspapers whose ostensible purpose was to encourage travel to the United States. The State Department accused the CIAA of trying to buy the allegiance of Latin American newspapers and their owners through attractive advertising contracts. There was also concern that contracts were being considered for newspapers sympathetic to the Axis powers. The complaints were sufficiently disquieting to force FDR to write a fairly blunt letter to Rockefeller, ordering his agency to seek State Department approval for all of its overseas activities.[64]

As CIAA operations fell into place, it became clear that inter-American cultural relations were far better served by "bringing *people* north to the U.S. and sending *things* south to Latin America."[65] Following that policy, the CIAA invited 140 newspaper representatives from the American republics for short-term stays in the United States. The fifth group of journalists to arrive was from Brazil. Representing the top bureau chiefs and newsmen from the nation's largest cities, they arrived in Washington on June 3, 1943, and toured the United States until July 17. A confidential report dated June 30, 1943, provides in addition to their names and press affiliations their ages, educational backgrounds, religions, marital status, attitudes toward the United States, and languages spoken. Perhaps not surprisingly, all of them were classified as admirers of or favorable to the United States. A few representatives were described as "white," while most seem to have eluded U.S. racial classification.[66]

The CIAA focused on four general topics around which materials for newspapers and other publications were developed: winning the war, the Axis menace to freedom, inter-American relations, and winning the peace. Frantz wrote to Jamieson that coordination committees in the twenty American republics could be especially helpful if they established press subcommittees to receive and disseminate CIAA articles, photographs, cartoons, and pamphlets.[67] He suggested that they could build friendly relations with editors and reporters and encourage local use of agency material. He also recommended that they hand-deliver CIAA publications and posters to individuals and shops. Frantz twice mentioned the importance of ensuring that *En Guardia*, the CIAA monthly magazine on U.S. military defense, be made available to libraries and universities. Styled after *Life* magazine, *En Guardia* was a free pictorial published in Spanish, Portuguese (*Em Guarda*), and French (*En Garde*) that quickly became one of the most widely read U.S. publications in Latin America. The initial run for the first two issues was 80,000 copies; by the end of the war, circulation of each issue had increased to 550,000 (Rowland, 46, 48).

Like other divisions, the Press and Publication Division constantly monitored the content and reception of its materials. In addition to *En Guardia*, it produced the biweekly *American Newsletter*, with a circulation around 13,000; spot news featuring information on conferences, the Brazilian war effort, and interviews; war posters and placards; news pictures and photographs of famous U.S. figures; news feature material on the United States; and pamphlets on Good Neighbor countries and inter-American relations for U.S. and Latin American consumption. An undated list of the circulation of CIAA materials to Argentina, Bolivia, and Brazil provides an idea of how many illustrated pamphlets were in circulation: Argentina had nine, at 53,450 total copies; Bolivia had fifteen, at 335,375 copies; and Brazil had sixteen, at 397,900 copies.[68] The most popular titles in each country were translations of pamphlets titled *Arms for Victory*, *Our Future—Free Men or Slaves*, and *Stories from Real Life*. The list indicates that more than 160,000 posters were sent to Bolivia and Brazil with titles such as "The Americans United for Progress and Victory," "Hitler Caged," "Hands off America," and "The Vision of Our Heroes." These and other pictorials were deemed vital to inter-American defense and hemispheric solidarity because of Latin America's large illiterate population.

Other Activities

In addition to the Motion Picture, Radio, and Press and Publication Divisions, the CIAA setup included a department for specific cultural and educational activities, directed by Robert Caldwell, the former dean of humanities at MIT. Initially, a plethora of U.S. goodwill ambassadors was sent to Latin America whose main purpose was to build good relations and support for the United States. Some cultural expeditionary forces like the Yale Glee Club were extremely successful. Between June 20 and August 11, 1941, the club gave seventeen public concerts, eight university performances, and two radio concerts. The group sang folk songs, ballads, hymns, and contemporary tunes as well as songs in Portuguese. Writing for Rio's *Diário de Notícias* on July 5, 1941, literary historian and critic Luís da Câmara Cascudo praised their performances: "From a country at which we looked as the one in which the machine and cement are supreme, our compatriots will now perhaps consider choral singing and the moral elevation that accompanies it as a fundamental value in education. For a few moments we may consider that the U.S. is not well represented by the cinema or 'swing.'"

Artist Jo Davidson's working tour, which produced bronze busts of ten former and current Latin American presidents and a traveling U.S. art exhibit, received equally favorable and widespread press notices. In contrast, movie stars had variable success as goodwill ambassadors. In 1940 Errol Flynn spoke on Rio radio at the invitation of the DIP. His incorporation of a few Portuguese phrases along with references to Brazilian hospitality, friendship, and Good Neighbors made a strong impression on listeners. However, Douglas Fairbanks Jr.'s 1941 trip to Latin America as special envoy at the personal behest of his friend FDR was a more complicated visit. Rockefeller biographer Cary Reich contends that Latin Americans did not regard Fairbanks an appropriate stand-in for the president of the United States (208). That was partly the case. In a May 16, 1941, letter, Claude Bowers, U.S. ambassador to Chile, wrote to Joseph F. Burt at the U.S. consulate in Valparaiso expressing his "embarrassment" and uneasiness with the forthcoming Fairbanks visit and his plans to carefully oversee the actor's appearances based on his reputation as "hot-headed and . . . saying things that will do more harm than good." But perhaps because of Bowers or because of Fairbanks's own diplomatic skills, the visit to the capital was a success.[69]

A confidential letter dated May 20, 1941, to Bowers from Norman Armour, U.S. ambassador to Argentina, dispelled certain concerns:

I am glad to state most emphatically that Fairbanks' visit has been a complete success. I must frankly admit before his arrival that I was not very sanguine as to accomplishments. I do not know whether you know these people here, but they are
extremely difficult to handle; thick-skinned and self-conscious to a degree. When it
comes to anything a little out of the ordinary run of things, they are apt to hold back
and hesitate to commit themselves. The fact that Fairbanks had apparently been
a real success in Brazil and that the Government turned out to receive him and to
show him even courtesy, far from having any influence here, had, I am afraid, just
the opposite effect. There is little doubt that the idea of a movie actor being designated by the President to come down on a special mission did not appeal to them.
The officials and the so-called Argentine society made little attempt to conceal
their feelings. So altogether the "ambiente" was not reassuring.

However, Fairbanks' personality, his simplicity, charm, and intelligence has [*sic*]
won everyone with whom he has come in contact. The visit which began slowly has
been in crescendo ever since his arrival, so that now, in true Argentine fashion, they
are tumbling over themselves to show him courtesies. . . .

He is a bear for work and is never so happy as when a heavy program is presented
to him. While he does not speak much Spanish, he reads a speech extremely well,
having a good ear, and has had great success with his radio broadcasts and the two
or three speeches he has made since his arrival. . . . He is looking forward keenly to
his stay in Chile and to the pleasure of seeing you all.[70]

Fairbanks's visit prompted the CIAA to consider other options for Good
Neighbor promotion.[71] Brazilian minister Oswaldo Aranha's quip "One more
goodwill mission and we'll declare war on the United States" (in McCann, 247)
may have been helpful in this regard. It was then that the agency began setting
up local coordination committees, which totaled seventy-six by the end of the
war, to build friendly relations and disseminate its propaganda (Reich, 250).
The CIAA published weekly reports that kept Rockefeller as well as local coordination committee heads informed of activities and special events throughout Latin America.

In 1943 CIAA cultural programs involving scholarships, libraries, the visual
arts, dance, and music in Latin America were transferred to the Cultural Division in the State Department. At the same time, the CIAA assumed greater
responsibilities in the areas of health and education—areas that became the
subject of several Disney shorts on topics such as hygiene, clean water, and malaria prevention. That same year the CIAA founded the Inter-American Educational Foundation to oversee educational conferences, technical support, and
teacher-training programs for Latin America. A Division of Inter-American
Activities was created under the leadership of University of Chicago professor

Walter H.C. Laves to establish inter-American centers throughout the United States. These centers served the public interests by offering classes in Spanish and Portuguese, promoting inter-American activities and exhibits, and organizing hospitality for Latin American visitors. By September 1944 there were eighteen centers in major cities that spanned the east to the west coast, and another five were under way in the South and Southwest. These centers worked in tandem with university-based inter-American institutes as well as professional and public organizations such as the National Educational Association and the Pan American Union (Rowland, 108, 111).

The success of the various CIAA initiatives might be measured by the fact that in 1945, the agency booklet titled *Some Specific Suggestions for Inter-American Programs* was in its fifth edition. The book's list of suggestions was fairly long, but the CIAA, ever mindful of its cultural relations enterprise, identified inter-American films, radio, news, and educational projects as priorities for any program. The full scale of what the CIAA achieved (or did not achieve) in its major divisions is the focus of the chapters that follow.

Chapter Two

ON SCREEN   The Motion Picture Division

> Of the three arms of psychological warfare—radio, news, and movies—the latter, from my point of view, has by far the greatest potentialities as it combines the impact of sight and sound. . . . [Film] is an industry that stands ready to produce the most potent instrument of war possessed by any nation in the world.
>
> Nelson A. Rockefeller to John Hay Whitney, May 1, 1942

Hollywood's Latin American Images

The popularity of 1930s Latin music in the United States was reflected in pre–World War II movies such as *Flying down to Rio* (Thornton Freeland, 1933), *In Caliente* (Lloyd Bacon, 1935), *Rumba* (Marion Gering, 1935), *La Conga Nights* (Lew Landers, 1940), and *Down Argentine Way* (Irving Cummings, 1940). But as critic Allen L. Woll and others have noted, the screen image of Latin America and its people was all too often demeaning, despite censorship by Joseph Breen's Production Code Administration (PCA) of negative racial and ethnic characterizations. At least two films, MGM's *Cuban Love Song* (W. S. Van Dyke, 1931), a musical featuring Lawrence Tibbett, Lupe Vélez, and Jimmy Durante that made "The Peanut Vendor" a hit tune in the United States, and RKO's *Girl of the Rio* (Herbert Brenon, 1932), a melodrama starring Dolores Del Río, Leo Carrillo, and Norman Foster, were so offensive to Cubans and Mexicans, respectively, that their governments demanded their suppression (Woll, 33). Writing from the American embassy in Buenos Aires, attaché Joe D. Walstrom reported that *Down Argentine Way*, the movie that made Betty Grable a star and introduced Carmen Miranda to U.S. audiences, still had not been exhibited because of its many ridiculous and disturbing images:

> Henry Stephenson is cast as a rich race-horse owner with an atrocious adopted dialect. . . . Don Ameche does a rumba in Spanish with castanets and talks about orchids, as rare in Argentina as they are in New York. Betty Grable does a conga with bumps. . . . The Nicholas Brothers do a tap dance in awful Spanish and add to the

Argentine impression that all Yanquis think they [the Argentines] are Indians or Africans. A colored person is seen in B.A. [Buenos Aires] as often as a Hindu in Los Angeles. . . . There are jokes like—"Whenever ten Argentines get together there's a horse race."[1]

According to historian Alfred Charles Richard Jr., six stereotypes of Latin America were rooted in the U.S. popular consciousness in the period prior to World War II: the banana republic with its wild revolutionaries; the Argentine tango dancer and gaucho; the jungle with its savages and deadly wildlife; the Panama Canal—oasis of civilization in a wild, tropical region; Devil's Island; and the exotic and sensual Caribbean (xxiii). Once the war began, the Motion Picture Society for the Americas worked to address this situation by producing movies that showcased Latin America's modernity and white middle class. The MPSA recognized that a light-skinned, sophisticated image appealed to Latin America's business elite who controlled the distribution of Hollywood films in their countries (O'Neill, 360).[2]

In 1942, at the CIAA's urging, Breen's PCA hired Cuban American Addison Durland to vet all scripts with Latin American subject matter—an oversight afforded no other ethnic or minority group in the history of Hollywood (Richard, xxviii). Critic Brian O'Neill contends that under Durland's supervision negative stereotypes of Latin Americans as greasers, bandits, and prostitutes were simply replaced with another, less obvious stereotype of a light-skinned, urbane people—although that image actually dates back to the silent period, with "Latin lovers" Ramon Novarro, Gilbert Roland, and Antonio Moreno. In 1933 *Photoplay* proclaimed Dolores Del Río to be the "most perfect feminine figure in Hollywood," praising her ivory-colored complexion, Spanish ancestry, and convent education—traits that seemed to belie her Mexican heritage.[3]

With the loss of European and Asian markets after Pearl Harbor, the region's more than five thousand movie theaters became not only venues for propaganda but also a major source of revenue for Hollywood. To bolster wartime commercial and political success, the United States moved to assure that most of those theaters complied with the CIAA ban of Axis productions; those that did not suffered financially and often went out of business.[4] At the same time, the CIAA began to monitor U.S. movies that were being shown in the Latin market, aiming to expunge unflattering images not only of Latin Americans but also of the North Americans who were appearing on south-of-the-border screens. The policy inevitably resulted in some heavy-handed, puritanical judgments.

An example of an objectionable film was RKO's *Mr. Lucky* (1943) with Cary Grant and Laraine Day; it was singled out by reviewer Helen Strudwick of

In Caliente stars Dolores Del Río and Leo Carrillo. Courtesy of the Library of Congress, Prints and Photographs Division.

the CIAA Motion Picture Division: "[T]he leading character is a draft dodger who steals exemption cards of dead crew members; he is owner of a crooked gambling ship and attempts to swindle [a] women's war relief organization (composed of silly, ineffective women). It is a travesty of all organization relief members." Actually, this film was a fairly typical Hollywood melodrama about a gambler who falls in love with the relief agent and reforms. Also consider a

June 18, 1943, communiqué from CIAA adviser Herb Golden to Francis Alstock expressing alarm over a typical B-movie titled *Mr. Big*, which deals with wayward youths: "Latin America can have very little regard for our judicial system when no one ever goes to jail in a picture except as a result of a frame-up. . . . [T]his type of film is spreading the idea throughout the world that there are no students in the United States but merely teenage-kids who go to school and college only as a locale for zoot suits, jitterbugging, and the production of amateur musical comedies. . . . Youngsters make fun of classes and successfully manage to evade any study except jazz."[5]

Occasionally, Latin politicians offered objections to the ways their countries were represented. At one point Chileans were alarmed that pretty-boy actor Robert Taylor (instead of Clark Gable) might be cast as their father of independence, José de San Martín.[6] Rockefeller received a more valid critique from Assis de Figueiredo, Brazil's assistant director of the DIP, regarding the Warner Brothers film *Now, Voyager* (1943), with Bette Davis and Paul Henreid. Figueiredo was displeased not only with the character of the "Brazilian" chauffeur, a bubble-headed Italian who speaks Spanish, but also with his dilapidated car, which suggested a less-than-modern Brazil. (In this context it should be noted that prior to entering the war in August 1942, Brazil censored Hollywood films about the conflict, especially when they were favorable to "liberal democracy." In fact, the very word "democracy" was taboo for Getúlio Vargas's authoritarian Estado Novo [New State] and was regularly cut from films.)[7]

The wartime Breen report to the CIAA on the activities of the MPSA contains a long list of Good Neighbor features. Musicals with Latin American scores and artists were popular in the United States and a specialty of MGM. The studio cast popular Cuban bandleader Xavier Cugat and his orchestra in several of these, including *Ship Ahoy* (Edward Buzzell, 1942), *Thousands Cheer* (George Sidney, 1943), *Bathing Beauty* (George Sidney, 1943), *Broadway Rhythm* (Roy Del Ruth, 1944), *Two Girls and a Sailor* (Richard Thorpe, 1944), *Anchors Aweigh* (George Sidney, 1945), and *Weekend at the Waldorf* (Robert Z. Leonard, 1945). Other MGM movies with Latin American themes were S. Sylvan Simon's *Rio Rita* (1942), with Abbott and Costello, John Carroll as a Mexican crooner, and Brazilian dancer Eros Volúsia; Vincente Minnelli's fantasy musical *Yolanda and the Thief* (1945), set in a studio-designed, subtropical, Catholic nation called Patria but populated by no Latin actors; and Richard Thorpe's *Fiesta* (1947), shot partly in Mexico and starring Esther Williams and Ricardo Montalban. The musicals fostered a sophisticated, luxurious image of Latin America while continuing to associate the world south of the U.S. border with rhythm and sensuality—qualities that were almost always subliminally connected to the myth of "primitive" cultures.

Latin American roles were also written into war dramas. Julian Rivero appeared as Miguel González in Columbia's *Underground Agent* (Michael Gordon, 1942); Cuban bandleader and singer Desi Arnaz played Félix Ramirez in MGM's *Bataan* (Tay Garnett, 1943); the Maltese actor Joseph Calleia was (mis)cast as a character named Rodríguez in MGM's *Cross of Lorraine* (Tay Garnett, 1943); and Anthony Quinn played Jesús "Soose" Álvarez in 20th Century Fox's *Guadalcanal Diary* (Lewis Seiler, 1943). Studios occasionally contracted Latin American consultants for films that were set there. The Argentine consulate assisted RKO with *They Met in Argentina* (Leslie Goodwins, 1941); Brazilian propaganda minister Assis de Figueiredo consulted on the Brazilian sailor sequence in Columbia's *My Sister Eileen* (Alexander Hall, 1942);[8] and Peruvian artist Renaldo

Dazzling with color, rhythm and song — lovely Lena Horne in the whirling "Brazilian Boogie Woogie."

GEORGE   GINNY
MURPHY · SIMMS

BROADWAY RHYTHM

"Brazilian Boogie Woogie" with Lena Horne, promotion for MGM film. Courtesy of the Library of Congress, Prints and Photographs Division.

Luza was technical adviser on United Artists' *Bridge of San Luis Rey* (Rowland V. Lee, 1944), an adaptation of Thornton Wilder's novel set in the Andes. In addition to trailers and publicity in Spanish and Portuguese, a special preview of 20th Century Fox's *Blood and Sand* (Rouben Mamoulian, 1941) was arranged for Latin American naval officers who were visiting the United States.

The Breen-MPSA report also contains titles of Latin-themed films that were shelved. These included *Don Q, Son of Zorro*, *Passport to Paradise*, and the Brazilian jungle film *Law of the Tropics*, which Durland rejected because the script used Spanish instead of Portuguese (O'Neill 367). *The Hardy Family in South America* and *Henry Aldrich, Good Neighbor*, featuring Hollywood's most popular film families, were apparently proposed but never came to fruition.[9] Welles's *It's All True* appears on the "shelved" list, though it was aborted jointly by RKO and the CIAA. Originally set in Cuba but deemed by the CIAA as counter to Good Neighbor interests, *To Have and Have Not* (Howard Hawks, 1944) moved its location to Martinique (McCarthy, 370).

Ramon Navarro, Antonio Moreno, Gilbert Roland, and Dolores Del Río were already major Hollywood stars when the war began. With renewed patriotic emphasis on Latin America, efforts were made to attract other Mexican performers to Hollywood. Charro (singing cowboy) sensation Tito Guízar appeared in *Blondie Goes Latin* (Frank R. Strayer, 1941), *Brazil* (Joseph Santley, 1944), the sequel *The Thrill of Brazil* (S. Sylvan Simon, 1946), and *Mexicana* (Alfred Santell, 1945). Guízar's charro compatriot Jorge Negrete, who had appeared in Mexican-U.S. co-productions in the 1930s, was cast in the earlier of two films called *Fiesta* (LeRoy Prinz, 1941). Popular leading man Arturo de Córdova starred in several movies, including *Frenchman's Creek* (Michael Leisen, 1944), *Incendiary Blonde* (George Marshall, 1945), *A Medal for Benny* (Irving Pichel, 1945) and *Masquerade in Mexico* (Michael Leisen, 1945). Other Mexican actors appearing in movies at this time were Cesar Romero, Anthony Quinn, Cantinflas, Esther Fernández, Carlos Ramirez, and Lupe Vélez, star of the popular "Mexican Spitfire" series. The "Queen of Technicolor" and Dominican actor María Montez was cast in numerous adventure films, beginning with *Arabian Nights* (1942), while Puerto Rico's Olga San Juan performed in musicals and the war dramas *Rainbow Island* (Ralph Murphy, 1944) and *The Conspirators* (Jean Negulesco, 1944).

But Hollywood's perception of Latin Americans as a homogeneous group led to miscasting. For example, Tito Guízar (and much later Ricardo Montalban in *Latin Lover* [1953]) played a Brazilian, while "Brazilian Bombshell" Carmen Miranda—who had the greatest success of any Latin actor in Hollywood—repeatedly appeared as a Spanish-speaking character with such names as Rosita,

"Mexican Spitfire" Lupe Vélez, promotion for RKO film. Courtesy of the Library of Congress, Prints and Photographs Division.

Chita, Carmelita, and Dorita. Miranda nevertheless became a symbol of U.S–Latin American friendship; between 1940 and 1945 she starred in nine 20th Century Fox musicals, including *Springtime in the Rockies* (Irving Cummings, 1942), whose "Pan-Americana Jubilee" finale is an explicit if lamentably Hollywoodish tribute to Good Neighbor cultural relations.[10]

The MPSA was involved in dozens of other activities that brought attention to Latin America. In 1943 Breen interceded on behalf of *Traveltalks* producer James FitzPatrick, whose short, theatrical travelogues were distributed by MGM, to request CIAA funding for a series on Mexico; the CIAA loaned documentary footage of Mexico City's airport for a new installment of RKO's popular *Falcon* series of B movies; and 35mm wartime shorts on Rio de Janeiro supposedly convinced David O. Selznick and Alfred Hitchcock to feature the Brazilian capital in the RKO production of *Notorious* (1946). In addition to Good Neighbor film productions, the MPSA sponsored studio tours and receptions for a long list of Latin American visitors that included dignitaries such as former Colombian president Eduardo Santos and Brazil's minister of war and future president Eurico Dutra.[11] The MPSA arranged gala public events, the first of which was a film festival in Mexico City in April 1941. Wallace Beery, Kay Francis, Desi Arnaz, Lucille Ball, and Johnny Weissmuller were among the stars who attended alongside Hollywood film magnates. The public turnout was so large that nearly two thousand officers were placed on duty to watch over the festival and its celebrity entourage.

There had been numerous collaborations between Hollywood and Mexico prior to the war, but the Mexico City festival was the beginning of a special partnership among the CIAA, the MPSA, and the Mexican movie industry. According to a report on a June 15, 1942, meeting of Jock Whitney and Francis Alstock with Felipe Castillo and Enrique Solis of the Coordinating Committee for the Promotion of the Mexican Moving Picture Industry, the CIAA agreed to extend assistance to Mexico in the form of equipment, technical aid, and money through Prencinradio, a clandestine CIAA corporation created in Delaware in 1942.[12] An agreement between Prencinradio and the Bank of Mexico was signed on March 23, 1943, and another agreement was made with the Mexican corporation Servicio Cinematográfico.

The CIAA rationale for creating Prencinradio was to encourage and facilitate friendly relations between Mexico and the United States and to "forestall the development of the film industry there by interests unsympathetic to the U.S."[13] There were other considerations: Mexican features regularly outsold Hollywood films in Mexico, film production in the country was relatively inexpensive, and Mexican movies were popular throughout Latin America.[14] Created to assist Mexican radio programming as well, Prencinradio was never mentioned in U.S. government hearings, and it operated covertly until outed by a May 18, 1944, exposé in the *Wall Street Journal*. By all accounts, Prencinradio enabled the CIAA to influence Mexico's film industry through direct payment, which, in turn, enabled Mexico to surpass "neutral" Argentina, whose industry was struggling because of the U.S. embargo on raw film stock. One might say that Prencinradio provided the gilding for what became the "golden age" of Mexican cinema.[15]

Besides gala events abroad, the MPSA sponsored Latin American film festivals in the United States, where pictures such as Chano Urueta's *El corsario negro* (Black Corsair, 1944), Ismael Rodríguez's *Amores de ayer* (Yesterday's Loves, 1944), and Bob Chust's *O brasileiro João de Souza* (The Brazilian João de Souza, 1944) were shown. (It also arranged a two-day exhibition of German propaganda films made between 1931 and 1941 that had been acquired and analyzed by the MoMA Film Library staff.)[16] By encouraging the use of Latin American music, whose rhythms were already popular with the U.S. public, the MPSA claimed credit in 1944 for the fact that some fifty Latin songs were featured in U.S. films.

Latin American reaction to U.S. popular music, on the other hand, was a topic of concern. A January 20, 1944, cable from Maurice Ries in the CIAA Motion Picture Division to the MPSA noted,

> [I]ndustry musicals not received with great enthusiasm [in Latin America]. Modest popularity of swing in night clubs of Rio de Janeiro and Buenos Aires deceptive as swing actually has had little influence on music of other Americas. Regarded as too strenuous and mechanical. Great preference is for music regarded as "highbrow" in this country. Viennese waltzes, operatic selections are "popular" music equivalent to swing in United States.[17]

The organization invited distinguished Brazilian composer Heitor Villa-Lobos to guest-conduct the Werner Janssen Symphony in Los Angeles—a major musical event that was broadcast to radio stations throughout Latin America.

To support MoMA's film operation, the CIAA bought footage on Latin America from newsreel agencies such as Movietone, Pathé, and News of the Day, as well as the National Geographic Society.[18] It entered into contracts for inter-American shorts with ERPI (Electrical Research Products Inc., which later became Encyclopedia Britannica Films), the American Film Center, United Specialists, and Hartley Productions, among others. By April 1942, just one year into its CIAA contract, MoMA had shipped 962 reels covering 42 subjects to Latin America. By April 1943 the number of subjects had jumped to 101.[19] MoMA prepared English-language versions of Spanish-language features that Rockefeller showed at regular Sunday-night gatherings in his Washington, D.C., residence.[20] According to Cary Reich, these Good Neighbor "culturefests" featured Spanish-language sing-alongs led by Rockefeller, who on one occasion enthusiastically belted out lyrics to a "Mexican ditty" about the Mexican government's expropriation of U.S. oil company properties (210–211).

Flying down to Rio: Redux

Some of the films made in the Good Neighbor period were especially important and deserve more detailed consideration. Unique among Hollywood studio releases, for example, were Walt Disney's *Saludos amigos* (1942) and *The Three Caballeros* (1945), produced by RKO. As we saw in chapter 1, Disney and his staff were commissioned by Jock Whitney to make a goodwill tour of Latin America, where they collected material for a projected series of twelve cartoon shorts. Four of these shorts were ultimately combined to make *Saludos amigos*, which premiered as *Olá amigos* in Rio de Janeiro on August 24, 1942, and shortly thereafter in major cities throughout Latin America, prior to appearing five months later as *Hello Friends* in the United States. The unprecedented opening of a Hollywood film outside the United States was an important Good Neighbor gesture, particularly toward Brazil, which coincidentally had just officially joined the Allied effort against the Axis powers.

Consisting of four animated shorts linked together by 16mm footage of Disney and his staff's travels by plane and on land, *Saludos amigos* has long been regarded as Hollywood's most successful film about hemispheric friendship and a brilliant piece of inter-American propaganda. In his detailed study of the film, critic Richard Schale points out that *Saludos amigos*'s main point was to "make North and South Americans feel comfortable with one another" by accentuating cultural similarities (45). He discusses Disney's use of maps and a travelogue format as devices that entertained and educated film audiences about hemispheric geography (44–45, 49). It should be noted, however, that at the level of its address to North American audiences, Disney's trip fits squarely within an older tradition of representations of foreign expeditions to Latin America dating back to the sixteenth century. Such expeditions persisted into the nineteenth century, when artistic and scientific missions from various nations, including the United States, explored and illustrated New World flora and fauna.

Cartography was central to this colonial exploration, and numerous colorful maps of newly discovered lands were produced and decorated with iconographies. Maps of Brazil featured figures of friendly as well as cannibal Indians, multihued parrots, and the commercially desirable trees known as brazilwood, often in an attempt to promote New World colonization. *Saludos amigos* has much in common with these earlier materials, whose main objective was to call attention to new and "exotic" commodities. The film makes liberal use of colorful, animated maps across which a tiny airplane icon traces Disney's explorations; in addition to lakes and mountain regions, the maps contain tiny cityscapes representing the major population centers as well as two little cows that come to life and scamper about as the tiny plane moves from west to east. Animated cartography turned the unknown worlds, in this case, Argentina, Brazil, Bolivia and Chile, into friendly and potentially profitable allies.

Animated maps with small, moving arrows were a regular feature in Nazi newsreels whose function was to indicate troop movement and conquered territory. As Siegfried Kracauer notes in *Propaganda and the Nazi War Film* (1942), the first German animated maps appeared in *Der Weltkreig* (World War, 1927),

Flying down to Latin America with Walt Disney, promotion for RKO film. Courtesy of the Library of Congress, Prints and Photographs Division.

whose designer, Svend Noldan, remarked on their ability "to give the illusion of phenomena not to be found in camera reality" (155). The propagandistic value of Noldan's maps was particularly evident in *Feuertaufe* (*Baptism of Fire*, 1940) and his own *Sieg im Westen* (*Victory in the West*, 1941), where they powerfully signified Germany's war might (Kracauer, 279). Hollywood recognized the importance of this sort of cartography and incorporated animated maps into wartime dramas such as Warner Brothers' *Casablanca* (1942), *Passage to Marseilles* (1944), and *To Have and Have Not* (1944). As *Saludos amigos* attests, Disney was equally aware of the power of "magic geography." While *Saludos amigos* was in production, Disney's former animator Reginald Massie was designing animated maps for Frank Capra's *Why We Fight* (1942–1945).

Like the maps, the narration in *Saludos amigos* has much in common with the older colonial discourse on the New World. *Ufanismo*, or "exaggerated rhetoric," was the Portuguese word for the ornate language used by navigators and scribes to praise the new lands and attract colonizers and investment. In Disney's film, the off-screen narrator employs a more down-home but no less hyped style, referring to "romantic" and "carefree" South America with its "amazing beauty," "glorious music," "quaint" and "colorful" marketplaces, and "hardy folks." Descendants of the early European artists who were enraptured by the New World, Disney animators are shown hard at work, transforming South American people and places into colorful illustrations.

What most attracted the original cultural and scientific missions to Brazil and elsewhere was the rural interior with its "exotic" animals, plants, and peoples. This is the case with three of the documentary subjects featured in *Saludos amigos*—the balsawood boats and colorful market people of Bolivia's Lake Titicaca region, the mountainous terrain between Chile and Argentina, and Argentina's pampas and gauchos. Indeed the Disney film is remarkable, especially in the context of Good Neighbor propaganda, in its almost complete lack of interest in the modernity of Latin America and its emphasis on a kind of folkloric Eden. The one exception is the final sequence on Brazil, which includes picture-postcard documentary glimpses of Sugar Loaf, Corcovado, and Copacabana beach life as well as several shots of costumed Cariocas dancing samba in the streets during carnival. Described in *ufanista* fashion as "Mardi Gras and New Year's Eve all in one," the carnival is linked with familiar U.S. celebrations but viewed as a panoramic spectacle without much attention to its people. (Technicolor carnival footage was possibly cannibalized from Orson Welles's incomplete *It's All True* minus the close-up shots of black celebrants.)

The film's protagonists, Donald Duck and Goofy, were well known to Latin

American audiences, and their antics as accidental tourists are the source of mostly benign slapstick.[21] Donald's safari-style pith helmet seems odd head-gear for traveling through Bolivia, but it serves to make him amusingly ridiculous as he struggles with a precarious balsawood boat and, later, a recalcitrant dancing llama. Similarities between the U.S. cowboy and Argentine gaucho are the subject of the cartoon segment starring "Texas cowboy" Goofy, who is magically transported from the United States to the pampas across an animated map. Although funny and endearing, "El gaucho" Goofy has none of the action-style bravado or complexity of Florencio Molina Campos's famous gaucho caricatures, which appear along with their creator in a documentary sequence that introduces the cartoon.

After viewing an early version of the gaucho segment, MPSA reviewer Luigi Luraschi, who is in charge of censorship at Paramount, expressed concern about its one-note content: "I don't think the Argentines will be pleased with it and they will be even less pleased after they see what a swell job was done for Brazil."[22] Molina Campos was so unhappy with the Goofy segment that he asked that his name be removed from the film as consultant (Schale, 46). Interestingly, *Saludos amigos* appeared in Argentine theaters not long after Lucas Demare's *La guerra gaucha* (1942), a landmark epic about the heroism of gaucho soldiers in Argentina's struggle for independence and an allegory of 1940s Argentina's need to resist foreign economic colonialization.[23]

Inter-American friendship is the theme of the final segment of the film, in which Donald meets his avian counterpart, José (aka Zé or Joe) Carioca, the umbrella-twirling, cigar-smoking "jitterbird" parrot who becomes ecstatic upon meeting the famous Pato Donald and invites him to "see the town."[24] The animation here is unparalleled in its fantastic transmogrifications of ex-oticized nature. In one shot an animated artist's brush drips dark chocolate sauce over the tops of bananas hanging from a tree, turning them into a giant, pendulous sundae; in seconds, the chocolate-covered bananas split apart to form the long, yellow beaks of tree-nesting toucans. The popular musical scores by Ary Barroso ("Aquarela do Brasil" ["Brazil"]) and Zequinha de Abreu ("Tico-tico no fubá" [Little Sparrow in the Cornmeal]) also contributed greatly to the success of the Brazil segment, which features Donald and Zé strolling through Copacabana, drinking *cachaça*, and dancing the samba—activities that suggest Brazil's relaxed, good-natured atmosphere and soothe the often frantic and bewildered Donald Duck.[25] In the final sequence Donald teams up with another Brazilian, whose animated and silhouetted figure is instantly recognizable as Carmen Miranda. The last animated sequence shows them dancing inside the Urca Casino, the landmark Rio nightclub where Miranda first became famous.

South of the Border with Disney

Although James Agee wrote disparagingly and perceptively in *The Nation* about *Saludos amigos*'s "self-interested, belated ingratiation" (29), audiences in both the United States and Latin America overwhelmingly approved of the film—a remarkable phenomenon given that its mode of address was to a North American audience. It appears to have been embraced in the south because it was essentially a colorful cartoon that appealed in certain ways to the national pride of each country depicted.[26] The film's popularity probably accounts for the fact that, just months after it premiered in the United States, Disney produced a half-hour documentary called *South of the Border with Disney*, a precursor of the "making of" documentaries so common in postmodern cinema. Centering on the Disney company's Latin American tour and artistic "research," this film was shown nontheatrically in many cities throughout the United States.[27] The only cartoon characters to appear in the short are the ones sketched by Disney's staff for *Saludos amigos*. The simple pencil drawings sometimes come to life on screen, as if they were just on the verge of becoming full-scale characters. These include the dapper Zé Carioca, Pedro the airplane, and a dancing llama, all of whom appear in *Saludos amigos*, as well as a tiny armadillo whose armor plates move to the sound of clinking tin cans.

South of the Border shows the Disney crew in eight countries as opposed to the four that were selected for the animated feature. The material on Uruguay, Peru, Guatemala, and Mexico later became the source for cartoon characters and footage that appeared in Disney's live-action and animated feature *The Three Caballeros* and in a few cartoon shorts. Like the feature film, *South of the Border* exudes ufanista prose, rhapsodizing about the size, color, and beauty of Brazil's wild orchids and the victoria regina, whose "individual blossoms are like whole bouquets." Disney highlighted the marvelous and fantastic native species, such as the "strange trees with roots above the ground," the anteater, the tapir, and various tropical birds. Not surprisingly, the parrot, one of the earliest symbols of Brazil, attracted Disney's attention, and Zé Carioca ultimately assumes a place of honor alongside Donald Duck and Goofy in *Saludos amigos*. Large, colorful, animated maps appear at intervals through the film and are festooned with nature icons, an approach in keeping with the colonial vision of Latin America as benign and largely pastoral—a paradise on earth with bountiful natural resources. No less than *Saludos amigos* and the art of the European explorers, *South of the Border with Disney* treats the south purely as a natural spectacle, but it gives less explicit treatment to the value of nature's commodities.

One of the major differences between Disney's documentary and the work of early foreign artists such as the Dutch Albert Eckhout and Frenchman Jean Baptiste Debret, who spent considerable time in colonial Brazil, is his approach to the people. Despite his resounding popularity, Disney seems little interested in the general populace except when people enhance the larger, picturesque setting through some kind of folkloric performance. One of the longest segments in the "making of" documentary shows several Argentine couples in traditional costumes dancing "el gato" and the "zamba"; other performances include segments on bronco-busting gauchos, Bolivians sailing their balsa-wood boats, a processional of solemn-faced Bolivian officials in traditional garb, and Mexican charros on parade.

Disney's approach here differs considerably from those of Eckhout, Debret, and other early artists who were attracted by the different racial types and produced thousands of drawings of Indians, blacks, and people of mixed race. Aside from brief glances of a few Latin artists, such as Florencio Molina Campos and two women who perform Latin dances with Disney and his staff, the film keeps local citizens at arm's length. The single exception is the segment on Argentina, in which an eighty-five-year-old gaucho dressed in his cowboy finery is treated on the order of an alien from Mars. As he sits astride his horse, the camera zooms in on his craggy face and descends for a close-up shot of his right foot, which is raised by a crew member to show the viewer that his leather boots are miraculously seamless. In the next shot, the old man stands like a store mannequin while a crew member removes his felt hat and proceeds to examine it as if it were an ancient artifact.

In an essay on Disney's Latin American films, Julianne Burton-Carvajal comments on this particular scene and its relationship to the segment on animals. As she points out, in his "zeal for appropriating the authentic exotic," Disney makes absolutely no distinction between humans and nonhumans, both of which are treated as objects (135). Humans interest Disney when they are quaint, picturesque, and colorful but not when they are black, which was in keeping with inter-American concerns about featuring blacks on screen. The only close view of a black face to appear in the documentary belongs to a small souvenir doll dressed in the regalia of a prominent Bolivian official.

Indigenous people occasionally appear in the film's segments on Peru, Bolivia, Guatemala, and Mexico, but the emphasis is on their status as models for their handmade and traditional commodities: the "riot of colors" created by their dress and market wares and the "plain, everyday food" that is "displayed artistically" in their markets. As the film's narrator, Disney says at one point, "Everybody agreed that this was the perfect type of research—entertaining and instructive." But the documentary turns everything into a touristic subject for Disney animators. In one scene we are instructed in the "delights" of plowing large, stony fields with oxen and a wooden plow—a sight that Disney hails as one of the most "picturesque" on their Latin American tour.

As an instrument of Good Neighbor propaganda, *South of the Border*, which is aimed almost entirely at U.S. viewers, attempts to convey the friendliness of Latin Americans and their hospitality toward Disney and his staff. Gestures of friendship include a birthday cake served to Disney by hotel waiters, who are invited to partake. Although the off-screen narration emphasizes this show of friendly accord, the waiters look uneasily at the camera as they eat their cake. At another stop in Argentina, we are told that a national holiday has been declared in honor of Mickey Mouse; schoolchildren surround a Disney artist who, in Good Neighbor fashion, tirelessly churns out sketch after sketch of Pluto for their eager hands. Friendship is also implicit in a barbecue held in honor of Disney and his crew on the pampas. Large slabs of meat are sliced and given to Disney as tokens of goodwill.

Early in the film Disney comments that everywhere they went, people gave them material to take back to the United States. The film's final segment turns these gifts into a joke as Disney and his crew are shown passing through customs before re-entering the country. An actor playing a daunted customs agent extracts an impossible number of sketches, paintings, and souvenirs from one small suitcase. When he pulls out spurs, a bridle, and a saddle, he turns to Disney and asks why they didn't pack the horse. A whinnying sound causes the agent to turn back in astonishment as the head of a real horse emerges from the luggage. With the exception of the startled customs agent, everyone in the scene laughs—no one more than Disney, and with good reason: according to Richard Schale, by the time Disney returned to the United States, the National Conciliator's Office had stepped in and resolved the animators' strike that threatened Disney's career, and *Saludos amigos* went on to gross $1.2 million, turning a handsome profit of $400,000 (108).

The Gift that Keeps on Giving: *The Three Caballeros*

In December 1942 Disney and his staff traveled to Mexico to promote better relations between the two countries and to begin preparation for cartoons with a Mexican background similar to the shorts used in *Saludos amigos*. The CIAA authorization for the project reads: "Disney expects to produce two pictures of the 'Saludos' type each year until the market is exhausted for this type of production."[28] In February 1943 the Mexican newspaper *Población* ran the article "Walt Disney nos visita" (Walt Disney Visits Us), accompanied by a cartoon image of a charro-like Disney sitting astride a saddled Donald Duck. The result of this trip was *The Three Caballeros*, which brought together Donald Duck, Zé Carioca, and the Mexican charro rooster Panchito in a combined live-action and cartoon feature, this time traveling from south to north with Mexico City as the final stop.

Initially titled *Surprise Package*, *The Three Caballeros* begins with Donald Duck opening a large box of birthday gifts from his Latin American friends. The first present is a movie projector and screen that provide the means for Donald to watch two cartoons on "Aves raras" (rare birds). In the initial cartoon, a South Pole penguin named Pablo decides to fulfill his dream of a tropical life by sailing his little iceberg-boat north to the Galápagos Islands. The second cartoon follows the adventures of a Uruguayan boy, Gauchito, who stalks a condor and ends up riding a winged burro to victory in a horse race. Other gifts include an animated pop-up book titled *Brazil*, which provides Zé Carioca and Donald entrée to a scenic tour of Salvador, Bahia, and an animated album on Mexico whose picture-postcard images become stops for Panchito, Donald, and Zé on a magic serape-carpet ride. As in *Saludos amigos*, animated maps highlighting themes of travel, discovery, and flora and fauna appear throughout. Folklore also plays a central role. Live-action segments show colorfully costumed couples performing traditional dances to musical accompaniments that include "Bahia" (originally titled "Na baixa do sapateiro" [In the Shoemaker's Hollow]) by Ary Barroso and "You Belong to My Heart," the English version of Mexican composer Agustín Lara's "Solamente una vez," which became a Bing Crosby hit in the United States.

Despite a budget ten times larger than that of *Saludos amigos*, *The Three Caballeros* was panned not only by Agee—"a streak of cruelty which I have for years noticed in Walt Disney's productions is now certifiable" (141)—but also by Wolcott Gibbs, Barbara Deming, and Bosley Crowther, who had praised the earlier film (Schale, 106). Latin audience reception, however, was favorable

because of Disney's popularity there. Brazilians especially liked seeing Carmen Miranda's sister, Aurora Miranda, who appears with Donald on-screen,
but they did not admire the film as much as they had *Saludos amigos*. A main
concern of U.S. reviewers at the time and a concern that continues to preoc-
cupy critics is Donald Duck turned loathsome lothario, an image unlike any

Walt Disney and Donald Duck in the news, in Mexico's *Población*. Courtesy of the
National Archives and Records Administration, College Park, Maryland.

projected in his other films. Indeed, for a Disney picture, this one is unusually sex-obsessed.[29] The ufanista rhetoric used in *Saludos amigos* takes the form of an exaggerated avian libido that looms whenever a live-action Latin woman appears.

First Donald chases after Bahian street vendor Aurora Miranda, who sings and dances as she sells her *quindins* (coconut sweets). Next, he breaks up a traditional dance in Veracruz to perform contemporary U.S. swing and jitterbug with a female performer. In Acapulco he ogles and literally dive-bombs sunbathing beauties who manage to keep him at arm's length; in later sequences he goes after Mexican dancer Carmen Molina and moons over singer Dora Luz. The scene in which Donald pursues Carmen Molina amid phallic cacti arranged à la Busby Berkeley is perhaps the most disturbingly risible moment because Donald acts more like a crazed stalker than a dopey duck. At one point he is so excited that he becomes momentarily oblivious to his surroundings and even kisses Zé Carioca. One critic has called him a "gay caballero,"[30] although the apparent intention of the scene is to suggest that Latin American women are so sexually stimulating to the duck that he becomes delirious.

Compared to colonial texts and its predecessor film, *The Three Caballeros* is caught up less in the portrayal of flora and fauna than in a sort of colonialist fascination with the indigenous female. Colonial documents frequently focused on women, who became not only objects of desire, as in Donald's case, but also the means by which Europeans populated the New World.[31] Unlike the colonial record, however, Disney's film completely erases Mexico's and Brazil's dark and racially mixed populations. Bahia's population is mostly black, and the turbaned Bahian street vendor is an icon of Brazil's slave past, but Aurora Miranda, who plays a Bahian, is white. In fact, all the women in *The Three Caballeros* are white or light-skinned—not unlike the virtually all-white casts in Hollywood movies of the period. By this means, *The Three Caballeros* promotes the idea(l) of Good Neighbor sameness.

Disney Theatrical Shorts

By the end of 1942 Disney had produced more government films than any other director (Gabler, 401). When *The Three Caballeros* was released in 1945, his output included the war feature *Victory through Air Power* (1943) and myriad propaganda shorts such as *Der Fuehrer's Face*, *Donald Gets Drafted*, and *Commando Duck*, which were partially financed by the CIAA.[32] Disney produced a series of CIAA educational shorts on agriculture, health, and literacy, including the highly acclaimed film *The Winged Scourge* (1945) about mosquito control and malaria prevention.[33] Most of these films were made with war needs and Latin America in mind, although they also were seen by and benefited people outside the Spanish- and Portuguese-speaking regions. As Neal Gabler has noted, Disney's educational films may in fact be his most important legacy from the war period (412).

Disney continued to explore U.S.–Latin American cultural relations, albeit in less prominent ways, in animated shorts based on materials from his 1941 goodwill tour. These included *Pluto and the Armadillo* (1943), *Contrary Condor* (1944), and *The Pelican and the Snipe* (1944).[34] After the war, Disney released the "Blame It on the Samba" segment in his compilation-style *Melody Time* (1948), which features Donald, Zé Carioca, and the zany woodpecker-like Aracuan, who first appeared in *The Three Caballeros*. *Pluto and the Armadillo* is built around the tiny Brazilian *tatu* with the charming, clinking armor in *South of the Border with Disney*; the film begins as Mickey and Pluto's Pan American Airlines plane stops for refueling in Belém, the capital city of Pará in the northern Amazon Basin, which the narrator describes in ufanista terms, hyping its "strange and exotic" flora and fauna. The plot involves Pluto's ventures in a nearby jungle and his inability to distinguish his ball from the armadillo, whose defensive, rolled-up posture looks exactly like the toy. Pluto plays rough with the armadillo, which occasionally unfurls, clinks her plates, smiles, bats her eyelashes, and winks at her pursuer.

The film's emphasis on the armadillo's femininity and Pluto's attentions is consistent with the gender politics of *The Three Caballeros*, in which Latin America is always feminized, while male figures symbolize the United States. But these cartoons have the zany transformations of folklore or myth and a more regressive style of sexuality. In one unusual scene, Pluto chases the armadillo underground, then pops to the surface with his head piled high with fruit, à la Carmen Miranda. (Miranda was often extravagantly impersonated by cross-dressing U.S. comics.) Although emphasis is placed on Pluto's rough masculinity, his sudden, androgynous, puppy-dog Good Neighborliness suggests a closeted, "underground" femininity—on the order of the Donald-Zé kiss in *Saludos amigos*. Perhaps to counteract his momentary loss of masculinity, Pluto proceeds to rip apart his ball; but then he fears he has demolished the armadillo instead and weeps enough tears to form a small lake. The armadillo's reappearance is the occasion for a celebration and Good Neighbor friendship. When Mickey calls Pluto back to the plane, Mickey grabs what he thinks is the dog's ball. As the plane takes off for Rio, the armadillo pops up as another "surprise package," and Pluto delights by giving her a fraternal, slurping lick.

In the tradition of his Latin American cartoons, Disney's 1944 *Contrary Condor* opens with a map of the Western Hemisphere showing the location of a condor's nest high in the Andes. This nest is the object of interest for Donald Duck, an eager ornithologist who wears ridiculous Swiss Alpine climbing attire to scale the steep mountain. The map and the condor's origins are the only specific references to Latin America in the cartoon, although the basic plot closely resembles *The Three Caballeros*'s sequence involving the character Gauchito, who pursues an Andean condor. However, unlike Gauchito, Donald is after the female condor's eggs, one of which hatches as he tries to carry the other off. In contrast to many Disney features, *Contrary Condor* has a mother figure who is protective of her young. Believing Donald to be another hatchling, she proceeds to instruct both "chicks" on the art of flying. Donald avoids taking the plunge and skirmishes with the jealous baby condor over the fraternal egg. When Donald gets hold of the egg, he is trapped by the mother, who wraps him and his now-pacified "sibling" in a nighttime embrace. Whether intended or not, *Contrary Condor* seems to suggest that not every Latin American commodity is a gift and, in some cases, is not even up for grabs.

Non-Disney Theatrical Shorts

Disney's CIAA-sponsored shorts constituted only a small portion of the 35mm theatrical "headliners" on Latin American topics that were produced during the war. All the major studios developed short subjects to instruct and entertain audiences about their neighbors to the south, although the largest studios, Warner Brothers, Paramount, and MGM, were especially active in the effort. The CIAA served as consultant on these films, frequently providing research and background materials as well as arranging for field photography in Latin America. But unlike Disney cartoons such as *Pluto and the Armadillo* and *Contrary Condor*, which are still marketed and reviewed and appear on the Internet and DVD,[35] the vast majority of MPSA shorts remain in archival vaults: still in their original form, the many films have yet to be commented on in any way. For the most part, they can be divided into musical short subjects and the travelogue, although a few along the lines of Disney's famous wartime cartoon *Der Fuehrer's Face* are patriotic propaganda about the war effort.

As much as or more than feature films like *Springtime in the Rockies* and *Broadway Rhythm*, the musical shorts emphasized the long-standing relationship between Latin American song and dance and the café society in cosmopolitan centers like New York. A curious example is the 1943 "headliner" *Copacabana Revue*, a Paramount production directed by Leslie Rousch in which a New York nightclub set serves as backdrop for a series of Latin American musical acts. The film employs two Hollywood starlets who carry large placards introducing the different musical numbers. The placards, designed in curlicue script, seem curiously old-fashioned for a nightclub revue, and so are the Little Bo Peep costumes worn by the young women, which contrast blatantly with the jazzy beat of the conga music played by the Cuban group Pancho and His Orchestra.

This strange mix of styles runs throughout the film. Following the fast-paced Cuban number, the revue segues into an Argentine tango performed by a couple dressed in formal attire; in the midst of the number, the image of two gymnasts running, jumping, and tumbling is gradually superimposed over the dancers, and the two couples appear and disappear into one another until the tango is finished. The follow-up act, "Six Samba Sirens," is equally bizarre: wearing picture hats and garden-party dresses, six Hollywood starlets carry fruit baskets around the set as a samba plays off-screen. Although not a Brazilian, singer Juanita Juárez gives a convincing impersonation of one in the film's next musical number; dressed like Carmen Miranda but without the rolling eyes or over-the-top headdress, bangles, and beads, she sings the samba "Aurora" in Portuguese and English.

Hollywood shorts like *Copacabana Revue* and Warner's *South American Sway* (1944)—a café musical stylishly directed by Jean Negulesco that features a swing version of a rumba called "When Yuba Played the Rhumba on the Tuba" and a white starlet performing "Negra baila la conga" (Black Woman Dancing the Conga)—mixed Latin American performers, rhythms, and styles with familiar Hollywood settings and motifs to ensure their success with U.S. audiences. That tango dancing and tumbling have little in common seemed less of a concern than how a slow, sophisticated South American dance might not be sufficiently entertaining unless coupled with a lively, "fun" performance. On the other hand, one could argue that a swing-style rumba or a garden-party samba were Hollywood's way of imagining a truly inter-American form of popular culture, an effect that is perhaps most vividly seen in 20th Century Fox's Carmen Miranda musicals and the repeated pairing of the dark-haired Brazilian with blond stars like Betty Grable and Alice Fay.

Nontheatrical Productions

In a 1943 article published in *American Cinematographer*, Staff Sergeant Alfred W. Rohde acknowledges the technical brilliance of German documentaries, which he argues were powerful weapons in the war of persuasion:

Coming in the guise of entertainment, these films could catch audiences unawares, and subtly implant the ideas their makers sought to spread. Dr. Goebbels felt that it was not necessary to get the foreign public to agree consciously that his ideas were good ones as long as the ideas were presented with realism and cinematic effectiveness. The idea, subconsciously implanted during an "off-guard" moment, was almost sure to take root and grow of itself. This is film propaganda in its most potent form. (11)[36]

To counteract the psychological effects of the well-established and prolific German documentary industry, Rockefeller contracted the MoMA Film Library (founded by Jock Whitney in 1935) to collect and underwrite appropriate 35mm and 16mm documentary films and footage for nontheatrical distribution in Latin America and the United States—a project that began in April 1941 under Film Library general manager and director John E. Abbott and curator Iris Barry.[37] The CIAA-supported project was announced in the *Bulletin of the Museum of Modern Art*'s October-November 1941 issue titled *The Museum and the War*, which included a series of images with captions to show the process of compiling films for exhibition.[38] World War II greatly expanded the use of 16mm, a less expensive stock used with more portable cameras that was introduced in the 1920s for mostly amateur home use. By the 1930s it had become the prime medium for newsreels and educational film production, the latter an up-and-coming industry that tied in perfectly with the CIAA Good Neighbor aims.

Besides contracting with Hollywood studios such as Pathé, Universal, and Movietone for newsreel footage, the CIAA signed agreements with East Coast operations including ERPI Classroom Films (Encyclopedia Britannica Films as of 1943), the American Film Center, March of Time Inc., the National Geographic Society, and the Smithsonian Institution, as well as with individual filmmakers Willard Van Dyke, Frank Donovan, Julien Bryan, and Herbert Knapp, among others.[39] The Motion Picture Division also received contributions to its film program in the form of waivers. For example, RCA waived sound-processing royalties on pictures distributed by the CIAA; the American Society of Composers, Authors, and Publishers waived royalties on its members' musical properties when used in CIAA films; and Columbia, Decca, and Vocalion Records each signed waivers for recorded music.[40] Walter H. Brooks, head of MoMA's CIAA 16mm film distribution, wrote to CIAA adviser William Benton, who was also vice president of the University of Chicago at the time, about other savings: "The film industry gives us everything it has at print cost. The big commercial and industrial film sources contribute the whole job, including prints. We provide prints and soundtracking for defense films and for desirable films that are originally available in English."[41]

In 1943 MoMA's Film Library received a special contract for twenty one-reel, ten- to twelve-minute documentaries on the life, culture, and industry of the United States for Latin American exhibition. The contract involved the Library's many resources, including its technical experts, projection and dubbing facilities, and access to its collection of 100 million feet of film (Miller

Iris Barry and John E. Abbott in the MoMA Film Library. The Museum of Modern Art Archives, New York.

8). Abbott worked with both studio personnel and independent filmmakers to come up with "good ideas and good scripts" that would have wide public appeal.[42] Among those with whom he corresponded was producer and scriptwriter John Nesbitt, whose *Passing Parade* radio program was made into a series of documentary shorts by MGM that appeared between 1938 and 1949. In a chatty, unintentionally amusing note Abbott received on January 31, 1944, Nesbitt refers to editing a shortened version of a film, *Art Discovers America*, for the movie matinee trade and wonders about its viability as a CIAA-MoMA project: "Do you think it would be mutually beneficial to tie this thing in with your culture shop . . . as a partial fulfillment of the Museum of M. Art promotion you've been needling me about? Do you think, further, that we could arrange to release it as one of the poverty-row documentaries in 16mm that we also have on the fire?" He touts the film's propaganda value abroad and proposes a comic introduction to the subject that would show on screen "the most horrible examples of what the U.S. millionaire bought from 1860–1910. Venus with the Alarm clock in her belly. Awful Genre subjects. The interior of the plushy Victorian house, etc." Other parts of the film would focus on changes in the national attitude toward art brought about by institutions such as the MoMA ("This would be your stuff—film shot in the Museum or specially shot for this purpose") and technical improvements in printing and design. Later in the letter, he discusses concerns about potential overlaps with OWI films as well as some progress made on the documentary front:

> I have been wrestling with the Documentary notions we discussed, but am currently filled with unhappiness over the apparent fact that the basic theme of these proposed doccies is precisely that which the OWI is already doing. The American Scene for example. How in the hell can we figure out something fresh and fairly bright if we don't know what is going on with other government inspired outfits?
>
> Despite above situation, I have made progress. Have found two excellent men to aid the work gratis. One a good editor & the other a producer. . . . Fitspatrick [*sic*] (the bidfarewellto beautifulWarsaw man) has said we can have any of his Technicolor outtakes free that we want.
>
> I have five outlines of subjects about ready. But in connection with these am disturbed by the matter first noted above. Can you get a catalog of other gov. stuff so as to avoid duplication?[43]

Among other Good Neighbor initiatives during the war, the Amateur Cinema League and the Harmon Foundation sponsored the film contest "Who Is Your Neighbor?" for the best movie about Latin America by a Latin American. An estimated 26,000 16mm projectors were available in schools and other public and private organizations throughout the United States, but schools and clubs in Latin America had a dearth of projectors, estimated at a little over 100 in 1942 for the entire region. Rockefeller purchased another 130 projectors to increase exhibition potential there; and in 1943 he bought a station wagon to supplement other modes of transportation—even horse and wagon during periods of gasoline shortage—for films showings in out-of-the-way towns in Brazil (Miller and Rowe, 7). Much of the exhibition in Latin America depended on this caravan-style approach, entailing crossing rivers in boats and transporting generators and other contingency equipment for the frequent periods of electrical outage.

In the United States, CIAA educational documentaries had tremendous significance as wartime propaganda,[44] and they were unquestionably a force in the agency's "soft power" program. By 1944 well over four hundred titles were in circulation in the form of "solid documentary films" and entertaining "fillers-in" (Miller and Rowe, 9).[45] In her essay "The Present as Past: Assessing the Value of Julien Bryan's Films as Historical Evidence," Jane M. Loy provides an overview of Bryan's twenty-three Latin American films, among them his much-heralded *Americans All* (1941), the first 16mm documentary produced for the CIAA. Although described by Loy as "not very exciting visually" (117), it was effective as Good Neighbor propaganda. Chief among Bryan's strategies here was shaping an image of hemispheric solidarity, common ground, and shared interests—themes explicit in the choice of the film's title, which became a signal trope in numerous later documentaries. But important historical antecedents to *Americans All*, such as the highly popular travelogues and newsreel shorts about Good Neighbor relations, opened the way for other educational vehicles.

To fully appreciate the work of Bryan and others who traveled south to make Good Neighbor 35mm and 16mm shorts, it is again helpful to view their productions in the context of the tradition of foreign expeditions that were sent to explore, describe, and illustrate New World people and places. Especially in the sixteenth century, when colonization efforts took hold, the Portuguese and Spanish wrote highly favorable accounts of the flora and fauna in their newfound colonies and hinted at the possibility of rich mineral sources. The Brazilian natives were initially described by Portuguese chroniclers as comely, clean, innocent, and prime subjects for Christian conversion; it was only after the colonization process was well under way that images of savages and cannibal acts emerged to justify eradicating rebellious indigenous populations.

Although the colonization process in the United States was distinctly different from that of Brazil and the rest of Latin America,[46] both continents were at

JULIEN BRYAN

Julien Bryan's South American articles and photographs will appear in LOOK in a series beginning January 1. Pathe RKO will soon release a series of 10 short Shorts of his pictures on South America as the best picture record available.

Just Returned from
SOUTH AMERICA
with two great motion picture lectures

"BRAZIL"

20,000 feet of film were shot to cover this great country—3,275,000 square miles—*larger than the United States*. The jungle of the Amazon. Gauchos in the north. 25-story buildings in Rio. Medical schools built with U. S. money. Impact of Pan Air. United States oil and automobile companies. Above all the potential danger of a million Germans in Southern Brazil. First complete story in photographs ever made of their churches, their schools, their factories, even a fully equipped airport and glider school run and controlled by young Germans.

"ARGENTINA"

Which way will Argentina turn—toward Hitler or toward the United States? Bryan's amazing photographs show not only the pampas and the great city of Buenos Aires, but probe deeper. Side by side with the Standard Oil Company, Pan Air, Goodyear, American packing houses, and American motion pictures are the equally open German and Japanese influences in newspapers, theatres, schools, sport clubs, rowing clubs, banks and great business houses, all openly German, and working directly with the German Embassy.

These two films added to his lecture on Mexico make a great trilogy on Latin America. He has just taken pictures of Avila Camacho, the new President.

*See in these
two lectures*

5000
feet of Movies
Actually
Showing
NAZI
Activities
in Brazil
& Argentina

Vividly Illustrated
by Julien Bryan
Hollywood Quality

MOTION
PICTURES

The only complete 35 mm. movies made of these countries in 1940

Poster for "motion picture lectures" of Julien Bryan. Courtesy of Sam Bryan.

one time European colonial territories and share a history of occupation and submission, followed by local rebellions, proclamations, and, in most cases, revolutions that led to independence. (Both continents were also colonized and conquered by exterminating indigenous populations.) Bryan's *Americans All* highlights a part of this shared history of colonization and struggle against oppression, which might also be interpreted as a metaphor for the wartime situation and the urgent need to keep the hemisphere free from Axis infiltration and occupation. As narrator, Bryan pushed home the point that the "twenty independent republics" of Latin America could not depend on European (German and Italian) commerce and that wartime economic well-being and prosperity were best addressed by inter-American trade to be facilitated by U.S. advances in overseas aviation, telephone and radio communications, and other industries—all of which the film promotes as mighty forces in the U.S. economic arsenal to defend the hemisphere.

Americans All is mostly about the need for U.S. audiences to recognize the rich cultural heritage and resources of Latin American countries; it shows that the southern neighbors are far more knowledgeable about northerners and the English language as a result of Hollywood movies, books, newspapers, and visits to the United States. The film introduced renowned artists Cândido Portinari, Florencio Molina Campos, and Heitor Villa-Lobos—all of whom were connected with the CIAA. In 1941 Portinari was commissioned to paint murals for the Hispanic Reading Room in the Library of Congress (where they remain to this day). Gaucho caricaturist Molina Campos worked with Disney on *Saludos amigos* and *South of the Border with Disney*, and composer Villa-Lobos was invited to teach and conduct in the United States.

In his tribute to the Americas, Bryan emphasized the role of young people in the progress and prosperity of their countries and the need for more schools to combat illiteracy and train and educate future generations in the areas of agriculture, heavy industry, aeronautics, and medicine. One shot focuses on the famous Oswaldo Cruz Institute in Rio, a center for tropical disease control, as the kind of modern facility needed throughout Latin America. Not coincidentally, a close-up of the institute entryway prominently features a plaque in honor of the institute's patron, the Rockefeller Foundation. While the film draws attention to issues of poverty, disease, and illiteracy in Latin America, it hastens to mention that there are similarly "backwards" areas in the United States. To offset any image of underdevelopment, the film makes frequent mention of Latin America's major cities, newspapers, and urban nightlife. Bryan adds a bit of humor in drawing other inter-American comparisons in his off-screen narration: "The bolero is the South American yo-yo," and "Debutante balls are as hard to crash in Mexico City as in Cleveland, Ohio."

Bryan's films subsequent to *Americans All* regularly contain commentary to link the North and South. In *Venezuela Moves Ahead* (1942) he points out that the giant Orinoco River is more important to the nation than the Mississippi River is to the United States. In *Colombia: Crossroads of the Americas* (1942) he notes that the country is the size of Texas and Colorado combined and that Colombians see the same Hollywood movies that audiences see in the United States, and he shows U.S. sculptor Jo Davidson at work on a bust of Colombian President Eduardo Santos. We learn in *Montevideo Family* (1943) that the middle class there is as powerful as in the United States, although a Uruguayan family generally has a maid but no car. The film provides still other comparisons, including the active role of women in public life; "familiar foods," such as the ones sold by a man "who once lived in Pittsburgh"; and moviegoing. A shot of a child's bedroom shows a toy stuffed elephant based on Disney's Dumbo atop a chest of drawers.

Unlike Disney and other filmmakers, Bryan was not hesitant to photograph dark-skinned people or to mention the topic of race. In *Venezuela Moves Ahead* he remarks somewhat naively that "there is no racial prejudice in this country," although his comment is clearly directed at discrimination in the United States. In *Colombia: Crossroads of the Americas* he is far more direct in his critique, pointing out that the country is "race tolerant far more than we are, for example, in the United States." He comments on the "new race" in Venezuela resulting from the mixture of indigenous, white, and black populations, and he proudly proclaims, "We are all Americans."

In 1942 the CIAA renewed Bryan's contract based on the high quality of films such as *Americans All* and *Colombia: Crossroads of the Americas*. His films were better than many produced for the CIAA and were widely used in classrooms and by private organizations like the YMCA. Bryan had a top-notch staff working with him that included photographer-director Jules Bucher, who had been part of Bryan's early documentary team in the Soviet Union in the 1930s; writer Miriam Bucher, who had been an assistant to Pare Lorentz; and photographers Francis Thompson and Kenneth Richter (Loy, 107). Bryan narrated most of his films, and their soundtracks featured diegetic music of local origin and nondiegetic music scripted by, among others, a young Norman Lloyd, who as an actor worked with Orson Welles, Jean Renoir, and Alfred Hitchcock. Jane M. Loy notes that the series was placed in more than 150 film distribution libraries throughout the United States and was widely used long after the war was over (109).

However, Bryan's association with the CIAA-MoMA ended on a sour note. Shortly after completing a five-film North American series titled *Small Town, U.S.A.* in 1944, he proposed to MoMA a second five-part series on *Secondary Schools of America* that he negotiated at $100 per subject. With the end of the war, the CIAA-MoMA contract was dissolved, and Bryan was offered $500. He refused the amount as inadequate for the treatments and demanded $1,000 per film to cover the research and scriptwriting. A mediator was brought in, and the dispute was settled in July 1945 in the amount of $2,187.50.[47]

Travelogues

Travelogues were prominent among the hundreds of CIAA shorts, and while some had considerable educational value, many were promotional vehicles prepared by local governments and distributed through CIAA channels. As mentioned earlier, CIAA investment significantly raised the profile of the Mexican cinema through contractual agreements that provided U.S. equipment, production, and distribution aids and technical expertise.[48] A good example of inter-American collaboration was the series of travelogues made by the Mexican government's Office of Tourism and narrated by Hollywood stars Joseph Cotten, Orson Welles, Tyrone Power, and Linda Darnell, among others.[49]

Directed at U.S. audiences to promote Mexico as a vacation alternative to off-limits Europe, the travelogues tended to focus on major metropolitan areas and large states. They emphasized a union of the traditional and the modern—what Alex Saragoza describes in the article "The Selling of Mexico: Tourism and the State, 1929–1952" as the country's attempt at the time at a cultural "reconciliation" of the old and the new (104). Consequently, towns on the order of Puebla and the much smaller Tehuantepec and natural sites such as Lake Patzcuaro were also featured. A common theme in *A Town in Old Mexico, Guadalajara, Vera Cruz*, and *Mexico City* is the availability of modern hotels for traveler comfort. After a brief historical introduction to the state, *Vera Cruz* focuses on the Mocambo Hotel, which was built in 1932 and gave its name to the fashionable Latin American–themed supper club that opened in Hollywood in 1941. Shots of the hotel emphasize its beauty and leisurely atmosphere, captured in a scene of a young woman lying in a tree-strung hammock and sipping a bottle of Coca-Cola. A marketing ploy for the U.S.-Mexican Coca-Cola partnership, this shot seems designed to persuade U.S. viewers that Veracruz, or at least the Mocambo Hotel, was a pleasant and "civilized" place to vacation.[50] Most audiences probably missed the irony, but follow-up shots of Jalapa, Ve-

Wartime poster by the Mexican Department of Tourism and the Mexican Tourist Association. Courtesy of the Library of Congress, Prints and Photographs Division.

racruz's capital city, feature "industrious and self-sufficient peasant women" carrying large water jars and hand-washing clothes in a stream.

Here and in other films, women are associated with the natural world (water, flowers) and domestic commerce (market foodstuffs, fashion, jewelry). In *Tehuantepec*, Linda Darnell tells viewers that there are five times as many females as males on the isthmus and that the women's remarkably straight carriage should be emulated by U.S. women. The conflation of women, nature, and beauty underscores the film's "male gaze," which, like Donald Duck's in *The Three Caballeros*, views Latin America as a haven for sensual and even sexual pleasure.[51] Darnell remarks that women are alone during the day while the male population works in fields outside of town where "only the vegetation is violent."[52]

Among Disney's many 16mm shorts is an animated and live-action film titled *The Amazon Awakens* (1944) featuring stops at river ports in Iquitos, Manaus, Fordlândia, and Belém. Ufanista rhetoric expounds on the size of the Basin's flora and fauna, a "botanist's paradise" that is "teeming with life," as well as the immensity of its famous river, which "discharges four times the water of the Mississippi River." To counteract stereotypic images of the Amazon population as a wild, fierce people, the film repeatedly calls attention to their "peaceful" nature. (The only fierce inhabitant encountered is a piranha, known as the "tiger of the Amazon.") Elsewhere the film promotes the modern character of places like Manaus, with its "up-to-the-minute, twentieth-century community," world-class opera house, excellent schools and hospitals, and Athletic Club "for the smart set." Fordlândia, named after Henry Ford and dotted with Ford rubber plantations along the Tapajós River, is another example of a "self-sufficient, modern community." The film goes so far as to suggest that "children from the big city may be envious of these happy, healthy children" of the rubber plantations, whose schools offer "scientifically balanced meals." The emphasis is on nutrition, not education, for these "future conquerors of the Amazon" (rubber tappers).[53]

The John Ford Mission and the Films of Gregg Toland

The strategic importance of Brazil, combined with the relative dearth of footage on the country, resulted in a unique CIAA–Office of Strategic Services (OSS) collaboration for a series of commercial and nontheatrical shorts supervised by one of Hollywood's finest directors, John Ford. Dubbed the John Ford Unit and later referred to in CIAA and OSS documents as the John Ford Mission, this group's initial reports from spring 1943 described its primary objectives as military and economic in nature. Footage would be shot of Brazil's navy, army, and aviation schools, the Brazilian Expeditionary Force—which was in combat training for the Allied movement into Italy—and strategic materials used in the U.S. war industry. Plans also included broad cultural overviews of the nation's capital cities, with emphasis on modern architecture, historic monuments, schools, churches, and scenes of daily life. A CIAA confidential report dated June 7, 1943, described the project as follows:

> Commander John Ford, U.S.N.R., one of Hollywood's greatest motion picture directors, has arrived in Brazil to supervise production of a series of motion pictures which will depict Brazil's contribution to the war effort and the role Brazil is playing for the cause of the United Nations. Associated with Commander Ford in this project will be some of the most important figures in the motion picture industry of the United States, including Lt. Cmdr. Gregg Toland, U.S.N.R., of "Citizen Kane" fame; Lt. Samuel Engel, U.S.N.R., one of the top producers and writers in Hollywood; Captain Bert Cunningham, U.S.N.R., "Ace" newsreel photographer and executive, in addition to a group of ten men who have occupied important positions as motion picture technicians. . . . The story that will be told in these motion pictures will not be a story with Carnival and samba, that [the] U.S.A. knows so well, but the story of rubber, quartz crystal, mica and other critical materials which are so vital to the support of the armed forces. . . . From the Rio Grande [do Sul] to the Far North these films will show every part of Brazilian life and will not only be shown commercially but will be made available in schools and churches throughout the entire United States, and will be supplied for showings in Brazil through the same outlets.[54]

Approved by the DIP and Brazilian Ministry of War, the mission was issued a four-month contract and began filming in early May 1943. Ford, who had just finished shooting scenes of Mexico's military efforts, stayed in Brazil for three weeks, then proceeded to another assignment.[55] With Ford's departure, Gregg Toland, the celebrated photographer of *Citizen Kane* and many other Hollywood pictures, assumed control of the project. Ultimately, the proposed fifteen-week job ran well over a year. After the first contract expired the CIAA assumed full financial responsibility with the expectation that, in addition to newsreel footage and nontheatrical shorts, the mission would produce a number of 35mm shorts to be shown and distributed theatrically by the major Hollywood studios.

Considerable archival documentation exists on the John Ford Mission, some of which describes timelines for approved subjects with occasional new ideas for films; among these was an educational short to be directed at young Brazilian women on the value of a nursing career.[56] Other archival materials

Cinematographer Gregg Toland with director John Ford. Courtesy of the Lilly Library, Bloomington.

reveal concerns and disagreements among those involved in the project. For example, the negative reference to "Carnival and samba" in the document quoted above was probably directed at Orson Welles's unfinished *It's All True*. Welles's experience in Brazil was unquestionably on the mind of his former cameraman Toland, who on September 29, 1943, received a letter from Engel, the 20th Century Fox editor of Toland's Brazilian footage. Engel wrote that he finally understood the overall aims of the CIAA project, which called for mainly 16mm nontheatrical shorts for U.S. and Latin American distribution—an understanding curiously at odds with the CIAA's decision to fully fund the mission based on its commercial potential. In his letter Engel advised Toland to shift from 35mm to 16mm filming, to keep a tight schedule to avoid a "dura-tion" project (undoubtedly another reference to Welles), and to highlight the country's modern manufacturing without overshooting scenes of industrial interiors. With respect to the mission's early decisions to focus strictly on the modern, Engel enjoined Toland not to slight "street types of people—their an-cient ways of travel . . . and the extraordinary things they truck on their heads." He added: "I saw four men carrying a baby grand piano—walking in perfect rhythm. It made quite a picture. I mention this because I believe we both were trying to present the nicer side of Brazil, and to underplay its ancient and poorer side. This is a good practice providing we don't rob our picture of a native flavor."[57]

Toland's barely tempered response to Engel on October 9 emphasizes his deep concern that the CIAA-OSS mission not fail. His eight-page letter forcefully points out the purpose and point of view the Brazilian footage would reflect: "It was our understanding that this mission was to be for the service of the Brazilian Government to present what they wanted to show the United States." As for robbing the pictures of a "native flavor," he commented: "I want to remind you again of [the] promise made regarding that phase of Brasil. We simply must adhere to certain assurances we both have made. I feel that if it is possible to follow scenes of native poverty with scenes of modern improvement, we have a reason. But I do not think we should depict such things as blacks and ancient modes of life and transportation just for a pictorial effect."[58] He argued in detail about the cost and quality advantages of using 35mm over 16mm Kodachrome, and he directly quoted from the project's initial authorization, which referred to both 35mm and 16mm productions.[59]

Brazilian official and public expectations of the John Ford Mission—not to mention the specter of Orson Welles—must have loomed in Toland's mind. He wrote: "[L]et's not forget our committment [*sic*] in this country to the Brazilians. This project simply must not be allowed to swerve far from its objectives. Remember the many, many nights of conversations and promises to Brazilians. And how suspicious [they were] of its completion (because of Orson Welles)."[60]

By January 1944 the number of mission film subjects had nearly tripled from ten to twenty-seven topics. Three separate units were at work at the time: one at the Natal air base, a second covering army troops maneuvers, and a third at the navy yards. On January 11 a rough cut of the mission's first completed film, *São Paulo*, was shown at the State Department. Russell Pierce wrote the following day to his boss Don Francisco in the Radio Division praising the film for its images of a progressive city and nation: "The picture showed modern Brazil rather than primitive Indians, houses with thatched roofs, etc. This reveals the great industrial and architectural developments which have characterized the amazing growth of Sao Paulo in recent years. . . . If other pictures are as well done and as well received as the one we saw yesterday, I should say that the project would be considered a success."[61]

In the meantime, Francis Alstock in Hollywood was increasingly nervous about the mission's ability to deliver more than one film. On February 25 he wrote to Brazilian Division head Berent Friele in Rio asking him to provide monthly reports on the mission's progress and to expedite, if possible, the completion of its assignment. Toland was aware of the surveillance and wrote to Alstock on April 8 providing a description of the progress made on twenty-seven projects, only a few of which were marked completed.[62] In his letter he urged Alstock to extend the mission's work until June, a plea he also made to Ford, who had written to Toland that he needed to finish in Brazil by May 1 to take up another assignment. Toland insisted in his letter to Ford that May 1 was impossible because of everything that needed to be done, including shooting last-minute scenes, packing equipment, and saying goodbye to Brazilian officials and colleagues. He informed Ford that he needed "at least two months rest and possibly hospitalization upon return [to the United States]," adding: "I'm in dreadful shape from many sources. Recently lost eight kilos with a severe cold and at the moment am a perfect 4F."[63] Toland pleaded with Ford to get him a copy of *São Paulo*, and it finally arrived in Brazil a month later.

The screening of *São Paulo* in Brazil was a major event. Foreign Minister Oswaldo Aranha, DIP representatives, and other officials saw the film in Rio in early May, and a few days later Fernando Costa-Federal, the Vargas-appointed governor, and three hundred guests viewed it at São Paulo's Palácio Campos Elíseos. Fourteen minutes long, the documentary is a superlative-filled paean to "the fastest-growing city in the world" and South America's "leading industrial city" blessed with "highly energetic and productive people." Toland was enthusiastic about the film in his correspondence with CIAA officials, and with good reason. It successfully blended visuals and commentary on São Paulo's vital wartime industries and commerce, its history in the struggle for independence, and its cultural riches, alongside scenes of what was described as everyday life. If Toland had any concerns about whether the film delivered what the DIP and others wanted viewers in the United States to see, *São Paulo* resolved those to his satisfaction.

The documentary greatly pleased the Brazilian government and São Paulo officials. In a congratulatory cable to Rockefeller on "the work of Commander Gregg Toland," Costa-Federal wrote: "This is a splendid undertaking which highly recommends the illustrious American technician. For my part I add to the congratulations my sincere thanks for the friendly and generous words which were used to relate to the listeners the progress of the Paulista capital."[64] The poet Guilherme de Almeida, who wrote for São Paulo's *Folha da Manhã*, gave the film a four-star rating, proclaiming that Toland had captured the entire city: "[The] São Paulo that thinks, São Paulo that studies, São Paulo that works, São Paulo that has fun (a little . . .) and São Paulo that hopes . . . that hopes to be able some day to pay back to the good neighbor all the good which has been said about him."[65]

What makes *São Paulo* especially effective as wartime propaganda is its emphasis on the city as a modernist utopia. Large industry exteriors are impressively filmed in wide shots that give them an epic countenance. Their grandiosity contrasts nicely with intimate, engaging interior shots of men and women at work, showing up-to-date machinery, efficiency, cleanliness, and quasimagical engineering achievements such as the transformation of a thin sheet of rubber into a plump, beautifully rounded tire. This is a world in which there is no trace of harsh, alienating labor and no sign of labor versus capital conflicts. The off-screen commentary oscillates between laudatory statistics ("Brazil is the largest coffee producer in the world") and patriotic rhetoric that is sometimes infused with wartime humor; for example, in a sequence on a shell-casing plant, the narrator proudly informs the viewer that "each casing is earmarked for the Axis." The film promotes the role of Brazilian women in wartime industries like the production of surgical supplies and pharmaceuticals. Propaganda that encouraged Latin American women to join the wartime effort fit CIAA objectives, and *São Paulo* shows a good many clean, modern workplaces that appear to be staffed exclusively by women. Stereotypes of the kinds of detailed work women have been traditionally assigned are apparent in close-ups of "nimble-fingered" tasks.

Similar to military documentaries and Hollywood-CIAA productions like *Saludos amigos*, *São Paulo* makes ample use of "magic geography" in its cartographic representation of the city. Aerial shots of the skyline, waterways, a major hydroelectric plant, and an enormous soccer stadium enhance the image of São Paulo's size and modern character. The film's shift from industrial to cultural commentary is seamless: a shot of a series of statues honoring the world's greatest inventors, including Thomas Edison and Brazil's Santos Dumont, leads into a segment featuring elegant neo-baroque façades of some of the nation's oldest churches. Faith and God were popular CIAA film tropes that promoted the importance of religion in the lives of all Americans, but the film's single greatest interest is São Paulo's modernist architecture, which appears in the form of spacious houses, high-rise apartment buildings, and trendy department stores.[66]

The elegant houses described as "typical" in *São Paulo* were actually part of the chic residential area called Higienópolis near the fashionable Jardins district, where embassy officials and other well-to-do residents continue

to live. We see idyllic, well-provisioned schools, libraries, and city parks. Although the OSS and CIAA were intent upon excluding the topics of carnival
and samba, both are mentioned—in particular samba in the soundtrack for
a supper-club scene indistinguishable from a New York café-society setting.
Here Brazilian middle- and upper-class couples are shown dancing in discreet,
ballroom fashion to a samba performed by a white singer and an all-white orchestra. Other "everyday" settings include a Hollywood-style "picture palace,"
the Teatro Municipal for patrons of world-class opera, and "exclusive shops"
for the "smart" set. The narrator ends by telling viewers that the slogan "bigger
and better and more" perfectly captures the Paulista spirit, and he predicts the
city's "brilliant future" in "an orderly and progressive Brazil."[67]

São Paulo elides urban poverty or *favelas*, and not a single black person appears anywhere in the documentary—the exact opposite of what Welles attempted to represent in *It's All True*, in an episode about poor fishermen who
made a dangerous journey to petition the government and originally in footage shot inside favelas. As is generally known, with the emancipation of the

Nelson Rockefeller sipping coffee in Brazil. Courtesy of the Library of Congress, Prints
and Photographs Division.

slaves in 1888 and the birth of the republic the following year, the Brazilian government launched a program of modernization, central to which was a desire to "whiten" the population by allowing only Europeans to enter the country to replace lost slave labor.[68] Although priding itself as a "racial democracy" from the 1930s until quite recently, Brazil continued to aspire to whiteness throughout Vargas's Estado Novo. Vargas disliked the image of a poor and black Brazil that Welles was creating in *It's All True*, and his preference seems to have determined *São Paulo*'s emphasis on white Brazil. This is implicit in Engel's September 29, 1943, letter to Toland, in which he recommended that only "a few types of men, women, and children" (my emphasis) be photographed. Toland's October 9 remark that blacks and poverty were not to be shown—at least not for pictorial effect—is an explicit rejection of Welles's approach and in keeping with the image desired and promoted by official Brazil.

It seems almost certain that *São Paulo* (like other CIAA Latin American–themed shorts) was directed more to Brazilians than to U.S. audiences. A tribute to a major cosmopolitan and industrial center, *São Paulo* expressed U.S. admiration for the city's rich culture and modern economy and was a celluloid hymn to the country as a whole and its Good Neighbor wartime effort. The film served as a template for later John Ford Mission films such as *Belo Horizonte* (1945), about the capital of Minas Gerais, which is touted as the "planned city with a plan." The documentary makes identical use of magic geography, aerial skyline shots, and still exterior shots, often low-angle, of monumental buildings and factories alongside interior views of men, women, and children working for the war effort. Emphasis is again placed on vital wartime materials in the region, especially quartz, mica, and iron ore. The state of Minas Gerais, with Belo Horizonte as its capital, was ranked fourth in world ore reserves, so the film strongly promoted the area's mineral bounty by showing an entire roadway made of iron ore.

Modernity is a major trope in the industrial footage of machines and manufacturing. The narrator takes care to address the absence of mechanized labor in excavation sites, observing that extraction often must be done by hand in order not to damage minerals such as quartz. To illustrate this point, *Belo Horizonte* features a few black workers in excavation and railroad scenes—most likely the descendants of African slaves who were brought to Minas Gerais to extract gold, diamonds, and other precious metals and stones from the fields. Like *São Paulo*, *Belo Horizonte* has shots of amenities supposedly available to the average *mineiro*, including luxurious, mansion-size homes, sleek high-rise apartments, and traveler comforts on the order of the elegant Brasil Palace

Hotel. There are no black children in scenes of Belo's "efficient and advanced schooling," but they are in evidence in shots of the Instituto João Pinheiro, a vocational training center for farming and animal husbandry "to improve the lots of underprivileged boys."

Slated to leave Rio within the week, Toland wrote Engel on May 20, 1944, that the John Ford Mission had shot a total of 160,000 feet of 35mm black-and-white footage and another 21,000 feet of 16mm Kodachrome, which when blown up to 35mm equaled another 52,500 feet of black and white. But much of his letter was about his passion for Brazil: "I do not relish the thought of returning [to the United States] and I have a thought that I may be able to come back here, I hope so. I am so thoroughly Brasilian at this point that our way of life seems rather dull."[69] In a report to Alstock dated February 2, 1945, CIAA official Tom Kilpatrick emended Toland's film figures, stating that after seventeen months of shooting, the mission had produced 182,500 feet of black-and-white film and 28,500 feet of Kodachrome but only six completed shorts. He added that from the unused footage, at most four more films might be made. Reasons for the small number were attributed to lack of studio space and services to make the films, the tendency of unused footage to duplicate what was already in completed films, and Engel's departure from the project in December 1944.[70]

On March 2, 1945, Toland wrote an uncharacteristically short and cheerful letter to Alstock from Phoenix, Arizona, where he was working with Disney on *Song of the South*. Toland talked about putting together a book of photographs on Brazil. He had just learned from the Brazilian naval attaché in Washington that Vargas awarded him *in absentia* the Order of the Southern Cross. However, his primary concern was the CIAA-OSS Brazil project and if and when it might be completed: "I want this project seen through to a finish if at all possible and if there is anything that I can do from this end I'm only to [sic] willing to offer my time."[71]

It is unclear if it was an initiative by the Brazilian government or a collaborative effort with Toland, but an album of snapshots of Brazil taken between 1943 and 1944 was given to Ford.[72] This was no ordinary album: oversized and leather-bound, it bears an official Brazilian medal commemorating the 1889 republic along with patriotic green and yellow satin ribbons. The hundreds of pristine black-and-white pictures are interesting to contemplate as part of the national imaginary that the Brazilian leadership (and Toland) wished to create.

Organized along the lines of a travelogue, the photographs start with images of Rio de Janeiro such as magnificent shots of modern buildings, new housing projects, and pictures of a "Cuban" floorshow at the fashionable Urca Casino.

Each photograph is dated and accompanied by a detailed description in English. For example, one caption reads "December 26, 1943. West side of the Ministério de Educação e Saúde Pública" (Ministry of Education and Public Health), and the image shows Lúcio Costa and Oscar Niemeyer's artful movable shutter arrangements on the building's exterior. Brazil's wartime preparedness is another theme: an "Army and Navy Section" contains several photographs of Brazilian soldiers in simulated war training, and one shows President Vargas reviewing military cadets smartly outfitted in dress-white uniforms. There are numerous aerial tourist shots of Rio's Corcovado and coastline, but the album contains just two beach shots and nothing on carnival.

Like the CIAA shorts, the photographic tour focuses on a modern, largely white, Brazilian middle to upper class at places like São Paulo's Jockey Club, the Fazenda São José [a large horse ranch], and the Edifício Ouro para o Bem de São Paulo, an ultramodern building with a curved design. The yacht club and casino in Oscar Niemeyer's Pampulha project are featured alongside a shot of the Morro Velho gold mine. The largely impoverished Northeast, whose fisherman-protagonists were filmed by Orson Welles just shortly before these photographs were taken, is shown as a land of bountiful natural resources (carnauba trees, cotton), majestic churches, and the home of "Brasilian author of fame" Gilberto Freyre, the only person other than Vargas to be specifically identified in the collection. The Amazon imagery touts the Manaus Opera House, the plentiful orchids, and "one of the widest sidewalks in Brazil." A photo of a riverboat on the Amazon River depicts well-heeled passengers on the upper deck while a steer's carcass dangles pictorially from the side of the boat. Those of lesser means, who ride on the darkened lower deck, are barely visible.

In 1941, two years prior to the John Ford Mission, the CIAA sent photographer Genevieve Naylor to Brazil. Among her hundreds of pictures are a few of an Amazon riverboat that seem remarkably similar to the one in the Ford album, except that her focus was on the passengers and strung hammocks on the lower deck. (See chapter 4.) By the time the John Ford Mission arrived in Brazil, the CIAA was more cautious and selective in representing Brazil as progressive, prosperous, and largely white—images that pleased government officials there and conveyed familiarity and friendliness to viewers at home.

Newsreels

In an essay titled "'Flash from Brazil'—1940s' Newsreels Present Latin America," historian Pennee Bender discusses the 1941 contractual agreements between the CIAA and MGM (and later with Paramount and Universal) for the production of newsreels on Latin America. She distinguishes newsreels that provided stereotypic views of Latin America as exotic, carefree, and carnivalesque from those that emphasized the region's military stability, wartime readiness, and leadership (often through shots of dictators and *caudillos*). The popular news documentary corporation March of Time worked in tandem with the CIAA to cover Latin America, but, as Bender notes, its format was longer and more detailed than most newsreels.

A case in point is *South American Front* (1944) about the roles of Argentina and Brazil in the war effort, half of whose footage came from the John Ford Mission.[73] Bender provides a good summary of this film, which juxtaposed commentary on "Bad Neighbor" Argentina, still neutral at the time, and "Good Neighbor" Brazil, the first South American nation to enter the war against the Axis powers. At about this time an editorial cartoon by Rollin Kirby appeared in the *New York Post* showing an Argentinian lolling unhappily outside a closed door. The sign above the door reads: "Conference of the Foreign Ministers of the American Republics."[74] The Manichean approach was used within the segment on Brazil to provide two opposing views of the country before and after its formal alliance with the Allied forces. Vargas in particular was regarded as "suspicious" and "distrusted by many Americans," while Brazil was a place where the "Army and Navy were sympathetic to Fascism" and "dangerous foreign groups" constituted "hot beds of pro-Axis activity," among them "one million Germans in southern Brazil" whose fidelity to German language and culture was on the order of the "Third Reich." On the other hand, the film praised the "good" Brazil associated with Foreign Minister Oswaldo Aranha, the "great and good friend of the U.S." As a result of Aranha's intervention, the Estado Novo was now regarded as a "benevolent dictatorship if not democratic then progressive and liberal."

The film goes on to tout the various social programs instituted by Vargas such as a doubling of the educational budget, free medical care for all schoolchildren, malaria prevention, government housing, and labor legislation. Its before-and-after narration accompanies a series of strangely ironic images. In representing the "distrustful" dictator the film shows scenes of Vargas smiling and laughing and Axis-sympathizing officers in dress whites talking and laughing over dinner. The "dangerous foreign groups" are represented by shots of a few mothers of Japanese descent with their children, and the southern "hot bed of pro-Axis activity" appears on-screen as small children at play, nuns and children entering a school, and a round-faced man cheerfully gazing from a second-floor window.

"Good Neighbor?" Drawing by Rollin Kirby, January 16, 1942. Courtesy of Lauren Post and Mrs. Rollin Kirby Post.

The follow-up segments on Allied Brazil focused on subjects seen in other documentaries and travelogues. A few shots are from Toland's *São Paulo* (the hydroelectric plant) and *Belo Horizonte* (an aerial view of the city's boulevard and scenes portraying the quartz and mica industries); and the soundtrack for some tourist-style shots of Rio is based on Ary Barroso's lighthearted "Brazil" that was used in Disney's *Saludos amigos*.[75] Where films produced by the March of Time company differ from other newsreel-style programs is in the emphasis on a wartime partnership: U.S. "know-how" and economic support of Brazil in the form of the Volta Redonda steel mill, blueprints for building destroyers, and naval and aviation training; Brazil's wartime contribution of quartz, tires, and other vital wartime supplies (through the U.S. naval base at Natal) across three continents; and Brazil's efforts to keep Allied shipping lanes open in the Atlantic. The film's final comment brings the whole discussion of the "South American Front" full circle but with a surprising recasting of hemispheric defense and wartime enemies: "Backed by a modern military force [the United States], Brazil no longer needs to feel the aggression of any of its South American neighbors [Argentina]."

Educating and Evaluating Audiences North and South

As we saw in chapter 1, distribution and exhibition of nontheatrical documentaries and newsreels were arranged through a system of CIAA-sponsored coordination committees in Latin American and corresponding inter-American institutes and educational bureaus in the United States. Printed film guides were available to accompany screenings and included on-the-spot "tests" to examine the materials' effectiveness as propaganda.[76] One of these guides was prepared for March of Time's aforementioned *Brazil*.[77] It includes a short summary of the film and nine questions to test viewer comprehension. The first question— "Who was the head of Brazil's Government during the war years, and when did he come into power?"—indicates that the guide was written in the immediate postwar period.[78] The guide's response to question one, "Getúlio Vargas. He assumed office on July 20, 1934," is only partially correct. Vargas was Brazil's leader throughout the war, but his term of office began much earlier as provisional president in 1930, following the October revolution, and ended in 1945 after a military coup d'état. The July 20, 1934, date refers to his presidential election following the promulgation of a new constitution.

Beyond this and other classroom-style questions such as "What city in Brazil is noted for innovations in architectural planning?" and "Why might Brazil have been a good spot for Nazis landing in the Western Hemisphere?" the guide suggested more sophisticated topics for "roundtable" discussion possibly by business or other adult groups. These are far from facile and seem designed to shape attitudes about inter-American relations. The following are two examples, numbered four and five, from the March of Time *Brazil* guide:

> On what products do you think Brazilians will concentrate in planning for the future of their export trade? What type of product do you think they will be most eager to import from the U.S.? What, in your opinion, is the case for and against U.S.

business companies setting up plants of their own in Brazil instead of shipping goods manufactured here?

What, in your opinion, are some of the most important contributions Brazil has made to the cultural life of the Americas? How would you compare her contribution in the fields of art, music, literature, and architecture with those of other Latin American countries such as Mexico, Chile, Peru, and Venezuela? (3)

The guide provides a bibliography of news articles and books on Brazil from *Time* and *Life* publications.[79] Despite the considerable attention given to culture in the film, nearly all the readings focus on wartime history, politics, and commerce. One notable exception is a review of Samuel Putnam's 1944 "Good Neighbor" translation of Euclides da Cunha's *Os sertões* (1902, *Rebellion in the Backlands*), also about warfare but of an internecine kind, still regarded as one of the most important works in Brazilian literature.

A similar guide was produced for ERPI's *Brazil (People of the Plantations)* (1943), about the *latifundio* or plantation system of producing coffee and sugar. Instructions include questions to consider and proper names and places as well as words and phrases to recognize before seeing the film (among them "highland terrain," "Latins," and "Santos"); a "test yourself" section with forty-eight true or false statements to be taken after the film; and a section titled "Other Interesting Things to Talk about and Do," followed by a short bibliography of readings directed toward schoolchildren. The film guide is actually more engagingly constructed than the documentary, which has none of the photographic appeal of a film such as *São Paulo*. One of the suggestions involves visiting the local weather bureau to get information on rainfall, temperature, and the seasons in Brazil, which would inform children about the different seasonal cycles in the hemisphere. Another suggests that students try to get samples of important products from Brazil, such as manioc, rubber, cocoa, and brazil nuts and find out how they are produced. Among the more theoretically provocative topics posed for discussion is the standard of living of the plantation worker in the film compared with that of the average American.

Besides educating film viewers through guides such as the two discussed above, the CIAA created "missions" to evaluate Latin American response to the motion picture program. A June 11, 1942, report from Richard Rogan to Rockefeller on the Motion Picture Division activities for Argentina expressed both enthusiasm and caution about theatrical materials directed there. Newsreels covering diplomatic visits and inter-American friendship and solidarity were labeled "outstanding," and special appreciation was given for films that featured Argentine army officers in training in the United States. But Argentine audiences tended to disapprove of newsreels that juxtaposed military shots with bathing-beauty parades, and they were not fans of the comedic feature films with military settings that starred Abbott and Costello or Fred Astaire and Rita Hayworth.[80] In an undated report, José Plaza, a "Latin-American with an acknowledged political background and record," administered surveys and two hundred personal interviews in various large cities and smaller towns in Chile, Argentina, Uruguay, and Paraguay between June 7 and December 7, 1945.[81] Interview questions invariably touched on Good Neighbor relations— for example, "Has the program awakened an interest in the United States? Has better feeling been promoted? Should the program be continued?" (2).

The perhaps predicable outcome of the assessment has all the earmarks of CIAA promotional literature, although the report's main point, "Never have so many Latin-Americans felt the United States closer, friendlier and trustworthier" (3), was undoubtedly more accurate than in any other time in the history of U.S.–Latin American relations. Probably the more important objective of the report was to confirm widespread Latin American support for the continuation of the Motion Picture Division's work, as indicated by interview responses: "The program has accomplished wonders considering its emergency character and its nature as a one-sided initiative; when in the post-war, this turns into a two-sided cooperation we shall have accomplished the full answer"; and "We have welcomed the United States war-time information program, we have not balked at United States propaganda; now let us turn this motion picture war-weapon into a peace-instrument for progressive and cultural education" (5).

The report's author, Plaza, was not hesitant to point out the infelicitous international consequences of curtailing the CIAA motion-picture project:

> From exponents of all walks of life the surveyor obtained the unanimous opinion that the suspension of the program would be of disastrous results to United States–Latin amity. It was unanimously pointed out that the program's best asset, its popular nature, would make suspension of it a continental shock. The ensuing accusation: branding the United States as the typical fair-weather friend would find continent-wide echo. (5)

Assuming (ultimately correctly) that future Good Neighbor relations alone were not sufficient to assure the program's continuation, the report laid out short-term as well as long-term considerations that would specifically benefit the United States, including an assertion that Latin Americans felt the United States was replacing France as the center of Western civilization and that a Latin America shaped by films representing "the American way" would be an important political and economic partner in the Western Hemisphere and world affairs (9). But to maintain the program, there were many needs, including better salaries for operators, new projection equipment and better repair facilities, greater inclusion of Latin American material in U.S. films, an increase in the number of prints, investment in transportation means, and better outreach to Latin officialdom (11).

In 1944, as the war in Europe began turning in the Allies' favor, the Hollywood-based MPSA proudly reported the elimination of derogatory or disparaging images of Latin Americans in U.S. films distributed to Latin America. Its proponents envisioned the region playing a greater postwar role in other parts of the world now that government officials realized the power of Hollywood movies. (This was a time when the major Hollywood studios were still vertically integrated and under government investigation for possible violation of the Sherman Anti-Trust Act; for the moment, it was very much in Hollywood's interest to become a friendly collaborator with government.) The MPSA offered to act as official contractor for all government documentary projects, to provide a research library on matters of joint government-industry interest, and to offer assistance in finding technical experts and authoritative information on foreign countries—thereby ensuring "accurate" portrayals of other nations.[82] But this vision of an international, politically connected, and politically correct MPSA was never realized, chiefly because government interest in culture would not outlast the immediate postwar years, when diplomacy became more militaristic and Hollywood began to collaborate with government in a different way, feeding cold war anxieties about alleged communists in the U.S. culture industry and government—some of whom, it was claimed, had worked with both the movies and the CIAA. The story of that political moment, however, is best reserved for my last chapter.

Chapter Three

ON THE AIR The Radio Division

> We will make radio not only more desirable from the quality of offerings, but more exciting, more varied, more colorful, and hence increase its efficiency in the sale of more sets, the greater use of sets, and as our audience builds, we will have a means of educating, influencing, and informing the peoples of the other republics.
>
> Radio Division report to Nelson Rockefeller, October 4, 1941

Unlike Hollywood movies, U.S. commercial radio was far from an international industry in the years leading up to World War II, and shortwave was used primarily for receiving foreign programs (Fejes, 56, 59). That situation changed dramatically with the war and the emergence of the CIAA and other information agencies, all of which recognized radio's ability to shape public opinion at home and abroad. The CIAA recruited major media figures to build a program of news and entertainment for domestic consumption and to provide Latin American listeners with alternatives to Axis radio—which, along with British radio, had gained worldwide prominence in the post–World War I years. Among the CIAA's chief administrators and consultants were advertising specialist James W. Young, the Radio Division's first director; Karl Bickel of the Scripps-Howard Radio Division; Lord and Thomas ad agency's Don Francisco, who became division head after Young's departure; J. W. G. Ogilvie, director of radio operations for International Telephone and Telegraph; and Merlin H. Aylesworth, the first president of NBC.

In 1942 the Radio Division had four separate bases of operations: the main office in New York City transmitted programs to Latin America in Spanish and Portuguese; a San Francisco base transmitted in English; a small Hollywood office recorded and broadcast a few shows on the West Coast; and Washington, D.C., had the administrative offices and broadcast programs not handled by New York (Rowland, 57). Programming was handled by two different sectors in the division, one for the United States and the other for Latin America. The domestic side was itself divided into two sections: the Contact Group, whose main duties were to deal with advertisers, artists, radio networks, and more than seven hundred local broadcasting stations to secure cooperation in the use of Latin American materials, and the Production Department, consisting of three separate units—for writing, transcription, and music (the last of these also served an advisory function for all U.S. radio shows that broadcast Latin American music).[1]

A War Department study titled "Propaganda Objectives in Axis Radio" provided information on Axis strategies, which were described along geographic lines.[2] In North America, for example, the enemy's chief aims were to ridicule the U.S. Army, criticize Roosevelt, expose supposed lies in U.S. news sources, and discourage military buildup; other objectives included fostering defeatism and confusion, alienating U.S citizens from Britain and the Soviet Union, promoting fascism in the United States, and splitting the United States from China by portraying the Chinese as weak and untrustworthy. The report's account of Axis radio objectives in Latin America was quite long and detailed. According to the report, Axis broadcast propaganda south of the border portrayed the United States as imperialistic, greedy, immoral, and anti-Catholic; it treated Roosevelt as a deceptive leader, repeatedly claimed that the United States advocated communism, and tried to exacerbate historical enmities between Mexico and the United States.

Unfortunately, some of the report's charges were supported by the official record. As Under Secretary of State Sumner Welles had pointed out in his 1935 speech on hemispheric relations, earlier U.S. policies such as the Big Stick and Dollar Diplomacy were wrong-headed interventions that produced resentment and bitterness in Latin America. Welles admitted that the United States was largely responsible for the overthrow of President Zelaya in Nicaragua, where Marines were stationed from 1912 to 1933. He also criticized the U.S. occupation of Haiti and the Dominican Republic and the heavy import tax levied on Cuban sugar—a result of the 1930 Hawley-Smoot Tariff Act—that nearly destroyed the Cuban economy. President Roosevelt's Good Neighbor policy, he argued, was vehemently opposed to those past actions and to any form of U.S. armed intervention in the Western Hemisphere (4–5).

Media historian Fred Fejes has written in detail about Rockefeller's negotiations with independent shortwave radio stations and with NBC, CBS, and other networks to create a larger, more powerful, and united radio communications system rivaling Axis operations. In addition to improving domestic transmission of Latin materials, the Radio Division worked with Latin American affiliates established by CBS, NBC, the Mutual Broadcasting System, and others to produce pro-U.S./Allied programming that would reach every possible citizen in their respective areas.[3] CIAA coordination committees founded in Latin American capitals, whose membership included U.S. expatriate businessmen and other citizens, supported radio programming efforts, while the CIAA funded broadcast training of Latin American personnel by U.S. communications specialists. Like the Mexican film industry, Mexican radio received considerable attention and support. Locally sponsored CIAA news programs like *Noon News Wire* and *La lucha por la libertad* (The Fight for Freedom) were broadcast alongside the highly popular *Amigos de México*, about famous Good Neighbor U.S. figures. *Programa cultural de la Biblioteca Benjamín Franklin*, another local favorite, featured interviews with famous Mexican artists, writers, and scientists. The largest CIAA-listening audience, estimated at one million, tuned in to the news program *El mundo desde México* (The World from Mexico) largely because of the popularity of announcer Félix F. Palavicini, a writer and intellectual associated with the Mexican Revolution.

In 1942 the Radio Division sent thousands of self-addressed paper surveys, or "listeners' reports," to Latin Americans to assess both the reception and quality of U.S. shortwave programming, and hundreds of handwritten responses were returned by diplomatic pouch to the CIAA's Washington headquarters. Besides commenting on individual programs, the respondents invariably noted unsatisfactory transmission in daylight hours. Their reports gave the CIAA at least a partial sense of the tastes and attitudes of the listening audience, though it was by no means clear if the responses were representative of the broad range of Latin Americans. Responses included complaints about programs devoted to women's issues, an objection to a certain "anti-Catholic commentary transmitted from Schenectady," and occasional irritation over "very noisy American music." A man from Santa Catarina in southern Brazil wrote that he enjoyed the Portuguese-language programs from the United States as much as the German radio shows from Berlin. A Carioca listener, on the other hand, disliked "the lies from German Radio"—a sentiment expressed by many others.[4]

Brazil's entry into the war in August 1942 followed shortly after the arrival of Brazilian journalists and radio personnel in the United States to inaugurate a nightly program transmitted point to point, from New York to Rio, and rebroadcast over eighty-nine Brazilian radio stations. Heading this group was Assis de Figueiredo, who, after two months in the United States, sent a letter to Rockefeller on the success and future of U.S.-Brazilian radio collaborations:

I would like to particularly emphasize . . . the fine reaction in Brazil toward the daily program from New York via point to point facilities to Rio at 7:30 P.M. . . . As you know these daily comments are a resume of the war activities in the United States interpreted through Brazilian eyes to Brazil. While these daily programs have been very effective in Brazil, I feel that it will be very helpful to complete the arrangements which are now under discussion for the broadcasting of an additional six fifteen-minute periods weekly from New York to . . . Rio and São Paulo . . . . These proposed programs will not be included in the Official Government Hour. I hope these plans will be completed shortly.[5]

The CIAA responded immediately to Figueiredo's suggestion. Don Francisco's June 1942 report to Rockefeller shows that the second fifteen-minute program titled *Brazilian Series* was on the air by May 25, 1942, and was being broadcast to eight stations in Brazil.

The use of foreign announcers such as DIP journalists Orígenes Lessa and Raimundo Magalhães in shortwave programs from New York was a successful communications strategy that not only strengthened inter-American cooperation but also increased substantially the number of listeners abroad.[6] The strategic importance of Brazil as both the largest country in South America and the only Latin American country to send troops to Europe was repeatedly acknowledged by the CIAA. In contrast, neutral Argentina was targeted for U.S. economic sanctions, although the CIAA employed sympathetic and veteran Argentine correspondents Alejandro Sux and Roberto Unanue in an effort to attract local audiences to U.S. broadcasts.

Starting in November 1942, various broadcasting methods were used to reach other Latin American audiences. Under a joint wartime lease by the CIAA and OWI, private and network companies began producing eight hours of shortwave programming per day in Spanish, Portuguese, and English—a significant increase over the half-hour weekly broadcast available in early 1941.[7] Major speeches by political leaders and special events programs were transmitted point to point for rebroadcast to specific countries by American Telephone and Telegraph, International Telephone and Telegraph, and RCA. Transcribed programs were distributed by CIAA coordination committees to smaller radio stations unable to broadcast live; located throughout Latin America, these committees also wrote and produced their own shows for broadcast on local stations and U.S. network affiliates.

As the agency invested in new and more powerful shortwave facilities, the Radio Division began collecting further information on audiences throughout the American republics.[8] In the beginning the division knew the approximate population and number of radio stations in each country but had no good data about the number of radio sets, the number of sets able to receive shortwave, the size of families, the number of sets per household, the local radio stations with the largest audiences, the listening habits of audiences, or the peak days and hours when listeners tuned in. Don Francisco traveled in spring 1941 to Latin America to assess the overall situation, which he outlined in an April 1941 report.[9] Based on his study, a July 1941 Radio Division proposal was drawn up to encourage radio manufacturers to produce and distribute 850,000 radios to support the estimated 3.2 million sets in Latin America—but this proposal was dropped as a result of Pearl Harbor and a sudden change of national priorities (Maxwell, 82).

On November 27, a *New York Herald Tribune* letter to the editor titled "Brazil's Good Will Needs No Stimulus: Sympathy and Understanding Better than Amateur Envoys" by Henry Hogg, a U.S. resident in Rio, criticized the CIAA for launching into radio program production when so few radio sets were available in Brazil. His deeper criticism was directed at U.S. exporters and banks: "The cause of such few radio sets in Brazil is an important one—the unwillingness of American exporters to grant credits to small importers. Large commercial and industrial concerns are in some cases protected by the Import and Export Bank credit facilities, but the smaller merchant receives no support, and consequently in the past had to turn to the European market for long-term credit"—a situation that, according to Hogg, gave the Axis powers a solid economic and political advantage in Brazil.

In some Latin American locations, mail and house-to-house surveys were conducted by trained specialists from the J. Walter Thompson advertising agency and Electronic Products, as well as by CIAA representatives, including coordination committee members. Prior to the U.S. entry into the war, surveys had tended to focus on the popularity of individual programs drawn from network archives to introduce Latin Americans to life in the United States. After Pearl Harbor, the division shifted into war gear and created new programs to address four basic themes: winning the war, with emphasis on U.S. production efforts and the importance of strategic Latin American materials; winning the peace, based on goals expressed by the Atlantic Charter's "Four Freedoms"; the Axis menace to democratic or quasidemocratic "freedom"; and the ideal of pan-Americanism, which placed great value on Latin America's role in the war effort.[10]

In practice, U.S. ideas of pan-Americanism were conflated with the growing inter-American cultural and educational agenda of CIAA radio. There was a strong belief that mathematical formulas should not be applied to carrying out the four major themes and that the division should be able to modify or eliminate programs in keeping with changes in the direction of the war. On balance, cultural programs were more plentiful than pure entertainment and, with few exceptions, were the most popular.

As well as top-level administrators, the Radio Division recruited some of the foremost names in broadcast writing. Among the contributors were Arch Obo-ler, who had written NBC's popular horror series *Lights Out*; Norman Corwin, who had worked at CBS and was the nation's most respected writer of socially critical radio drama; Clifford Goldsmith, the creator of *The Aldrich Family*; Stuart Ayers, an NBC veteran who wrote the *Land of the Free* series; and distin-guished writers from Dupont's *Cavalcade of the Americas*, including playwright and journalist Maxwell Anderson, poet Stephen Vincent Benét, and Pulitzer Prize–winning novelist Sherwood Anderson. One of the most active among the agency's contributors was poet, antifascist dramatist, and Library of Congress head Archibald MacLeish, who directed the short-term Office of Fact and Fig-ures (OFF) and Committee on Information (COI) and then became assistant director of the OWI. MacLeish wrote and narrated many programs for, among others, *NBC Inter-American University of the Air*, a series that provided informal instruction to listeners to increase awareness of hemispheric relations.

Latin Americans were also an important part of the Radio Division. Chil-ean Daniel del Solar, a writer for March of Time and the Associated Press, who produced scripts for the series *Estamos em guerra* (*We're at War*); Colom-bian George Zalamea, who wrote for *Radioteatro de América* (Radio Theater of America); and Brazilians Orígenes Lessa, Pompeu de Souza, and Raimundo Magalhães, who produced material for the DIP's New York–to-Rio program *Hora do Brasil* (*Calling Brazil*). Undoubtedly the most exciting and flamboy-ant broadcast contributor, however, was Orson Welles; back from filming in Brazil, he wrote and narrated the CBS *Hello Americans* series, which blended instruction with entertainment and featured Hollywood personalities such as Carmen Miranda and well-known actors from Welles's Mercury Theater. Ever interested in better relations with government, the Hollywood MPSA regularly loaned out celebrities for radio dramas, interviews, and special programs—many of which were broadcast from Hollywood. Film star Joan Blondell greet-ed listeners in Portuguese in her December 1942 interview with poet and Bra-zilian Consul Raul Bopp, while Welles was busy writing and broadcasting *Hello Americans* from the same West Coast office.[11]

Library of Congress director Archibald MacLeish. Courtesy of the Library of Congress,
Prints and Photographs Division.

Wartime Dramas and News Programs

One of the earliest and most influential radio programs on winning the war
was *This Is War!* (1942). Written by Norman Corwin and narrated by stars Raymond Massey, Robert Montgomery, and Paul Muni, among others, the thirteen-week series was produced at the urging of MacLeish's OFF and was broadcast by four U.S. networks (Blue, NBC, CBS, and Mutual). The weekly program
was picked up by the CIAA for transmission to the other American republics
and was the inspiration and template for a CIAA weekly Spanish version called
Estamos en guerra, which began shortly after the last airing of *This Is War!* on
May 9, 1942. *This Is War!*'s popularity was derived from a formula that combined uplifting news commentary on war production and military technical
advances with dramatic portrayals of average citizens played by well-known
actors.[12] Sound effects—powerful aircraft motors, machine-gun fire, the clash
of bayonets—gave immediacy to commentary on battles being waged in Europe and the Pacific. The initial February 14, 1942, broadcast referred to these

sounds of war as the "new American slogan," and narrator Lieutenant Robert Montgomery called out to Hitler, Mussolini, and Hirohito, asking how they liked the sound of the U.S. war-machine buildup. Winning the war required that listeners know the facts and "truth" about the Axis powers, whose early protestations about interest in territorial takeovers was revealed to be the "big lie." To give greater reality and force to that lie, actors playing German, Italian, and Japanese leaders were heard professing their support of nonintervention-ist treaties—this in their respective languages and translated into English. A typical program focused on patriotic accounts of what citizens from all ranks of society were doing to support the war effort. In the March 26, 1942, show, for example, John Garfield plays a factory worker who is working as hard as he can and who provides suggestions to increase production efficiency; Henry Hull, a factory owner, has switched from making cash registers to machine guns; and housewife Katherine Locke has joined the workforce while also finding emergency housing for refugees. (The last of these characters is especially sig-nificant. Although there were no women executives in the Radio Division or the whole of the CIAA top administration, the topic of women in the workforce was regarded as vital for radio listeners in the United States and especially in Latin America, where middle-class women tended to stay at home. As we shall see, whole series were designed for Latin female audiences around the theme of women and war.)

Estamos en guerra followed the This Is War! format by employing a narrator, a supporting cast of more than a dozen actors for the dramatized scenes, a full orchestra, and rich sound effects.[13] A typical broadcast brought together head-line news and dramatizations of victories in the war. The December 20, 1942, show, for example, featured news of Allied troop movement into Burma and the government's use of U.S. colleges as sites for military training; added to this were dramatizations of scenes from the African front, including the cut-ting apart of General Rommel's legendary army, and from the Pacific front, describing the exploits of Claire Chennault's volunteer Flying Tigers in China. These shows sometimes featured Latino characters; all were directed toward Spanish-speaking Latin America but were also transmitted locally to Spanish-speaking minorities in the United States. The agency's management was sen-sitive to discrimination against Latinos, particularly in the Southwest, and aware of the need to safeguard against racist acts or state laws that would re-flect badly on the nation. The Spanish-language radio broadcasts offered a way of acknowledging the service of the country's Latino populations and keeping them involved in the war effort.[14]

Other radio series built specifically for the winning-the-war theme were *Tributo a los héroes* (Salute to Heroes), *La epopeya de América* (American Epic), and *La marcha del tiempo* (*March of Time*), all of which were transmitted in both Spanish and Portuguese and designed to make Yankees and Latin Americans appear to belong to the same community. The weekly fifteen-minute *Tributo a los héroes* featured stories about the patriotic deeds of contemporary figures throughout the Americas, most of them famous people but some of them average citizens. For the December 20, 1942, show, for instance, a U.S. citizen named Mrs. Romero was recognized as the first "gold-star" mother in the war.[15] *La epopeya de las Américas* featured stories about heroes but with an emphasis on famous names from history; among those profiled were John Paul Jones, Andrew Jackson, José Antonio Paez (a military leader in the Venezuelan war for independence), and Bernardo O'Higgins (another independence leader, this one from Chile). Connections were repeatedly made between revolutionary wars in North and South America, thus promoting a pan-American ethos and creating an allegory of the contemporary struggle for liberty. *La marcha del tiempo*, adapted from the original NBC half-hour program, featured dramatized news stories about U.S. war production together with reports on strategic military projects such as the construction of the Alcan Highway, which, as part of the transcontinental Pan-American Highway, would serve as a cultural and commercial link between the Americas after the war.

Many shows about the winning of the war were more escapist in nature and aimed at young people or a lowbrow audience. *La marca del jaguar* (Mark of the Jaguar), a typical adventure program, showcased the daring exploits of a Latin American known only as Alberto, who, in the style of Zorro, leaves his distinctive liberator's mark on Axis opponents. The opening pages of the initial March 19, 1943, script (my translation from the Spanish) provide an idea of its straightforward, pulp-fiction style:

> Announcer: *The Mark of the Jaguar!* Wherever his claw prints appear, the enemies of liberty tremble! *The Mark of the Jaguar!*
> (Music)
> Announcer: Columbia Broadcasting System, the Americas' Network [Cadena de las Américas] presents the first episode in the series *The Mark of the Jaguar*. The events and people in this series are purely imaginary. Nevertheless, the action is based on dramatic events that could be happening at this very moment in one or another of the occupied countries in Europe. *The Mark of the Jaguar* represents the unending battle against tyranny and oppression, the history of a people who refuse to be enslaved.
> (Music)

Sound: A telephone is ringing.

Woman's Voice: (Answering testily.) Gestapo General Headquarters. Yes! (More kindly.) Oh, excuse me, Inspector Hans! . . . Today we're all running around like crazy. The Chief is in a foul mood! It seems something has gone wrong. I can hear him shouting from here.

Gestapo Chief: (Annoyed and shouting) I said it and I'll say it again, friend Biemler, this situation can't go on any longer! As Gestapo Chief, I will not tolerate the Mark of the Jaguar making the entire police force of the Reich look ridiculous! Either you capture the man or there'll be a radical cleanup in France! . . . beginning with you!

Biemler: I can't do anything more! I've exhausted all resources. This infernal Mark of the Jaguar has mysterious powers. I give up . . .

Chief: (Furious) And you dare to admit it! This is completely undignified for a son of the Reich! Are we going to announce that the Gestapo is impotent? No, not while I'm Chief! And you'll see! . . . Ludwig! Ludwig!

Ludwig: At your service, Chief.

Chief: Has the order been prepared?

Ludwig: Yes, here it is.

Chief: Read it.

Ludwig: As Chief of this zone, and in the name of our Führer, I ORDER AND COMMAND all Chiefs, Inspectors, and Agents of the Gestapo in France . . .

Chief: That includes you, Biemler!

Ludwig: . . . that using all means and without the least delay, the capture of the criminal, saboteur, and enemy of the Reich known as the Mark of the Jaguar, be tracked down and captured immediately . . .

Chief: Just what you most fear, my dear Biemler!

Ludwig: The Chiefs in each district will be personally responsible for any misdeeds committed in their regions by said individual or his gang.

Chief: Do you now understand, my dear Biemler?

Biemler: Yes, sir.

(Telephone ringing)

Chief: Speak! (Beside himself) What? The Mark of the Jaguar just attacked again? An explosion? . . . A truck destroyed? . . . We'll be out there immediately! (Transition) Did you hear that? That scoundrel did it again!

Biemler: It's incredible!

Chief: Huh! Incredible! I'm going to take charge of this personally! Come with me!

Biemler: At your service. Heil Hitler!

Chief: Let's go! Let's go!

(The sound of motorcycles and sirens)[16]

Although various entertainments focused on the enemy's "true" nature, few were as successful with Latin American audiences as the satiric *El Baron Eje* (Baron Axis, *Barão Eixo* in Portuguese), whose declared purpose was to "explode all Axis untruths."[17] The only CIAA program in Spanish and Portuguese that used the word "Axis" (Radio Division officer John White reported that words such as "Nazi-fascists," "dictators," and "totalitarian powers" were preferred in Latin America),[18] the fifteen-minute *El Baron Eje* featured a muddle-headed Nazi announcer called Eje, possibly modeled on the Axis commentator Don Juan, who makes a fool of himself when he tries to broadcast propaganda, as when he echoes Berlin's insistence that Rommel will hold the line at El Agheila in Libya when it was already widely known that Rommel had defied Hitler's orders and withdrawn his forces.

Another dramatic program, *Contraespionaje (Counterespionage)*, which concerned the unmasking of enemy spies in the United States and was commissioned from the outside by the division, came under internal CIAA criticism. Radio Division staff member Alis de Sola reported in late 1942 to assistant director Russell Pierce that the series was not especially worthy because of its quality. Her description of the December 15 show, titled "La muerte de O'Brien" (The Death of O'Brien), is brief and dismissive: "Melodramatic account of the trapping of a female spy by unorthodox means. Only point of value is the disclosure of the protective coloration so frequently assumed by foreign agents."[19] In another Radio Division report, the show was faulted for giving the impression to long-term Latin American listeners that the United States was "rife with such vermin." The report added: "The situation can be improved if an appropriation is made to cover the cost of original scripts to be written under direction of the Radio Division."[20] The series was nevertheless maintained, although its focus was shifted to the Pacific once victory in Europe seemed certain.

Written to address all four CIAA themes, the first sixteen broadcasts of the hour-long Sunday night *Radioteatro de América* focused primarily on the enemy and, like *El Barón Eje*, was satiric, indeed almost cartoonish. In the show titled "Tragicomedia Roma-Berlin" (Rome-Berlin Tragicomedy), Italian and German leaders, bored with conferring with one another, send their wartime doubles to discuss strategy at a conference held in the Alpine Brenner Pass; instead of deliberating peacefully, the stand-ins heatedly argue and end up shooting across the conference table until the frustrated "real" leaders arrive and intervene. The show emphasizes the two dictators' disregard for one another and Germany's heavy-handed treatment of Italy; it also suggests, on the basis of little evidence, a growing public disaffection toward Mussolini and Hitler within their own countries.

With Allied wins building in the war, *El Barón Eje* underwent a shift in emphasis and tone in 1943, when its dramatizations began to focus on the war's impact on the home front, the personal experiences of fighting men, and cultural topics.[21] Meanwhile, *Mirando al horizonte* (Looking to the Horizon) was among the programs designed to promote winning the peace, a theme that led to such topics as the preservation of democratic institutions, the annihilation of fascism in order to achieve a secure postwar society, and the promotion of enlightened (or at least friendly to United States) pan-American leadership. Winning the peace also meant a focus on improvements in daily living. The educational program *Hacia un mundo mejor* (Toward a Better World) was especially concerned with such issues and offered several shows describing medical advances and the role of science in improving the health of impoverished communities around the world.

The Sounds of Music

Among the programs concerning cultural "ideals" of the Americas, the single most powerful weapon in the CIAA Good Neighbor arsenal was music. As we saw in chapter 2, Latin American rhythms were already popular in East and West Coast café society and in Hollywood musicals of the prewar period. As the international language, music was a fairly inexpensive way to build hemispheric goodwill.[22] Availing themselves of free prewar recordings made by the Coca-Cola Company in Latin America, CIAA musical shows for the U.S. audience required little scripting, although problems arose when U.S. listeners received insufficient information about the music.[23] In a 1943 essay for the CIAA publication *The Inter-American*, music reviewer Joseph R. Hellmer singled out a Chilean folk music program for critique, arguing that while the songs were very good, the lack of commentary left audiences unable to appreciate fully what was being played (39).

Overall, musical programs dominated CIAA radio offerings in the United States and Latin America. During the week of April 26, 1942, for example, 70 of 127 programs, or 55 percent, were exclusively musical—a proportion that remained fairly constant until 1945, when music began supplanting "winning the war" programming. Despite the Good Neighbor rhetoric of sameness and compatibility, there was a sharp difference in the listening tastes of audiences north and south. U.S. audiences enjoyed the big-band sound of rumbas and congas as well as traditional folk music. The Radio Division played to these preferences with programs such as *Rumba Rhythms, Xavier Cugat's Rumba Band, José Bethencourt's Rumba Band, Tunes from the Tropics, Andrini Continentales—Rumbas and Folk Music, Charro Gil Trio,* and *Tropicana.* In addition to Cugat and Bethencourt, other radio big-band leaders were Alfred González,

Pancho (of Pancho and His Orchestra), Maya (of Maya and His Pan-American Orchestra), and Eric Madriguera. Cugat's name and face were already familiar because of his nightclub performances and cameos in MGM "Latin" musicals. The radio broadened his popularity. Dubbed "The Rumba King," he and his band could be heard as often as two or three times a day. Folk music was also popular. Brazilian singer Olga Coelho, a specialist on the subject, had her own program of folk tunes that complemented several other folk broadcasts from South America. Thirteen programs in the series called *Let's Be Neighbors* showcased a range of Latin music recorded in Mexico City.

Latin American preferences for music from the United States tended more toward classical and jazz. One of the most popular shows was *NBC Symphony Orchestra*, whose conductor, Arturo Toscanini, made a widely publicized and acclaimed Good Neighbor tour of South America in 1940. The program showcased Latin American composers and guest conductors, including Brazilian Francisco Paulo Mignone, who was famous for his *choros*, *modinhas*, and waltzes. *The Chicago Symphony* was another listening favorite; it combined performances of composers such as Debussy and Ravel with conductor commentaries that were transcribed and broadcast in Spanish and Portuguese. Cuban-born operatic star Emma Otero had her own half-hour show that was broadcast in the afternoon and evening. Among the popular and jazz programs were *Music of Manhattan* and *Concertos da música popular* (Popular Music Concerts); the latter featured, among others, Duke Ellington and his orchestra at Carnegie Hall. Commercial radio contributed to CIAA efforts with programs on the order of *Your Hit Parade*, which was simultaneously broadcast in Spanish and Portuguese, and *Old Music Hall* with Bing Crosby.

Music was central to U.S. domestically broadcast variety shows that regularly touched on one or more of the war themes. *Brazilian Parade* was a collaborative project of the DIP, Mutual Broadcasting, and the CIAA to promote Brazil's contributions to the war effort. Narrated by Puerto Rican actor and Hollywood star José Ferrer, its weekly musical guests included Tito Guízar, soprano Nadine Conner, and cabaret singer Hildegarde and were backed by a thirty-eight piece orchestra. A hyperbolic yet condescending description of the show by division member William A. Hillpot on June 2, 1943, indicates the degree to which music was presumably the means to achieve friendly relations as well as the chief message-carrier on winning the war: "The music is essentially Brazilian in the hope that our people will learn as a result of the folk songs and ballads of Brazil, a better understanding of the 'little people' of Brazil who are following their leaders so loyally in the world effort to defeat the Axis powers."[24] Building on the success of the Disney film, the U.S. radio show *¡Saludos, amigos!*, hosted by José Ferrer and broadcast at home and abroad, combined Latin music with commentary about Latin Americans' work and sacrifice in the war effort. The broadcast starred major film and radio singing personalities, among them Bing Crosby, Deanna Durbin, Nelson Eddy, Kay Keyser, and mezzo-soprano Gladys Swarthout, backed by some of the country's biggest orchestras. Like the Disney movie, *¡Saludos, amigos!* was popular and widely regarded as a successful tribute to Latin American friendship and generosity.

Wartime Educational Programs

In a sense all CIAA broadcasts were intended to be educational, but from a purely instructional standpoint one of the most original and ambitious CIAA shows, seldom free of dramatized material, was *NBC Inter-American University of the Air*. Its organizing committee of prominent figures included Pedro de Alba, assistant director of the Pan American Union; John Begg, assistant chief of the State Department's Bureau of Cultural Relations; Mary McLeod Bethune, president of the National Council of Negro Women; Willard Givens, former secretary of the National Education Association; Carlton Sprague Smith, chief of the Music Division in the New York Public Library; Walter Lippman, writer and political commentator; and Preston E. James, chief of the Latin American section in the Office of Strategic Services.

Directed by Sterling Fisher, a specialist in public opinion and radio, *Inter-American University* was a distance-education program devoted primarily to topics in history and music. Designed in consultation with educators in the United States and Latin America, the program was broadcast in English and transcribed and rebroadcast in Spanish and Portuguese to supplement classroom instruction throughout the hemisphere.[25] In the words of a promotional flier for Spanish-speaking audiences, its objective was "enseñar delectando," or "to teach while giving delight." Preston James's *Latin America* was the series' official textbook, and listeners could write for program booklets with transcriptions of the shows and bibliographies.

The preview show for *Inter-American University* was broadcast on June 28, 1942, with the program's general supervisor, James Rowland Angell, serving as announcer and backed by the NBC Symphony Orchestra conducted by Frank Black. In his introduction Angell discussed the role of the "ethereal university" for the "spiritual defense of the Americas" as a "permanent agency for mutual understanding based on the finest cultural thinking."[26] Several prominent figures helped to launch the show. Speaking from Washington, D.C., Nelson

Rockefeller talked about the program's objectives, including opening new intellectual horizons and bringing higher education in reach of everyone; he called it a "free university as opposed to those in totalitarian countries whose cultural vitality was crushed and sapped." Assistant Secretary of State Adolf Berle noted the program's high level of scholarship and literacy aims, while J. T. Thorson, Canada's minister of War Services, spoke about the program's ability to bring closer understanding among the Americas. Actor Vincent Price read poetry by Walt Whitman and Archibald MacLeish and was followed by the song "America" performed by the Voices of America choir. A roundtable with U.S. and Latin American representatives discussed the new radio university as a medium for promoting the democratic spirit, raising the living standard of people through education and teaching as entertainment. The program concluded with an announcement of its first series, called *Land of the Free*.

The stated premise for *Land of the Free*'s projected twenty-seven broadcasts was "mutuality" based on four characteristics supposedly shared by the Americas: republican forms of government; democratic principles derived from constitutions or bills of rights; a stake in world economic and political life; and an expressed common desire to maintain political, economic, and cultural independence.[27] The first four shows, or "chapters," laid the foundation for the series. Aired on July 6, 1942, chapter 1, "The Search for Freedom," focused on the Atlantic Charter and New World immigrants who fled from religious and political persecution at home. Such historical dramatizations, as always, serve as allegories of contemporary wartime struggles. For example, comparisons were made among persecuted Huguenots, Irish, French, Germans, and others who escaped to the New World and U.S. residents in Europe imprisoned by the Nazis and then shipped back to the United States through Lisbon.[28]

Chapter 2, "The Few and the Many," begins with the voices of two fictionalized Nazis who scoff at the idea of representative self-government. One of them asks: "Where can we find it today?"—as if democracy were passé. A second voice jubilantly replies: "That, my friend, is a blessing of the Western Hemisphere!"—a declaration followed by a narrative on the colonial struggle for representative self-government in the Americas. "Freedom of the Common Man" was the subject of chapter 3, about Spanish priest Bartolomé de las Casas, who preached against the mistreatment of Indians and later African slaves in sixteenth-century Mexico. Chapter 4, on "Freedom of Trade," begins with a conversation between two Brazilian coffee growers concerned about their product reaching U.S. markets because of enemy ships in the Atlantic. Maurício says to João: "Freedom of trade is the very life of our nations!" João replies:

"We will have it again, Maurício. Some day when the war is over." This brief dialogue serves as the basis for a dramatized account of the history of colonial trade in the New World.

Praised by radio reviewers for its quality and originality, *Land of the Free* was renewed for the 1942–1943 broadcast season. Besides shows on New World discoveries, exploration, and settlement, three other topics were given miniseries treatment. *The British Colonies* looked at charters such as the Mayflower Compact and the lives of colonial leaders Lord Baltimore and Roger Williams. MacLeish narrated the March 14, 1943, program on Lord Baltimore, "The Story of the Founding of Maryland," which dramatized the struggle for religious freedom by Protestant and Catholic settlers. A second series, *Caste and Society*, looked at problems faced historically by women, blacks, and racially mixed or mestizo populations in the hemisphere. A third series focused on Canada, a nation often sidelined in CIAA Good Neighbor projects and rhetoric; it featured topics such as "Canada Comes of Age" and "The Road to Alaska" and was written by Canadian playwright Elsie Park Gowman.

Inter-American University was awarded a Peabody honorable mention for top educational programming in 1943. Its 1942–1943 season featured a new series titled *Music of the New World*. Scripts and scores for the projected three-year program were prepared by John Tasker Howard, curator of the New York Public Library Music Division's Americana Collection; Gilbert Chase, Library of Congress Latin American music specialist; and Ernest La Prade, author of the music primer *Alice in Orchestralia* (1925). At the time, NBC's reference collection was limited to music for daily broadcasting needs. Producing *Music of the New World* required extensive knowledge not just of the field but also of the archives where compositions could be found. The programmers' collective musicological expertise resulted in the playing of little-known compositions as well as older, once familiar but rarely heard songs (Chase, 93–94).

Like *Land of the Free*, *Music of the New World* was organized chronologically, beginning with pre-Colombian material and ending with contemporary compositions. A summary of the first program reads:

> The year is 1100 AD, the scene Lake Titicaca in Bolivia. Pan pipes, drums and other blow whistles of the period will be featured. Llamas, Indians, the civilization of the high Andes before the white man appeared. Possibly a bit of the story of the famous drama, Ollanta, would be enacted. The chief thing, however, is the musical note, and sound predominates from beginning to end.[29]

Other shows focused on "Music of the Catholic Church: 1500 to 1560," "Viceregal Music: 1600 to 1750," "Minority Sects and Their Music: 1735 to 1835," "Italian Opera: 1825," "The Modern Orchestra: 1860 to 1914," and music inspired by "Skyscrapers: 1929 to 1941." To give a sense of the quality and variety of these broadcasts, "Modern Orchestra," for example, presented scores from Antonín Dvorak's *New World Symphony* (1893), which he composed while visiting the United States; Edward MacDowell's "Indian Suite" (1892); Henry F. Gilbert's "The Dance in Place Congo" (1908); and selections from patriotic compositions by Argentine Julius Aguirre and Brazilian Alberto Nepomuceno. One show was dedicated to Canadian music performed by the Toronto Symphony Orchestra. Among the few surviving recordings from *Music of the New World* is a program titled "The Expanding Frontier" about the 1848 Gold Rush. Featuring nearly a dozen songs, it describes how eastern minstrel tunes were picked up by the "forty-niners" and transformed into frontier hymns. One of many examples is black minstrel James Bland's "Carry Me Back to Old Virginnie," a soulful, nostalgic song that evoked homelands left far behind.

Two years after *Inter-American University* was launched, Archibald MacLeish wrote and narrated a new series for the curriculum, titled *The American Story*. Once again, the basic focus was the similarity of the Americas based on shared history of European discovery and exploration, crown-appointed governments, and more general attributes such as the lure of the frontier and the "infection of freedom."[30] A combination of narration and dramatization, the half-hour evening broadcasts used colonial documents from the Library of Congress and other archives as source texts for the scripts. Aired on February 5, 1944, the first show was a template for those that followed. After a solemn musical opening, MacLeish tells listeners that hemispheric differences, such as the lingua franca, are real. But he immediately reverses direction and poses the rhetorical question: "What is it that binds men more closely than speech?" He replies: "Experience . . . our history," a theme that assumes the status of a mantra.[31] MacLeish then draws from colonial sources for a dramatic account of Columbus's life and voyages that serves as a model for what he calls the "single record" of New World discoveries by the French, Germans, and other Europeans in the late fifteenth and early sixteenth centuries.

What makes MacLeish's program compelling is not only the quality of the script but also the performances by him and radio personality and stage and screen star Arnold Moss, who appeared throughout the series. In many ways, this and other series in the *Inter-American University* anticipate *You Are There*, the popular CBS radio and later television show whose dramatizations brought together figures from the past and present. The February 12 broadcast anticipates by several decades critic Hayden White's commentary on the relationship between literary and historical narratives: MacLeish challenges those who say that an American literature has yet to be achieved by referring to the wealth of historiographies (correspondence, reports, and personal journals) written by New World discoverers. An early explorer of Peru who wrote about his experiences, Francisco Pizarro, is one of the subjects dramatized in this show, while Amerigo Vespucci is both subject and "star" of the February 19 broadcast.

A handbook for the series, titled *American Story*, was published in 1944 by U.S. poet and pan-American advocate Muna Lee, who devoted herself to inter-American activities throughout the war.[32] Each chapter begins with a quotation by MacLeish that might be one or two lines or a much longer statement on a subject taught in the series. For example, the section on Amerigo Vespucci opens with MacLeish's "And how do you find the new worlds anyway? By sailing to them? By crossing the mountains? Or perhaps by believing in them?" (Lee, 15). The chapter titled "The Settlement" uses a MacLeish poem that conveys the solemn majesty, simplicity, and quiet heroism of a hemispheric community of "the People."

Whatever was truly built
    the People had built it.
Whatever was taken down
    they had taken down.
Whatever was worn they had worn—
    ax handles: fiddle bows:
Sills of doorways: names for children:
    for mountains:
Whatever was long forgotten
    they had forgotten—
Fame of the great: names of the rich
    and their mottos
The People had the promises:
    they'd keep them.

Muna Lee's fifty-nine-page handbook provided transcriptions of historiographic materials used in the program, a bibliography, and the list "Books for the General Reader." Among the many source texts featured in the handbook are Inca Garcilaso de la Vega's *Royal Commentaries of the Incas* (1609), Bernal Díaz del Castillo's *A True History of the Conquest of New Spain* (1632), Alonso de Ercilla's epic poem *La Araucana* (1569–1589) about the conquest of Chile, and the U.S. Declaration of Independence. Both the radio show and the handbook were tributes not only to Good Neighbor relations at the time but also to a largely unknown history of the Americas that has only recently received the attention that MacLeish felt it deserved.

The Female Listener

On April 29, 1941, Rockefeller received a letter from Heloise Brainerd, president of the Comité de las Américas (Committee of the Americas) in Washington, D.C., an affiliate of the Liga Internacional Femenina Pro Paz y Libertad (International Women's League for Peace and Freedom) in Geneva, Switzerland. Brainerd had been given suggestions by Gabriela Mistral, the Chilean consul in Brazil, for a series of radio programs for and largely about women. A gifted poet, activist, and later Nobel Prize winner, Mistral was deeply interested in international women's issues and asserted that radio could serve what today might be called a protofeminist function, producing a better understanding between the women of North and South America. Her suggestions as summarized by Brainerd, with Brainerd's parenthetic observations, were as follows:

> 1) Short biographies of women here [United States] who are prominent in science, literature, reform movements, journalism (she especially mentioned Dorothy Thompson), and politics; 2) Resumé and criticism of the best books by women, and of women's journals; 3) Messages from U.S. school children. Description of social work done by children here for the children of Latin America (I suppose she refers to the Junior Red Cross); 4) Transmission of religious music of the United States; and 5) Interesting descriptions of the country, especially of rural life and customs, rural schools and health work.[33]

The CIAA eventually responded to Mistral's call with several shows designed for female listeners, some of them highlighting career women or social activists, others concentrating on domestic themes and soap-opera emotionalism. Both the Spanish-language *La tribuna femenina* (1943–1944) and the Brazilian *Página feminina* (Woman's Page, 1944–1945) consisted of war news and interviews with Latin American women visiting the United States. (Interviews for the Brazilian version were conducted by the well-known writer Lúcia Benedetti.) *La mujer de los Estados Unidos* (1945), a fifteen-minute radio segment on the lives of famous U.S. women, profiled figures such as suffragist Susan B. Anthony, novelist Harriet Beecher Stowe, and, most interestingly given that Nelson Rockefeller was the head of the CIAA, teacher and journalist Ida Tarbell, who had written one of the most celebrated muckraking exposés of the century, *The History of the Standard Oil Company* (1904), documenting John D. Rockefeller's ruthless business practices.

Among the first CIAA radio programs broadcast in Mexico, *Charlas femeninas* (Women's Chats) featured the wives of U.S. officials stationed in Mexico who discussed the various wartime activities of U.S. women (Ortiz Garza "Propaganda," 10).[34] *Comentario de Margot Bottone* (1944) was primarily a news commentary show about women's political and wartime activities, reporting on public figures such as Commander Florence Jepson, the U.S. military's first female diplomat, but also on private citizens who had unique and often emotional or sentimental stories; one show, for example, describes the heartrending farewell between a departing soldier and his nearly blind mother. The year 1944 also saw the advent of *Comentario femenino*, a series of twenty shows on topics such as the League of Women Voters, North America's Voluntary Services Organization, and the role of women in postwar peace conferences. Lighter fare was offered in *De las mujeres* (By Women), which featured advice on cooking, beauty care, and topical wartime practices such as clothing conservation and food rationing.

Where women's drama was concerned, the "conversational" dialogue and the personal letter—forms long associated with women's writing—were appropriated by radio to apprise female listeners of current events and the active role that women in the United States and elsewhere had assumed in wartime. Although no fighting took place in Latin America and only Brazilian troops entered combat in Europe, there was a growing demand for labor in the region to produce the raw materials and other items vital to winning the war. Women in the United States, Europe, and Asia were already contributing to that effort in significant ways; CIAA-sponsored shows drove home the point that despite different upbringings and expectations tied to the home, Latin American women were equal in patriotic drive and could do the same.

Among the radio dramas was *Cartas a las mujeres* (Letters to Women), which ran from July 21, 1945, to November 17, 1945. This program consisted of dramatizations of scenes growing out of a supposed correspondence between a young woman in New York and her friends in the United States and other parts of the world. The stateside correspondents included Harriet, a young Washington State housewife whose husband was gone to war and who felt a patriotic duty to take up war work. Other letters arrived from women in war-ravaged countries. Marion, a member of the French underground resistance, wrote: "I sometimes think it's the strength of her women that will carry France to victory. And the women of the Americas will have to work very hard to keep up the pace which is being set by women in France."[35] A communication arrived from Alice, a Philippine nurse who described rescuing a female bombing victim in Bataan; later

Alice joined the local resistance and was rescued by the same woman whose life she saved.

The twenty-six shows of *Diálogos femeninos* (Feminine Dialogues) in 1944 were even more like the popular Latin *radionovela*, or radio soap opera. The shows dramatized the daily lives of two young Uruguayan roommates in New York City: Angélica, a thirty-something student who had lived in the city for some time, and her recently arrived friend, nineteen-year-old Olga. In contrast to most CIAA programs but in no less calculated fashion, *Diálogos* episodes were sometimes as much about the differences as the similarities in North and South. Olga's youthful excitement is quickly tempered when she learns that Angélica has neither a cook nor a cleaning lady—domestic help common to even modest-income families in Latin America. Brought up in a traditional Uruguayan household, Olga is surprised by the number of U.S. women employed in war work and by the many women's organizations that support the war ef-

Ad for a Spanish-language radio program on women in the United States. Courtesy of the National Archives and Records Administration, College Park, Maryland.

fort. Like all soap operas, *Diálogos femeninos* largely centered on friendships and love interests. Inter-American relations are quickly established with the introduction of Kitty, Angélica's recently married U.S. friend, and Kitty's brother Bob, who becomes Olga's admirer and boyfriend. War, however, is always a prominent and recurring theme intertwined with the romantic episodes—as when we learn that Paco, Angélica's Latino boyfriend, is about to be stationed overseas.[36]

Radio Personalities

Like all radio listeners, World War II audiences regularly tuned in to hear their favorite broadcasters. Among the Radio Division's most popular Spanish-speaking personalities was Alejandro Sux, whose fifteen-minute NBC morning news program, *Alejandro Sux habla* (Alejandro Sux Speaks), was broadcast three times a week throughout Latin America. Born in Buenos Aires, Sux was a member of a radical "anarchist" literary movement, and like other modernists (including Archibald MacLeish), he had moved to Paris in the 1920s. His literary career involved both fictional and journalistic writings, the latter of which appeared regularly in Argentina's *El Mundo* and Mexico's *Excelsior*. After leaving Paris to tour the United States and Latin America for a book about the Americas, Sux settled in New York City, where he contributed to the New York–based review *La Nueva Democracia*. Sux's program was especially important because it featured a pro-Allied Argentine during a period when Argentina, under President Ramón Castillo (1940–1942) and his successor, the dictator Pedro Ramírez (1942–1944), refused to declare war on the Axis powers.[37]

A compelling commentator, Sux had a mellifluous voice, a calm yet authoritative demeanor, and, in the words of division head Don Francisco, an "unusual ability at striking the unique in the news."[38] In his first show, on May 17, 1942, he gave a forceful and dynamic talk on why the war had to be won. For his second show, on May 19, he offered his own life story as an example of *panamericanismo*, stressing his European ancestry, his status as a Latin American who called the United States his home, and his pride in being "an American." He emphasized the absolute necessity of inter-American solidarity, telling his listeners at one point: "Don't give up anything (as in Europe) to appease the oppressor." In later broadcasts he combined the personal and political in emotion-filled commentary about the arrival of destitute European refugees in New York, the "abominable situation in Europe," and events such as the 1943 Cairo Conference where the "Big Three" (FDR, Churchill, and Chiang Kai-shek) met to discuss the war against Japan.[39]

Other top radio personalities included Roberto Unanue, former foreign news editor for *La Nación* and a member of Argentina's wing of the Associated Press. His CBS news program from New York provided Latin Americans with concise commentary on world events and was praised by listeners in fan letters to CBS.[40] According to a radio survey conducted between July and September 1943, 72.18 percent of Mexico City radios were tuned to Félix F. Palavicini's locally produced *Interpretación mexicana de la guerra* (Mexican Interpretation of the War).[41] Writer, politician, diplomat, and newspaperman, Palavicini was a famous figure in Mexico. With Emilio Rabasa he founded the daily newspaper *El Universal* in 1916 that carried his pro-Allied editorials during World War I, and he was a radio pioneer. Mexican radio historian José Luis Ortiz Garza has been critical of Palavicini for purportedly selling out to the CIAA Radio Division, arguing that Palavicini reported what the United States wanted Mexicans to hear and that his show's "title was deceptive because there was no such 'Mexican' version of the war" (*La guerra*, 104). Even so, Ortiz Garza acknowledges that Palavicini's program was the most popular and important in Mexico during the war (103).[42]

The much-anticipated New York arrival of Brazil's CIAA-DIP radio team of Júlio Barata, Orígenes Lessa, Raimundo Magalhães, and Pompeu de Souza in August 1941 was covered by *Time* magazine and the *New York Times*, among other publications. Appearing as part of *Hora do Brasil*, the Brazilian government's official one-hour radio program, the five-minute news show had a built-in following.[43] The show spawned a fifteen-minute spin-off for which Lessa, Magalhães, and Souza wrote Good Neighbor scripts about their experiences in the United States and their discovery of U.S. citizens' admiration for Brazil. A major novelist, Lessa wrote and narrated programs about the latest development in U.S. literature and dedicated one entire show to an interview with John Steinbeck. His scripts also addressed wartime realities; in "The Moon Is Down" he described the widespread human suffering in occupied Europe. These and other reports and interviews were later collected in his book, *O.K. América* (1945).[44]

There were a number of up-close and personal programs about Good Neighbor relations. In NBC's *Americanos todos* (Americans All), Argentine journalist Eloy "Buck" Canel, who years later broadcast the Mets and Yankees games to Latin America, used the first-person voice to acquaint Latin Americans with the United States. In his March 3, 1944, show from Washington, D.C., he gave his audience a sense of the nation's bustling capital by describing his arrival at Union Station—a "madhouse of travelers . . . where everyone seems to know where they're going."[45] Trying to figure out how to get to his hotel, he commented on helpful station aids, the cadre of smartly uniformed porters, and the "absolute order" of long lines waiting for cabs. His hotel reservation having been misplaced, he shared his experience of trying to find a room in a city whose hotels are fully booked as a result of a population explosion from a prewar 350,000 to more than a million. Canel was only one of several narrators for this daily and quite popular fifteen-minute program that featured dignitaries and persons of newsworthy interest, all of whom spoke in Spanish on inter-American topics.

Among the many CIAA radio personalities broadcasting in English was NBC newsman Leon Pearson, brother of the famous *Washington Merry-Go-Round* columnist Drew Pearson. Describing himself as "your gringo guide," he talked informally about the contributions of the other twenty American republics to the war and commented on subjects as diverse as Simón Bolívar and the Pan-American Highway. By summer 1943 his transcribed program was being carried by 310 local U.S. stations during peak listening hours. Leon Pearson was following in the footsteps of brother Drew, whose *Washington Merry-Go-Round* syndicated column had been promoting Good Neighbor relations and Brazilian coffee since December 1940. Correspondence between Drew Pearson and Oswaldo Aranha about this program's coffee advertisement was high spirited, and Pearson sent Aranha copies of congratulatory telegrams he had received from Vice President Wallace and Nelson Rockefeller on the show's Good Neighbor initiative. In one letter he wrote:

> In order to meet the needs for Brazilian coffee, I made an arrangement with the best coffee manufacturer in Washington to roast a new brand of "Good Neighbor Coffee—100% Brazilian." I am enclosing a bag which you will note features Brazil and good neighborliness. You will be interested to note the demand for this good neighbor coffee has been even beyond our expectations. I enclose one letter from a wholesale dealer in Virginia ordering twelve hundred pounds. . . . We have also arranged a window display in Washington featuring Brazil and coffee.[46]

One of the most recognized U.S. voices on radio belonged to Orson Welles, whose CBS *Hello Americans* series with his Mercury Theater players was sponsored by the CIAA. As goodwill ambassador, Welles had traveled throughout Latin America for the unfinished *It's All True* and gathered a wealth of information in the region. In the spring of 1942, while still working on the film (or at least hoping to save it from being destroyed by the CIAA and RKO Pictures), he broadcast two radio shows from Rio's most famous nightclub, the Urca Casino, to celebrate the Pan-American Conference being held in Rio and the birthday

of Getúlio Vargas. Welles was a great admirer of the samba, and the real subject being honored on his programs was the music. Besides singer Linda Batista, whose voice he preferred over Carmen Miranda's, Welles introduced U.S.
listeners to the music and to the various instruments such as the *reco-reco*, the
surdo, and the *ganzá* that were used to play samba. Welles was at his playful
best in his "Anatomy of Samba," pronouncing the name of each instrument
in Portuguese and describing in often humorous detail its distinct physical
characteristics.[47]

Back in the States, Welles introduced radio audiences to his *Hello Americans*
series on November 15, 1942.[48] He began the first of the weekly half-hour shows
with what he would often describe as "dramatic license"—in this case, the illusion he was speaking from Brazil, the first stop on a Latin America tour. "An
Introduction to Brazil" was a variation on the pan-American salute that he had
broadcast from Rio with Linda Batista, but with a few important differences.
This time his co-star was "North Americans' South American favorite," Carmen Miranda, who sang—and even induced Welles to sing in Portuguese—her
trademark song, "O que é que a baiana tem," (What Does the Bahian Woman
Have?).[49]

A variation on this script was prepared in Portuguese but never broadcast to
Brazilian audiences. Instead of a single cranky "telephone caller" motivating
Welles's patriotic introduction to the English-language show, the Portuguese
version had two callers who complained about the mistreatment of largely
black and poor samba composers at the hands of whites in Brazil. It is doubtful this script would ever have passed the censors in New York, chiefly because
of the emphasis on race and social class that was pure Welles:

> Voice 2: [The white composer Noel] Rosa often published songs written by others
> there [in the favelas, or slums] without any attribution. And many lesser-known
> composers bought these poor peasants' works for scant sums and then put them
> on the market as if they were their own. I'm a Brazilian and an authority on samba
> and I know what I'm saying. . . .
>
> Voice 1: That's right, Mr. Welles. [And] the musicians were often arrested by the
> police, who were threatened by the noise they made late at night in the city. That's
> why they fled to the hillsides, where the police couldn't reach them.[50]

The Portuguese script has a lengthier discussion between Welles and an
unnamed Brazilian character about the importance of topics beyond carnival
and samba—a discussion that was undoubtedly intended to appease both the
Brazilian government censors and the CIAA. Welles's repetition of the word
"true" during this conversation may have been a subtly playful reference to *It's*

Orson Welles on CBS radio. Courtesy of the Lilly Library, Indiana University, Bloomington.

All True or perhaps his way of calling attention to the subjectivity of truth, especially in relation to government propaganda:

> Brazilian: You are here on a specific mission, right?
> Welles: It's true.
> Brazilian: You're a Good Neighbor ambassador.
> Welles: That isn't quite the truth. There's a more appropriate word to describe me—I am an interpreter.
> Brazilian: And don't you think that it would be a misdeed to give your people the impression that people in this country only laugh and sing?
> [At this point Welles makes a short speech about the importance of laughter in wartime.]

Welles: . . . I'll talk about your beautiful schools, your factories, your magnificent
cities—and I'll do this not just in one broadcast; this is part of a whole series . . .
I hope that this is an explanation.

Brazilian: Yes, it is. And I'm counting on your promise that you won't forget the
rest of Brazil in your broadcast.

Dramatizations of historical events and people were not new to radio, but
in *Hello Americans* Welles was a master at creating a sense of immediacy. The
show featured the Mercury Theater's Edmund O'Brien, Agnes Moorehead, and
Ray Collins, and an important part of its success was the music, which in the
first show was based on the work of Brazilian composer Carlos Gomes and performed by Bernard Hermann's orchestra. The second week's show, "Christ of
the Andes," is a striking example of the programming at its best. At the opening Welles seems to be flying over the 1904 monument built high in the mountains to commemorate the continental commitment to internal peaceful relations. From this unique vantage point, he informs listeners that one can see
"all of the nations of our hemisphere."

Welles's chief theme, freedom from oppression, allowed him to focus on
the South American wars of independence and the heroic deeds of famous lib-
erators, among them Francisco de Miranda, Simón Bolívar, and José de San
Martín. He elaborates the theme through a dramatized "conversation" with a
housewife, a salesman, a truck driver, and a little girl—characters described
only in terms of their occupations or social status. The dialogue morphs into
a quiz, a device often used in CIAA radio programs. While the three adults
struggle to respond to Welles's questions about the Andes, the little girl pipes
in with an amazing list of facts and figures that sound like she is reading an
encyclopedia. A new character called simply "the man with the facts" suddenly
intervenes in the conversation and adds more specifics on the region. Following a dramatic pause, Welles asks his audience, "Do facts tell the story?"—a
question that implicitly, if not ironically, challenges the truth-in-information
approach adopted by the CIAA and other wartime agencies (most notably the
OFF). The show then proceeds to a dramatic recounting of conquests by con-
quistadors and struggles for liberation that defined the character of the Andes
and South America as a whole. At the same time, although to a much lesser
extent, the program repeats the CIAA's mantra on the similarities among the
Americas. Welles compares Bolívar and his army's struggle across the snowy
Andes to the suffering of Washington's troops at Valley Forge, and he ends the
show with a reference to the "common destiny of the Americas."

"Christ of the Andes" was a model for subsequent shows including the final program, on "Pan-Americanism," which aired on January 31, 1943. Once again Welles tests the public's knowledge of a subject, in this case, "Pan-Americanism," which he describes as a "big word and a big idea." The question-and-answer on the topic springs from a story about having discovered as a child his grandmother's treasured souvenir silver spoon from a pan-American exposition. By dramatic license we hear their conversation: "What does pan-Americanism mean, Grandma?" Like the adults in the show about the Andes, the grandmother is vague and uncertain in her reply. Moving forward in time, Welles talks about his schoolboy memorization of information about Latin America, such as the size and population of Brazil—facts that evoke the little girl's encyclopedic recitation on the Andes in the earlier show. Advancing further in time, he adds humorously and perhaps for ironic effect other kinds of knowledge he gained: "Much later I learned about the tango, gauchos . . . then the rumba, Latin lovers, jungles, and tamales . . . hot tamales."

The program's second half is often rambling. Welles briefly reintroduces the CIAA rhetoric on the similarities among the Americas: their shared heritage, traditions, democratic ideals, and destiny. He knew how to deliver phrases like "We cut our teeth on the Declaration of Independence" without sounding corny, but perhaps more importantly in this show, he departed from the standard rhetoric to point out the individuality of the American republics—differences not simply between North and South but among the various nations. He provides a long list that includes the differences between samba and swing and between artists Cândido Portinari and David Siqueiros, as well as the variety in Hollywood entertainment in the form of Walt Disney and Mickey Rooney. Welles sums his attitude by stating with considerable verve: "Thank God for the differences."

Speaking at a moment when audiences were inundated with messages about truth and hemispheric sameness, Welles was refreshingly complex. Although CBS dropped his series after his salute to pan-Americanism—and cancelled the *Ceiling Unlimited* show, sponsored by Lockheed, that he began with the salutation "Hello Americans"—he continued to speak about world affairs in his *Radio Almanac* series and in guest spots for the roundtable-style *The People's Platform*, the dramatized *Cavalcade of the Americas*, and numerous commercial programs hosted by Hollywood stars.[51] He remained a forceful advocate of Good Neighbor relations and was active in Roosevelt's reelection and in war-bond drives, but his association with the CIAA had ended with the loss of *It's All True* and the qualified success of *Hello Americans*.

Travel, Adventure, and Hollywood Entertainment

Hello Americans was only one of several programs to use a travelogue format. NBC's *Pan-American Holiday* was a dramatized series about Don Ricardo, a U.S. professor who becomes infatuated with his Mexican tour guide, Margarita, while on a tour of South America. Their driver Pedro supplies humor and advice as Richard's attempts to woo Margarita are repeatedly foiled by the unexpected appearance of rivals on each stop on the road. In the August 15, 1942, show, Richard's competition is Jorge López, who accompanies the trio to the Tucumán province in northwest Argentina, the birthplace of the country's independence. Discussions of local customs and historic sites are accompanied by musical numbers that include tangos and folk songs. To ease Richard's frustration at Jorge's constant presence, the driver Pedro launches into a romantic song in Spanish about a young girl in love. Margarita translates the lyrics into English for Richard, who is heartened by her attention. In Good Neighbor fashion, everyone joins in the song, and listeners are offered a copy of the lyrics upon submitting written requests to the studio.

Pan-American Holiday* was inspired by an earlier NBC program called *Down Mexico Way*, the brainchild of Vice President Henry Wallace following his 1940 trip to Mexico. The simple story of U.S. boy meets Mexican girl and falls in love is filled with music and song as the young couple travels each week to a different city. A Latin American enthusiast, Wallace promoted songs as an excellent way to learn Spanish. While there is no record of any gains in their language proficiency, listeners liked the music and wrote to local stations for copies of the song lyrics in Spanish with English translations. A March 16, 1942, article in *Time* reported that the previous week's program drew as many as 1,700 requests. A later CIAA report confirmed *Down Mexico Way*'s widespread popularity: "[T]he mail response as a result of these broadcasts has succeeded that of any sustaining feature ever broadcast over the [NBC] facilities."[52]

The success of *Down Mexico Way* and *Pan-American Holiday* prompted a spin-off in Spanish called *Allá en los Estados Unidos* (Over There in the United States). In this show, a young South American named José Zaragosa comes to the United States to work on his musical career and study the language and customs. His guides are Professor Whitlock, a friend of his father's, and Whitlock's niece, Phyllis, who provides the young love interest. Music and song are central to the show as the trio travels to popular tourist sites such as Niagara Falls and Chicago as well as to small, remote towns such as Titusville, Pennsylvania.

Although most dramatic and musical programs were designed with the family in mind, the CIAA also sponsored a children's weekday serial, *Adventures of the Sea Hound*, which combined tales of intrigue on the high seas with lessons for children, including facts about Latin America (an "educational" approach that Welles's *Hello Americans* often disparaged). The fifteen-minute dramatization on the Blue Network was a hit with young audiences and, although initially scheduled for thirteen weeks, ran from 1942 until 1951.[53] Featuring the adventurous Captain Silver, his sidekick Tex, the boy Jerry, and the Chinese scholar Kukai, the program's basic wartime plot involved tracking down spies and other foes of the Americas. A good example is the episode titled "The Envelope." Sailing in the waters off the coast of Guayaquil, the *Sea Hound* has been sent to pick up a physician who has been studying medicinal plants in the Ecuadorian jungle. In the interim, Axis agents have forced Silver's friend and Guayaquil leader Señor López into hiding. López's daughter, María, has brought Silver news of her father's plight and enemy submarine activity in the area. The episode ends just as Silver casts off in the Spray Hound, his powerful auxiliary skiff, to rescue López.

Children's edification in this episode takes two forms: at various junctures Kukai (whose character and voice are reminiscent of Charlie Chan) offers wisdom and morale-building advice in the form of ancient Chinese proverbs such as "He who rejects iron cannot make steel." More obvious pedagogical efforts come in the form of lessons on Latin America woven into the action. In "The Envelope," Jerry mispronounces the word "tomorrow" in Spanish as "manana" instead of "mañana." Pausing in his dramatic rescue preparations, Silver replies:

Silver: "What did you say?"
Jerry: "Manana. That's Spanish. It means 'tomorrow.'"
Silver: (Laughs) "Don't try that on anyone in Ecuador, Jerry."
Jerry: "Why not? They speak Spanish, don't they?"
Silver: "Yes, but you don't."
Jerry: "But I read that."
Silver: "There was a little mark over the first 'n' when you read that, wasn't there? A mark like the letter 's' on its side?"
Jerry: "Yeah, that's right. I showed it to Tex and asked him what it was."
Silver: "Tex wouldn't know."
Jerry: "He called it the lazy 's.'"
Silver: "Well, the lazy 's.' Tex would call it that. Someday I'm going to have to take his cowboy stories away from him and see that he gets different reading. That little mark, Jerry, is called a tilde."
Jerry: "Tilde?"
Silver: "Yes. It changes the sound of the letter 'n.'"

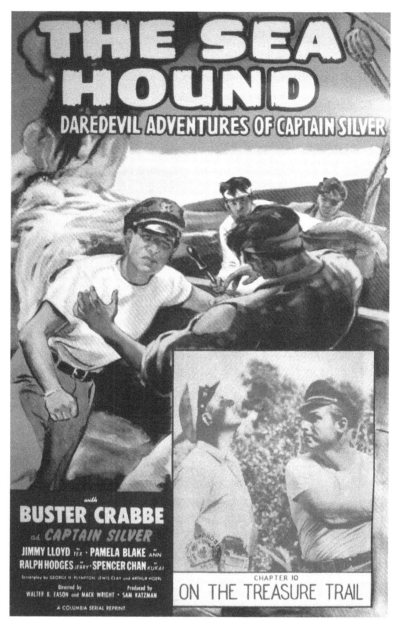

The *Sea Hound*'s Captain Silver on "The Treasure Coast." Poster for 1947 film, in the author's collection.

Jerry: "Oh . . ."

Silver: "It gives the letter 'n' the sound of 'ny.' Instead of saying 'manana,' you should say 'mañana.' "

Jerry: "Mañana."

Silver: "Yes, that's more like it. Now you're on course again."

Jerry: "Mañana. Gee, I'm glad I got that straight before I went out on a reef."

Silver: "Then you could say 'hasta mañana.' "

Jerry: "Hasta mañana? What's that mean?"

Silver: "'Until tomorrow.' Well, you might say it means 'goodbye' or 'so long, I'll see you soon.' "

Jerry: "Gee, I wonder how long it will take for me to speak Spanish."

Silver: "Not very long. Anyone who can learn to speak English can certainly speak Spanish. It's a lot more regular."[54]

Following this language lesson, the action resumes as Silver begins the dangerous mission to protect Guayaquil from an Axis takeover. In a June 2, 1943, report to Rockefeller that short-listed several popular broadcasts, William A. Hillpot wrote that more than 135,000 requests had been received for the "Captain Silver Sea Chart" that the series offered to listeners over a three-week period.[55] Hillpot noted that individual requests ranged from a single chart to as many as 6,500 for distribution to students in the Brooklyn school system. The chart was a 24-by-36-inch color map of Latin America on which children could track the captain's sea exploits. Its lavish iconography of natural resources, national flags, and major heroic figures provided information on the region.

Free offers of items such as sea charts and sheet music were an important part of radio culture—a strategy used liberally by the CIAA to attract and retain listeners. While Captain Silver stopped occasionally to tutor Jerry in Spanish, other CIAA shows were dedicated entirely to language learning. The 1943 program *Let's Learn Spanish* offered thirty-nine lessons over a thirteen-week period and sponsored a proficiency contest to award the best student-listener.[56] According to *Time* magazine, the winner was a Long Island housewife, and the prize was a "beige fur-felt Mexican sombrero with a hummingbird [decoration]."[57] Coordination committees throughout Latin America launched radio instructional programs on English. In Mexico City the committee broadcast a fifteen-minute, twice-weekly program in cooperation with the Biblioteca Benjamín Franklin, an institution funded by the CIAA. In Rio the committee sponsored *English Lessons*, a thirty-minute program aired twice a week.

In addition to dramatic, musical, and educational programming, the CIAA made full use of its Hollywood connections to promote Good Neighbor relations. The fifteen-minute *Habla Hollywood* (Hollywood Speaks) was an inside-Hollywood-style program whose Peruvian announcer, Alberto Rondón, interviewed stars and reported news on celebrities in the armed forces. The show's slogan, "¡Belleza, gloria de la mujer! ¡Libertad, gloria de las naciones! ¡Defendemos ambas!" (Beauty, the glory of women! Liberty, the glory of nations! Let us defend both!), was typical of a paternalistic patriotism that defined the nation-state's need for protection of the feminine. This view of women was not at all typical of CIAA-sponsored programs, as they in general rallied women to enter the workforce on behalf of the Allied cause.

The Hollywood office recorded and broadcast special one-time programs as well. A CIAA report for December 18, 1942, lists among Hollywood broadcasts that week a fifteen-minute program titled "Christmas at San Gabriel," which combined a dramatization of the first Christmas with references to Good Neighbor connections between the cultures of "Spanish California" and Latin America.[58] Another show was a half-hour radio interview with Lockheed-Vega airplane plant workers hosted by Latin star Rosita Moreno, who began her career opposite Richard Arlen in *The Santa Fe Trail* (1930). The men and women interviewed included test pilots, Pearl Harbor widows, and gold star mothers whose testimonies on the U.S. war buildup were translated by Moreno into Spanish for broadcast to Latin America. Recordings for a series titled "How an Argentine Artist Views the United States" with gaucho caricaturist Florencio Molina Campos were also made that week. Other shows included a thirty-minute interview conducted by Rosita Moreno and Jinx Falkenberg with five Latin American journalists on a CIAA tour of the United States and a special that featured Walt Disney and songs from the *Saludos amigos* soundtrack performed by André Kostelanetz's orchestra and soloist Tito Guízar. Preparations were made but never completed for an interview with James Cagney and Hollywood Victory Committee chairman Kenneth Thomson, to be translated into Portuguese for the Brazilian radio series. Orson Welles was scheduled to narrate a broadcast on Mexico City from Hollywood the following week, but the program was cancelled by CBS.[59]

Assessments and Reactions

The Radio Division considered various methods of measuring audience reactions to programs both domestically and abroad. One report listed six possible approaches and recommended that at least one or more be adopted to assess listeners' likes and dislikes.[60] The most popular was the "telephone coincidental check" to be conducted while programs were on the air. It was estimated that 350 to 400 dialings would have to be made in the United States to achieve the one hundred interviews required to secure adequate listener feedback. The report notes that more calls were likely needed for Latin America because of the prevalence of servants and the difficulties of getting past them to speak to the woman or man of the house. Interviewers were to receive training on being cordial, quick, and accurate in their interactions with the public. The division specified that interviewers cover a wide geographical area and different income groups.

Direct mail surveys were used from the beginning of the division's operations. The U.S. National Archives II contains boxes filled with hundreds of reports based on these surveys, catalogued by city and country.[61] For example, in Mexico from July to August 1943, *Defensa nacional* (National Defense), a program that combined dramatizations about the war with military band music, achieved a 99.42 percent approval rating, while *Radioteatro de América* scored 60.85 percent and *El Hit Parade* a remarkably low 4.02 percent.[62] Another method of gaining information relied on letters and telephone calls from listeners. Fan mail for NBC and CBS shows poured into stations for certain radio hosts and specific programs and sometimes reported problems with reception and scheduling. Based on these listener reactions, the Costa Rican coordination committee contacted the CIAA to complain that, unlike the BBC, shortwave news programs from the United States came in too long after events had happened.[63] Buying newspaper space for short questionnaires to be returned free of charge by post was another strategy for obtaining audience feedback. The most direct form of acquiring information was through interviews with businessmen and laborers at work or as they arrived and left their jobs. There was, however, a gender bias in these interviews, a presumption that only men worked in businesses and factories and that conversation with women should be confined to the home, the church, or the marketplace. Although trained investigators were required for most of the interviews with men, those with women could be conducted by "upper level school boys and girls or college students."[64]

By 1942, U.S. shortwave kilowatt (kw) power had increased substantially from an average between 25 and 30kw to 50kw or more, although radio beams continued to be too broad (20 to 60 degrees to Latin America) in comparison to London's and Berlin's narrower and stronger beams (6 degrees) (Maxwell, 87). As a result, reception throughout the Americas continued to be a problem. By 1943, with more quality programming (resulting in large part from transcriptions and local coordination committee production) and an East and West

Coast reorganization (whereby stations covered less territory with stronger beams), responses to surveys showed significant improvement. By late 1943, U.S. radio was twice as popular in Peru as British radio, which historically had dominated the Allied airwaves. Colombians were also pleased with programming. CIAA radio publicity by this time was at its peak, with between 125,000 and 150,000 printed schedules being sent monthly to Latin America, as well as full-page ads that appeared in the Spanish and Portuguese versions of *Reader's Digest*, *Time Air Express* (Maxwell, 88–89), and *En Guardia*. Radio continued to be a formidable media force after the war, but there was nothing before or after to compare to its importance at this particular moment in U.S. and Latin American history, and there has not again been such a rich cultural exchange in the air between nations.

IN PRINT   The Press and Publication Division

Established in October 1944, the Press and Publication Division assumed the work that had been carried out under the CIAA's Communication Division (1940–1942) and Department of Information (1942–1944). Most press activities after 1944 took place at the division headquarters in Washington, D.C., although a subsidiary office continued to operate in the former headquarters in New York City. Despite the various name changes, the unit's aims remained the same: to prepare and distribute throughout Latin America feature news articles, booklets, magazines, pictures, cartoons, and posters designed to strengthen inter-American cultural ties and encourage wartime cooperation and solidarity (*Federal Records*, 241).[1] The division subsidized the publication of more than two hundred translations of literary, historical, and scientific works from Spanish and Portuguese into English and from English into Spanish and Portuguese. This project resulted in a minor but important surge in literary translations that anticipated the publication of Latin American Boom writers in the United States by two decades.[2]

The Features Unit

The Press and Publication Division's main task was to write feature stories about U.S. and inter-American news for distribution to Latin American papers. Donald W. Rowland has observed that because of the high costs of feature services prior to the war, only about one hundred Latin American newspapers carried these general-interest items (51). However, by mid-1942, as a result of special cost-saving feature services, an estimated five hundred Latin American newspapers were publishing CIAA stories and photographs on a weekly basis; by 1945 the number of newspapers had jumped to well over a thousand (51, 53). An October 20, 1941, memo by Harry W. Frantz, assistant to division head and Pulitzer Prize–winning journalist Francis A. Jamieson, pumped up excitement about inter-American press possibilities:

Working newsmen of domestic wire services without exception agree that the United States national interest in Latin American topics is greater than ever before, and more Latin American date-lines are moving out of New York on general wires. . . . A significant development in Inter-American journalism during the past year has been the reciprocal growth of North American and South American interest in feature article material. The Coordinator's offices in New York and Washington undoubtedly have made a great contribution to this trend. . . . For the first time in history, many "ace" writers of the United States are giving serious attention to Inter-American topics. . . . In the long perspective, the greatest service which the Coordinator's Office may render to Inter-American journalistic relations will be the creation of United States interest in Latin American topics. . . . [This] operation is comparable to "sub-soil" fertilization in agriculture.[3]

In its attempt to reach a wide audience, the CIAA placed articles as well as ads in Spanish and Portuguese in the tabloid *Boletín Linotípico* (Linotype Bulletin), which subsequently supplied them to newspapers throughout Latin America. One example, of no special relevance to Latin America, was a feature on Irving Berlin that included a cartoon illustrating his rise as one of the world's great songwriters. The CIAA also worked on technical innovations to get the news as quickly as possible to the region. Besides matted illustrated articles ready for reproduction, the agency developed plastic printing plates to accommodate smaller Latin American operations without expensive printing technology. The CIAA introduced microfilm as a means of sending features and photographs inexpensively by air mail.

The press clippings file at the National Archives II has numerous examples of CIAA articles in Latin American newspapers. For example, on August 12, 1942, Argentina's *La Acción* reported on the University of Louisiana's Casa de las Americas, an Americas Center established in the home state of Jefferson Caffery, who was U.S. ambassador to Brazil at the time. A June 24, 1942, article in Argentina's *La Gaceta* focused on a major U.S. book exhibit touring Latin America and featured best-selling titles published in the previous decade. The Bolivian newspaper *Noticias* ran stories about the other Americas' recognition of U.S. Independence Day (in the July 11, 1943, issue), the radio transmission of symphony concerts to Latin America (September 28, 1943), the increase in women factory workers for the war effort (May 3, 1944), and a stateside summit in which U.S. women hosted members of the Latin American Women's Commission (April 20, 1944).

A letter to Rockefeller from the Brazilian Division, a special unit created in Rio de Janeiro to oversee CIAA materials and their local reception, enthusiastically noted that in the April 17, 1944, issue of *Vanguarda*, "all but two of the articles are Inter-American." It goes on to describe *Vanguarda* as "an evening newspaper with two editions [that] enjoys a reputation of considerable importance. The owner and publisher, Dr. Ozeas Motta, who has a great deal of influence in political and social circles, has been a loyal and constant friend of this office."[4] The letter proceeds to list other topics that appeared in the newspaper: the importance of Brazilian mica to the war effort; the translation of one hundred U.S. books in nine months in Brazil; Thomas Jefferson and the Declaration of Independence; the North American educational system and its international influence; and finally, how people should be judged by who they are and not by their racial make-up.

There was some debate about the pros and cons of running items such as women's fashion news during wartime. In a May 30, 1942, memo to his boss Jamieson, Harry Frantz offered that "such materials would attempt to lighten the weight of our general feature report and give greater diversity of materials to editors." He added that their content "corresponds to the editorial interests of Brazil, Argentina and other countries." But Frantz was concerned that "the processing and distribution of such material could invite criticism on allocation of 'boondoggling'" and that "a prejudiced critic obviously could make the point that some of our publications might not be immediately contributory to the war effort."[5] He recommended that Rockefeller and the CIAA's content committee review and comment on such material. Two fashion stories were published in Argentina a few months later, suggesting that the various CIAA officials came to agree on topics other than the war—especially if they increased readership interest and circulation.

Frantz was eager that Latin American–based coordination committees be proactive in creating a favorable climate for CIAA press activities. His lengthy list of suggestions for those committees included establishing friendly personal relations with newspaper editors and reporters; directly disseminating publications such as the magazine *En Guardia* to individuals and libraries; keeping the agency informed of any plans for Latin American journalists to visit the United States; reporting monthly on the materials' reception and topics of local interest; and, whenever possible, forwarding any Axis publications so the CIAA might examine and refute their content.[6]

The degree to which U.S. newspapers reported on CIAA inter-American activities can be partly determined by clippings information from MoMA's Department of Public Information scrapbook for the years 1941 and 1942. Although most of the articles are from New York newspapers, a few appeared in places such as the New Orleans *Times-Picayune*, the *Dallas Morning News*, and the *Los Angeles Examiner*. While several early articles focused on the CIAA's creation of the Motion Picture Division, the vast majority provided information on Latin American and U.S. artists and traveling art exhibits. A number of articles reported on the CIAA-sponsored exhibit of 289 U.S. paintings and its enthusiastic reception by audiences in Mexico City, Buenos Aires, Montevideo, and Rio. This was one of the CIAA's most widely publicized cultural initiatives; Rockefeller himself facilitated it in conjunction with MoMA and the Metropolitan Museum of Art. (Chapter 5 presents a discussion of this exhibit, and the final chapter gives an account of the U.S. government's changed attitude about modern art in the postwar years.)

Although Frantz was eager to get U.S. papers to carry Latin American news, a statistical survey by Leonard W. Doob on Latin American datelines published between October 1941 and July 1942 was not reassuring. In an August 31, 1942, memo to Frantz, he concluded that on average less than one story per day about Latin America appeared during the survey period, that there was considerable variability in the amount of coverage each month, and that Latin American news was mostly limited to large-city newspapers. His breakdown of the different newspapers by region and the number of stories printed shows the mid-Atlantic region with the highest average, or eight stories per month, while New England had the lowest, with five. Not surprisingly, the *New York Times* led all other newspapers with a high of fifty-three articles in a single month, followed by the *New York Herald Tribune* (39), the *Los Angeles Times* (34), and the *Los Angeles Examiner* (29). The *Washington News* printed ten stories in January 1942 but ran only one story each in November 1941 and June and July 1942.[7]

A September 3, 1942, memo from Frantz objects to Doob's survey and recommends that it be discontinued:

> When the survey was suggested, it was intended that the one major effort of the Press Division would be to expand the North-bound flow of materials from the other Latin American Republics to the United States. With the coming of war, it became imperative that the preponderate effort should be to develope [*sic*] materials for the other American Republics, and to expand the South-bound flow of all manner of newspaper, magazine, and radio materials. We do not therefore have the anticipated need at present for a statistical yard-stick on materials carried in United States papers.[8]

Frantz's pique on this issue was symptomatic of the fact that U.S. newspapers, then as now, have rarely covered Latin America except in periods of dubious clandestine or openly military interventions. A February 12, 1942, confidential report to Rockefeller from the Princeton team of Hadley Cantril and Frederic Swift indirectly attested to this lack of coverage in their survey of U.S. public opinion about Latin America.[9] They reported that the public knew too little about Latin America to give any opinion whatsoever, that people were so little informed that they rarely absorbed any new information provided on the region, and that because of these problems, respondents felt survey questions posed were "cold and aloof."[10] The division staff might have felt some small modicum of satisfaction in one set of statistics indicating that what little information respondents did receive about Latin America came largely from newspapers, followed by magazines, radio, books, and movies.

On the other hand, as I have already noted, press clippings show that a wide range of U.S. topics was being reported in Latin America—not only the opening of the Americas Center at the University of Louisiana and the traveling U.S. book exhibit across Latin America but also such pictorial items as U.S. fashions based on the Cuban rumba style and Deanna Durban wearing South American furs. Many articles focus on the increasingly public role of U.S. women: women substituting for men in factories, women receiving members of the Inter-American Women's Commission, women as war heroes, and women's preference for slacks over skirts.

The Press Division's continued interest in female readers and their role in the public workforce can be seen in the copy for a January 13, 1943, feature article in Spanish titled "A los 21 años, una señorita de Costa Rica abre nuevas rutas para las mujeres latino-americanas" (At 21 years of age, a young woman from Costa Rica is breaking ground for Latin American women).[11] The article praises Carmen Venegas, a scholarship student who specialized in aeronautics and engineering at Virginia Polytechnic Institute. According to the article, she was the first Latin American woman to receive an electrical engineering degree, the first woman from Central America to earn a pilot's license, and apparently the first woman ever to operate a locomotive. This sort of attention to women's education, work, and achievement continued to appear in Latin American newspapers, including reports on scholarships created by women's clubs in Washington, D.C., and on Eleanor Roosevelt's effort to raise the working wage of women throughout Latin America.

Frantz was concerned about the speed, quality, and effectiveness of feature articles sent to Latin America.[12] On June 18, 1942, he wrote to Jamieson about the desirability of a Latin American writers unit that could produce articles directly in Spanish and Portuguese as well as supplement general CIAA news by shaping it according to regional interests.[13] Frantz was of the opinion that a few individuals in the translation unit, which was adequately staffed, would make good writers. However, there were obstacles to the plan involving national security (Press Division writers had to be U.S. citizens, for example) and even journalistic style: "The difficulties attending a special unit of Latin American writers would arise especially from possible difficulty in clearing their materials, and the fact that in many cases their editorial method usually would be rather discursive and personal."[14] Frantz's idea for a special unit did not materialize; nonetheless, the many journalists who visited the United States supported the CIAA mission by writing about inter-American cultural relations and the war effort for newspapers back home. Local coordination committees were especially active in assessing the number and reception of CIAA articles featured in these newspapers.

For a time in 1942, Doob was conducting weekly quantitative analyses of the Latin American press based on opinions about international affairs expressed in editorials, features, and regular columns. His February 13, 1942, report to Jamieson, Frantz, and former Rockefeller Center architect Wallace K. Harrison, who was Rockefeller's right-hand man, estimated that 74 percent of the opinions were "friendly" to the United States and that these opinions referred mainly to "policies and actions involving a Latin American country or the actual progress of the war." Doob concluded that the small percentage of unfriendly comments tended to concentrate on the cultural dissimilarity between the United States and Latin American countries. He described this angle of reportage as the "use of Hispanidad or wedge tactics."[15]

Another memo sent from Doob to Jamieson and Frantz on the same day quotes an unnamed Yale anthropologist in the employ of the CIAA who was conducting research in a small town in Costa Rica. His comments about the local culture emphasized the importance of getting print news to communities in the remote interior:

> Apart from the radio, the newspaper is the great source of information and the radio doesn't really compete with it. Besides the houses that receive their own papers, the pulperias (grocery shops) commonly have their copies out on the counter all day as public reading matter. Most people, to be sure, may not be careful readers. But those who are careful readers may spread their information widely. . . . [I]t would take a very small sum in the form of translators in the United States to see that such material was available from the United States, provided the original publishers didn't want to be paid, and perhaps some form of subsidy would work if they did want to be paid.[16]

One month later, Doob filed another report based on this same colleague's observations on the importance of maps to Good Neighbor relations and the war effort:

If the United States should have some money to spend on promoting a better knowledge of war events in these parts of the world, it could do no better than to print up huge quantities of good maps of the world and distribute them widely (which isn't done with other free publications sent out by the United States, as contrasted with the British). Believe me, there is a hunger for knowledge of this sort, and the maps in the bookstore windows in San Jose gather crowds. . . . I can't think of any single type of propaganda that would be better calculated to put over the idea (which many but not all people already have about British propaganda) that the propaganda of the United States is directed at making the truth known, regardless of whether palatable or not. On such a map distances should be marked in kilometers, and not in miles (of which people have very erroneous notions here, and which may never have been heard of in some other countries). Although En Guardia is beautifully done and deserves a much wider circulation if it can be afforded . . ., I am absolutely certain that the same amount of money would be far more valuable if put into maps.[17]

The CIAA had excellent working relations with large U.S. firms and entities such as the National Geographic Society and provided them with inter-American materials for their publications. A photograph sent to National Geographic on June 1, 1942, via the coordination committee in Rio shows a copy of the magazine sticking out of the back pocket of a construction worker there. But the real magazine success story was *Seleções*, the Portuguese version of *Reader's Digest*.[18] According to Brazilian historian Antônio Pedro Tota, this magazine was introduced into Brazil in 1942, the same year as Coca-Cola and the country's famous Kibon ice cream (59). Published monthly in Pleasant-ville, New York, *Seleções* contained colorful advertising alongside stories that promoted the "American way of life." The very look of the magazine fascinated Brazilian journalist Argemiro Ferreira when he was a youngster: "I was not able to read it but I can remember being impressed with those charming, sophisticated ads, all put together in the last pages of each edition, right after the articles" (162).

It was estimated that in 1941, around eighty U.S. cartoons were regularly featured in Latin American newspapers. The publication that year of the first South American comic strip in the United States, which appeared in the New York–based left-wing tabloid *PM*, was considered a major breakthrough and picked up by the CIAA for general press release. The central cartoon character, an Argentine Indian called Patoruzu, was described in the newspaper as a philosopher, humorist, and Good Neighbor fellow as well as a combination Paul Bunyan–Popeye figure who was prone to accidental adventures. His creator, Dante Quinterno, who began the strip in Argentina in 1928, was hailed as Walt Disney's counterpart in South America.[19] *PM*'s publicity campaign for the new comic strip announced weekly cash prizes for readers who submitted the best verse to complete Patoruzu's weekly "Good Neighbor" limerick. The contest began with the following lines:

> Was La Mancha a pompous old fake?
> Or the work of a royal mistake?
> Patoruzu, a-thirst
> To discover the worst
> . . . .[20]

In his letter to Rockefeller shortly before returning to Brazil, Assis de Figueiredo urged the coordinator to publish a cultural magazine for Brazilian readers that would fill the gap created by the wartime loss of European magazines. He cited *Seleções* as an excellent model. The transcription of a 1944 conversation between Franz and Conrad Wrzos, head of Brazil's Inter-Allied Agency (Serviço Interaliado), was considerably more detailed and frank about what

The South American comic strip's U.S. debut in *PM*. Courtesy of the National Archives and Records Administration, College Park, Maryland.

the CIAA should do to ensure the quality and effectiveness of its propaganda in Brazil. While Wrzos was generally positive about the Portuguese-language *Em Guarda*, he felt that the issue with portraits of American republic presidents should have used a larger picture of President Vargas and placed it alongside Roosevelt's. He pointed out major grammatical errors in Portuguese on CIAA war posters; Brazilians' less than favorable reaction to CIAA materials written in Spanish instead of Portuguese; the lack of local interest in printed speeches by U.S. politicians (with the exception of Roosevelt and Hull); and the questionable importance of anti-Japanese materials in Brazil when Brazilian troops were fighting in Italy and the country as a whole was focused on the European front. (He did not mention Brazil's large population of Japanese immigrants and their descendants.) To resolve these and other problems, Wrzos suggested that CIAA publications slated for Brazil be translated in Rio as opposed to Washington. He pointed out that "a more perfect publication would represent a gift happily received by Brazilians." He added, "Given the current transportation difficulties, this [approach] would reduce unnecessary expenditures."[21] Unfortunately, Wrzos's suggestion was never implemented.

En Guardia and Newsletter Publications

Although military production and readiness were regular themes in CIAA documentary shorts, the Press and Publication Division devoted much more attention to wartime issues, including the size, training, and superiority of Allied troops, the growth and inventiveness in Americas' industrial production, and the much-touted "moral elements of victory," which, according to the division's editorial policy, entailed a spirit of "international unity" and the "tradition of tolerance" demonstrated by free peoples everywhere.[22] Under its banner of "We Are Winning the War," the division countered German propaganda by highlighting in its materials the Axis powers' moral and material weaknesses and their "menace to freedom."

Its most important publication in this regard was the monthly photo magazine *En Guardia*, begun in 1941 and styled after *Life* with the aim of providing Latin Americans with a comprehensive view of U.S. wartime defense and military readiness. As Donald W. Rowland has pointed out, the idea for the magazine originated with Karl A. Bickel, who worked under Jamieson when he was the division's head in its early days (40). Over 50 percent pictorial, *En Guardia* ran articles by both North and South American writers and journalists and was distributed throughout Latin America as well as to Spanish-speaking communities in the United States and Canada. *En Guardia* was one of the highest-quality publications ever produced by the U.S. government: it featured the best newsprint available with matte, glossy, and textured finishes, black-and-white and four-color images, facsimiles of major documents such as the Atlantic Charter, and special booklet-style inserts with entire speeches by FDR and other important figures. Realizing the impact of the magazine on Latin American readers, the Axis powers released a copycat version of the publication that they called *De Guardia*.

Distribution of *En Guardia* in Latin America was handled chiefly through direct mailings and regional CIAA coordination committees. As the magazine matured, individuals wrote directly to the CIAA to request the free publication, and the agency secured and routinely updated additional mailing lists. In his study Rowland discusses the problems of maintaining up-to-date lists and the general concern over possible resentment from Latin American publishers, who were struggling because of a wartime lack of newsprint. He comments on some officials' feelings that *En Guardia* was too expensive and misdirected toward the middle and upper classes rather than the poor and working classes that constituted a much larger population. However, Rowland notes, counter-arguments prevailed: it was claimed that anything less than a quality publication for the region would offend Latin Americans; that the literate population to whom the magazine was addressed constituted those who had the most power; and that radio shows, films, and posters were already being produced for the largely illiterate rural and working-class populations (49).[23]

There is no question that *En Guardia* was popular with its targeted audience. It had a continuous run between its inception in 1941 and 1945, when the last issue was printed, and demand for the monthly magazine soared from an initial forty thousand in 1941 to more than a half-million by 1944.[24] In an essay about the Good Neighbor years in Brazil, journalist Argemiro Ferreira has remarked on the magazine's popularity there, noting that each new issue passed through the hands of at least five readers (164). Although it may be difficult to imagine how a defense magazine could attract so much interest, the sheer physical size of the publication and its full-page photographic spreads were probably more than sufficient to capture attention. Like its physical dimensions, which were enlarged after the second issue, its stylistic approach to military matters was grandiose and oversized. U.S. airplanes, battleships, and artillery were photographed in close-up and from low angles, giving them an air of beauty and indestructibility. Color provided a sense of vitality to photographs illustrating the firepower of battleship guns. Overall, the magazine offered a visually compelling pictorial of war power—not unlike images that

Cover of the popular wartime magazine *En Guardia*.

Cover of *Axis* magazine modeled after *En Guardia*. Courtesy of the Franklin D.
Roosevelt Library, Hyde Park, New York.

attracted millions to Hollywood wartime movies during the period. Indeed, *En Guardia* ran occasional photographs of Hollywood stars such as Lana Turner, who posed alongside smiling soldiers in the magazine's debut issue.

Along with military might, *En Guardia* focused on individual troops in the war effort, showing them in battle training as well as in leisure shipboard activities such as sunbathing, eating, and drinking and in domestic settings with family members. One unusual photograph shows a smiling Annapolis cadet and his date in formal attire, seated side by side on what appears to be a terrace. The nighttime setting looks like an open-air nightclub but is actually a ship. We know this because jutting out of the darkness over their heads is the enormous barrel of a battleship gun.

There were obvious thematic similarities between *En Guardia* and the films sponsored by the CIAA. The magazine touted military readiness and hemispheric friendship and solidarity; its articles featured headers such as "America Means: 21 Nations," "United for Victory," and "Nations for Liberty Fight the Axis Powers." Considerable attention was given to the raw materials essential to the wartime effort, and maps and charts were used repeatedly to point out their locations, their increases in production, and their overall superiority to European materials. As the publication gained readers, more space was given to Good Neighbor relations. A section titled "Interamerican Friendship" provided information on Latin American dignitaries visiting the United States, and starting with the fifth issue an entire page was devoted to the schedule of U.S. shortwave news programs transmitted in Spanish throughout Latin America. The May 1942 issue featured impressive full-page photographs from Mexico and Brazil in recognition of their decision to enter the war against the Axis powers. Perhaps most importantly, the magazine gave attention to individual Latin Americans training in the United States, with captioned photographs identifying them by name and country of origin.

Like the CIAA motion-picture documentaries, *En Guardia* regularly included commentary on U.S. women in the war effort. Photographs showed enlisted nurses, civil defense volunteers, factory workers, and women tracking troop movements on maps and donning gas masks for practice air raids. To ensure as wide a readership as possible, the magazine focused on children as young wartime citizens and future leaders of the Americas. Just as Lana Turner turned out for the soldiers, a teenage Shirley Temple was photographed alongside smiling Latin American children at a birthday party.

As the number of photographs and stories from the battlefront increased in the magazine's pages, more attention was given to the arts, which achieved a level of government recognition never before or again seen in U.S. wartime. Good Neighbor relations were at the center of this cultural reportage and attractive imagery: Cândido Portinari's murals in the Library of Congress, Mexican actor Arturo de Córdova in a scene with Joan Fontaine from the film *Frenchman's Creek* (1944), and distinguished visitors to the States, including Chilean pianist Claudio Arrau and a delegation of Latin American women journalists. One issue of *En Guardia* covered a story about the myriad European art treasures that had been looted by the Nazis and were being recovered by the Allies as they made their way across Europe. Literacy and reading habits were other important topics. One of the magazine's final issues claimed that people in the United States were reading more books—not best-selling fiction but rather volumes about the problems facing the postwar world.

In his May 3, 1942, letter to Rockefeller, DIP official Assis de Figueiredo wrote appreciatively of the magazine: "During my conversation with Mr. Frank Jamieson and others in your New York and Washington Offices, I have been impressed with the type of material included in the magazine 'Em Guardia' [*sic*]. It seems to me that this magazine has served a very useful and valuable purpose." But he also stated the need for other kinds of magazines, especially those of a cultural and scientific nature, to replace European publications no longer available or distributed in Brazil. He added: "Therefore, my suggestion that a cultural magazine from the United States, put in circulation in Brazil, will receive wide acclaim and a great reader audience." He gives *Seleções*, the Portuguese version of *Reader's Digest*, as a model for what the CIAA might produce: "[The magazine] started a circulation in Brazil only four months ago with a planned circulation of 50,000 copies each month. Today this circulation has jumped to over 200,000 copies. This is fully an indication of the interest the Brazilian reading public has on cultural matters."[25]

In addition to condensed versions of books, *Seleções* ran a section titled "Barracks Talk" that gave Brazilians information about U.S. military customs and build-up. The magazine contained eye-catching ads for U.S. consumer goods such as Zenith radios, Caterpillar diesel tractors, and RCA record players pictured alongside battleships and tanks as wartime necessities.[26] A frank assessment of *Seleções* content and reception in Brazil is provided in a February 24, 1944, transcription of remarks by Conrad Wrzos of Brazil's Inter-Allied Agency in a conversation with Harry Frantz, who had become head of the Press and Publication Division after Jamieson's promotion to CIAA assistant coordinator:

> I sincerely consider [U.S.] propaganda almost perfect. However, there are aspects from an editorial point of view that leave a little to be desired. . . . Brazilians don't like to be compared to the less important nations of South America, for they consider themselves first in the line of nations after the major global powers. From my point of view it would have been preferable to stop the presses and produce a magazine issue expressly for Brazil that would include more information about the country. . . . Try to avoid showing heads of state from other nations arriving in mass in Washington. . . . Don't forget that Brazilians are very proud and patriotic.[27]

Less costly than *En Guardia* and less widely read were the various newsletters published by the CIAA. Begun on September 29, 1941, and published every two weeks with versions in Spanish and Portuguese, the *American Newsletter* supplied information about the Americas not generally covered by U.S. radio programs or the national press. Initial issues tended to have a business focus, although following the December 9, 1941, issue with FDR's war proclamation, the newsletter began to stress wartime mobilizations and sacrifices. For example, the March 3, 1942 issue discussed modifications that clothing and styles would undergo: "Simple frills will be eliminated. Women's dresses will be without metal decorations. Silk stockings are replaced by cotton and rayon hosiery. Reused wool and rayon will be woven into new clothing."[28] Greater emphasis was placed on hemispheric relations, such as cultural exchanges involving musicians and athletes (March 17, 1942), the visit of Peruvian President Manuel Prado to the United States (May 26, 1942), Brazil's entry into the war, the readiness of its Força Expedicionária Brasileira, and statements of solidarity from leaders both North and South (September 1, 1942).[29]

For primarily domestic consumption, the trimonthly *Special Feature Service* newsletter and *Inter-American Economic News Service* provided updates on the other Americas and were sent to some 1,500 U.S. outlets and designated individuals overseas. The *Economic News Service* publication ran articles on the order of "Mexico Boosts Mining Output to Record Levels" and "Dehydrated Foods May Help Supply Amazon Workers" (June 6, 1943). According to a letter from John M. Clark to Jamieson, reception of the *Economic News Service* by CIAA supporters in Chile was less than lukewarm: "[U]nanimous enthusiasm for En Guardia, unanimous boredom for the Economic Newsletter" (in Rowland, 53n48). In contrast, *Special Feature* combined economic with cultural news and had broader appeal; its commentaries covered a range of material under headlines such as "U.S. Publishers Honored by Peruvian Association" and "Pan-American Theater Brings Broadway to Mexican Stage." News on women's adoption of slacks and sportswear was covered, as proclaimed in 1943: "The Ladies Wear the Pants in Uruguay" and "'It's All the Rage in New York': Murmur the Ladies in Other American Republics." *Special Feature* ran U.S. comic strips in Spanish, including "Henry," "Mandrake," "Felix the Cat," and "Blondie and Dagwood," which became "Pepita y Lorenzo."

Identifying and securing outlets for dissemination of magazines and newsletters abroad was particularly challenging. Shortwave radio was used for daily transmission of some 25,000 words of time-sensitive news that added up to an average of forty-four hours weekly of broadcast time.[30] In April 1942 it was estimated that all fourteen shortwave radio stations on the East and West Coasts were transmitting CIAA news materials to Latin America.[31] The CIAA 16mm industrial documentary *Brazil Gets the News* (1942) describes a day in the life of *A Gazeta* in "busy, bright, brisk São Paulo," the "home of fine, modern newspapers." The objective of the film was to show similarities in U.S. and Brazilian news production, as indicated by one of its title cards: "São Paulo, the Detroit of Brazil, or is Detroit the São Paulo of the U.S.?" As the camera follows a low-angle exterior view of *A Gazeta*'s tall, modern office building, the narrator says, "Let's go inside and look around," after which we glimpse the editor's office, the reception room, the library, the advertising department, and the city room. The narrator calls attention to a workroom for a special children's edition of the newspaper: "U.S. newspapers, please copy."

Subtle language lessons in Portuguese are introduced by focusing on door nameplates for each room, such as "Sala de recepção," or reception room. The quick cutting between areas suggests both energy and efficiency, and a similarly rapid montage shows the working of the press from the arrival of a wire story on the sinking of an airplane carrier to its publication in the finished newspaper. Along the way we see modern machinery; men skilled in linotype, castings, and printing; and crews loading large rolls of paper onto presses and bundling the newsprint copies. The quick beat of light Brazilian music on the soundtrack suggests the "speed and accuracy [that] make possible the modern newspaper." The ten-minute short concludes by returning to the similarities of São Paulo and U.S. cities: "São Paulo is energetically alive with progressiveness and looks like Chicago." The film reinforces the importance of the U.S. press to Latin America: "They need brisk, up-to-date journalism and they get it—sent by air and train to all parts of South America." The entire film has a swiftness and lightness, and the final animated scene adds humor by showing myriad newspaper bundles moving back and forth in what looks like a dream sequence; finally the bundles arrange themselves to spell out the word "FIM." The narrator makes sure that U.S. viewers know this is Portuguese for "the end," but his pronunciation needs some fine-tuning.

Pamphlet Publications

The CIAA issued a series of booklets in Spanish, Portuguese, and English to inform readers in the American republics about one another and about inter-American efforts to protect and defend the hemisphere. Approximately sixty pamphlets in various editions appeared from 1941 through 1945; the first was titled *Por que nos armamos* (Why We Arm Ourselves) and featured six speeches by FDR dating from 1936 to 1941. Among other early publications was *Brazil: Introduction to a Neighbor* (1941), the first in a series that highlighted each nation in Latin America. Here as elsewhere, Brazil was prioritized to demonstrate U.S. recognition of its hemispheric importance and gain its support in building wartime relations. The booklet was a template for the other publications in the Americas series, among them *Venezuela, Land of Oil* (1943); *Rural Haiti* (1943); *Chile, Land of Contrasts* (1944); *Nicaragua, Lakes and Volcanoes* (1944); and *Bolivia, Storehouse of Metals* (1944). Brazil had a special designation as a "neighbor" rather than being defined by its topography or a commodity.

The exaggerated rhetoric or ufanismo associated with CIAA film narrations can also be found in the booklets, as exemplified by the opening sentence of the *Brazil* pamphlet: "Brazil is many things—most of them spectacular." Other commentaries give nativist exuberance an interesting twist by lauding aspects of Brazil that are superior to the United States: "The land is vast—greater in area than continental United States. . . . It has a water fall 40 feet higher than Niagara. . . . Rio de Janeiro and São Paulo are big, modern cities which were in existence a half-century before the Pilgrims sighted Massachusetts Bay" (n.p.). A full-page illustration with outline maps of Brazil and the United States touts the former's greater size in square miles. Although an accompanying chart shows the U.S. population to be larger, another graph shows the Amazon River to be much longer than the Mississippi. A recurring motif in the narrative is Brazil's importance to the United States as a source for raw materials, as a buyer of U.S. goods, and as a strategic partner in hemispheric defense. Emphasizing the latter point is a two-page cartographic spread with the northeastern city of Natal at the center and arrows linking it to Dakar in the east and North America to the northwest.

Other cartographic drawings in the booklet show the predominance of the Portuguese language in South America and major air and land routes and waterways. Another two-page spread focuses on the variety and location of agricultural products and natural resources, with cattle and coffee icons mingling with those of manganese, iron, and quartz crystal deposits—minerals vital to the war industry. Graphs show the quadrupling of the Brazilian population in the previous seventy years and the size of different European immigrant groups that contributed to this rise. Another chart records the large increase in the number of children attending primary schools. That numerical information dovetails nicely with a pictorial image representing the many social services created by what the pamphlet author refers to as Vargas's "New Deal" government.

Accompanying the maps, charts, and graphs are hand drawings of a baroque church, various indigenous plants, landscapes including the mountainous terrain between São Paulo and the port of Santos, and a tuberculosis sanitarium in Salvador. Public health in Brazil had improved as a result of a U.S.-Brazil project funded by the Rockefeller Foundation in the 1920s and 1930s; the U.S. government would add to its funding in 1942. This collaboration led to the almost complete eradication of malaria in Rio and the Amazon, as well as the creation of the University of São Paulo's School of Hygiene and Public Health and a Special Bureau for Public Health.[32] The emphasis given to disease control in *Brazil* was an obvious way to celebrate the achievements of an early inter-American initiative and the Rockefeller family's role in the public-service sector. (The CIAA under Nelson Rockefeller pushed for further improvements in public health education; among its most notable arms was a popular series of animated shorts on disease prevention and hygiene produced by Walt Disney.)[33]

The vast quantity of Good Neighbor materials sent south was regarded as wartime cultural diplomacy, but as Antônio Pedro Tota has pointed out, much of the material constituted a "seductive imperialism," infusing the "American way" into all aspects of national life.[34] Many of the forty "special theme" CIAA booklets outside the Americas series were focused on history and had a somewhat paternalistic quality. A popular title among Spanish-reading audiences was *Hombres de las Américas que lucharon por la democracia* (Men of the Americas Who Fought for Democracy), which describes the U.S. role in the lives of four famous Latin Americans—the Venezuelan Francisco de Miranda, who fought for Spanish America's independence and met with George Washington during his exile in the United States; Ecuadorian patriot and later president Eloy Alfaro, who introduced plans for a U.S.-style railway system in his homeland; Argentine president and author Domingo Faustino Sarmiento, who modeled his country's educational plan along the lines of Horace Mann's plan for universal public education; and Puerto Rican journalist Eugenio María de Hostos, editor of the New York newspaper *The Revolution*, who introduced North American educational and health reforms into the Dominican Republic and Chile.

Hombres de las Américas was illustrated with drawings that showed Miranda dining with Washington, Alfaro studying U.S. railroad construction plans, Sarmiento visiting Mann in his Boston home, and Hostos attending a Fourth of July celebration in New York. An outline map of the United States pinpointed the large metropolitan centers where they stayed as well as smaller cities and towns visited by Sarmiento (Ann Arbor), Mexican President Benito Juárez (New Orleans), and Cuban poet and revolutionary José Martí (Tampa).

Another historical booklet, titled *Americas United* (1943), tracks the historical trajectory of pan-American conferences and describes wartime sacrifices and economic challenges overcome through inter-American cooperation. Unlike most pamphlets, *Americas United* has only one illustration—a cover image of two interlocking rings superimposed on an outline map of the North and South American continents, recalling Harold D. Laswell's early idea for an insignia based on a circle with a double "A" to represent the two Americas united. There is no question that U.S. financial investments enabled the hemisphere to defend itself during wartime, and much is made in the pamphlet of U.S. negotiations that transformed and improved import, export, and other aspects of trade within the Americas. However, as time has shown, the increased U.S. presence in the Latin American economy has had long-term consequences, and today the pamphlet's interlocking rings seem more a sign of economic penetration than of Good Neighbor friendship.

A pamphlet titled *The Americas Cooperate for Victory and Peace* (1945) summarizes the history of wartime mobilization in the Americas. The narrative is balanced in its discussion of pan-American efforts, although significant space is given to favorable commentary on the increased presence of U.S. films, radio, and news in Latin America. One of the CIAA's more unusual and detailed pamphlets is *La marcha fúnebre, estilo nazi* (The Funeral March, Nazi Style, n.d.), about the German occupation of Poland and the atrocities experienced by citizens of Warsaw. Purportedly based on anonymous eyewitness accounts, the descriptions of suffering are interspersed with quoted commentaries that give the narrative authenticity and an intimate, urgent appeal. One statement describes Nazi soldiers filming the conquered Poles for the purposes of newsreel footage to tout the invasion in German movie theaters.

This and other actions by the Germans are illustrated in drawings by a "former Polish Army officer during the first days of the occupation." Images depict a man lying in a street, the victim of Nazi soldiers; a German military band playing in front of a toppled statue of Chopin; a despondent and destitute family huddled in a cold and sparse kitchen; and a cart piled high with skeletal corpses from the Jewish ghetto. The last few pages describe the Polish resistance and its tactics such as clandestine radio messages and publications and outright killing. All of the drawings have captions. The last image in the booklet portrays two men, one standing with a gun while the other, a Nazi officer and Hitler look-alike, is sprawled on the ground. The caption reads: "Los Nazis no se atreven caminar solos por las calles" (Nazis don't dare walk the streets alone).

The CIAA pamphlets went through various editions, suggesting if not their success with readers at least their widespread distribution by U.S. inter-American centers and coordination committees in Latin America. An undated CIAA distribution document for Argentina, Bolivia, and Brazil shows that nearly three-quarters of a million pamphlets were in circulation in those countries alone.[35] Another undated report based on feedback from the coordination committee in Guayaquil, Ecuador, lists the most popular pamphlets there with a short note on each:

Héroes verdaderos (True Heroes) "15,000 distributed, which did not half-cover the demand"

El sueño alemán (The German Dream) "Published in series in the newspaper, as allotment received too small to start covering the demand"

Tres hombres en una tina (Three Men in a Bathtub) "Also series published in newspaper specially appealing to children"

Nuestro futuro: Hombres libres o esclavos (Our Future: Free Men or Slaves) "Tremendously appealing to South Americans, who are born unruly, and have a deeply ingrained feeling for freedom and race-consciousness"[36]

Héroes verdaderos was one of two cartoon-style pamphlets about war heroes, while *El sueño alemán* described the Nazi dream of ruling the Americas, and *Nuestro futuro* used pictorials to demonstrate what would happen in the hemisphere should the Nazis prevail. The CIAA report noted the Guayaquil committee's enthusiasm for *Héroes verdaderos* and its members' suggestions for additional publications:

The pamphlet Héroes verdaderos had such a raging success in Ecuador, specially on the coastal region of the country. The Guayaquil Committee's office suggested that a series be worked out on the basis of this pamphlet, inasmuch as it was observed that many children, who are in the habit of reading the adventures of CAPTAIN MARVEL, and other similarly imaginary heroes, went to sleep with HEROES VERDADEROS in their hands . . . [I]t is thought that, no matter how much it may affect private Syndicates from a commercial point of view, if popularity with Latin American publics is sought for, there is no publication that will attain such a tremendous popularity, among both grown ups and children, as this publication would. Besides, regarding children, the educational viewpoint should be considered, as it is a well known fact that what is instilled in a child's mind, is bound to grow up and develop into a very definite ideology.[37]

The committee further recommended the publication of "musical" pamphlets based on the anthems of the South American republics: "They would make a

most suitable present for schools, universities, labor unions, and other important organizations. Also for radio stations."[38]

Pamphlets were the means to educate the U.S. public about works by Latin
American authors. *Neighbors, a Self Portrait* (1943) surveys representative major authors whose writings told the region's story from colonial conquest and
independence to contemporary times. The booklet features nearly forty novelists, short-story writers, and poets whose works were available in English.
The short preface explains that only translated writers are profiled, and not
surprisingly about half of them are part of the CIAA project to translate Latin
American authors into English. (This pamphlet features a multipage bibliography, an unusual feature for any CIAA publication, giving interested readers additional information.) The CIAA co-sponsored, with the Pan American Union,
a series of history booklets on the Incas, the Araucanas, Spanish explorer Ca-
beza de Vaca's Narváez expedition, Argentine liberator José de San Martín, and
Francisco Pizarro, called the "founder" of Lima. Among other pamphlet subjects were a snake farm in Butantã, Brazil, that served as a testing ground for
medical research with viper venom and the Guano Islands, an avian paradise
off the coast of Peru. Besides all this, the CIAA supported publication of inter-
American educational bulletins and textbooks, such as Helen Follett's *This
Way to Latin America!* (1943).

Graphics

The CIAA's graphics unit sent pictures in print, mat, and plastic format to Rio
and Buenos Aires on a daily basis and from there on to other South American
cities. Up-to-the minute photographs of the D-Day invasion and other critical
events were transmitted by radio from New York to Latin America. Another
essential part of the press and publication North-to-South initiative was the
distribution of illustrated materials including posters and cartoons for the
largely illiterate population. In the area of poster art, a Hemisphere Solidarity Poster Contest was launched by MoMA as part of a CIAA arts initiative in
1942. The competition required the use of one of twelve slogans in English,
Spanish, and Portuguese, such as "Hands off the Americas," "21 Republics—
1 Destiny," "Unite against Aggression," and "Fight for a Free America." Prizes
totaled $2,500. MoMA received 473 entries from Latin America and 382 from
the United States and Canada.[39]

Thirty-four prizes were distributed, half to Latin Americans and half to U.S.
and Canadian entrants, and there were nineteen honorable mentions. The
two largest prizes ($500 each) went to José Renau from Mexico City and Stan-

ley W. Crane from Woodstock, New York. Renau's "Unite against Aggression" was judged the most visually compelling and hard-hitting poster: colorful flags of the twenty-one republics form the backdrop for a powerful image of three hands that together plunge a sharpened stake into the body of a large, writhing cobra. MoMA published a pamphlet with illustrations of the prize-winning artworks and distributed 13,708 copies in North America and another 6,000 in South America.[40] The contest was written up in major magazines and newspapers, including *Newsweek* (November 2, 1942), the *New York Times* (October 21, 1942), and the *Christian Science Monitor* (November 7, 1942, with color images). As if addressing the CIAA's earlier concern about lightweight stories on fashion in wartime, *Vogue* magazine (February 1, 1943) ran a full-page color ad in which fashion models were artfully posed against a backdrop of the prize-winning posters.[41]

By 1945 the CIAA boasted that it had the world's most extensive collection of Latin American photographs, covering a broad range of subjects. Many of these pictures were taken by professional photographers contracted to travel to Latin America. Arguably the most important among them was Genevieve Naylor, a highly talented Works Progress Administration (WPA) and Associated Press photojournalist who traveled to Brazil in October 1940 with her soon-to-be husband, the artist Misha Reznikoff. According to historian Robert M. Levine, the DIP restricted Naylor to subject matter that emphasized Brazil's modernity and largely white, middle- and upper-class population; among the Rio subjects she was allowed to photograph were buildings, homes, and beachfronts in the fashionable Zona Sul (Southern Zone), yachting and golf club settings, and commercial shops along the historic downtown Rua do Ouvidor (38). The Vargas government prided itself on its reform measures, and as a result Naylor was encouraged to photograph various social services, including a newsboys' foundation and a school for children of fishermen, which also became the focus of a CIAA documentary, *Boys' Fishing School* (1945).

Naylor and Reznikoff traveled widely in Brazil for nearly three years, trekking into the interior and as far north as Pernambuco, and despite the limits imposed by the government, Naylor was often able to break free and photograph less officially approved subjects.[42] Still in her twenties, she had studied under Berenice Abbott at the New School for Social Research in New York, and her work is very much in the tradition of the socially conscious, Depression-era photographs of the New Deal's Farm Security Administration and the street photography of the New York Film and Photo League. (Famous names from these schools include Walker Evans, Dorothea Lange, Ben Shahn, and Helen Levitt.)

José Renau's entry in 1942 hemisphere poster contest. Courtesy of the Library of Congress, Prints and Photographs Division.

Entry in 1942 hemisphere poster contest. Courtesy of the Library of Congress, Prints and Photographs Division.

Entry in 1942 hemisphere poster contest. Courtesy of the Library of Congress, Prints and Photographs Division.

The power of Naylor's black-and-white images derives partly from her poor or working-class subjects, who are captured in daily yet dramatic motion: a newspaper boy walking in a chiaroscuro afternoon in downtown Rio, passengers clinging to the outside of a crowded trolley, street performers dancing the northeastern Brazilian *frevo*, young and old enjoying the beachfront, crowds celebrating carnival, and hundreds gathering for a religious festival. Significantly, several of her photographs disclose the intimate physical proximity between the poor and the well-to-do. We see a black fishermen hauling in nets while a Zona Sul luxury high-rise looms in the background; in another shot, first-class passengers loll on a riverboat's comfortable upper deck while third-class travelers ride on the deck below, where an enormous side of beef on a hook dangles against a backdrop of strung hammocks.

Naylor showed candid scenes of Brazil at war: soldiers boarding a train, street actors comically miming Hitler and Mussolini, and profascist graffiti on a wall—this last a reminder of fifth-column activity in Brazil. She frequently veered away from the DIP's approved subject matter but was never actually prevented from recording the country's poverty. In one photograph weary adults

Trolley car in Rio de Janeiro. Photograph by Genevieve Naylor. Courtesy of the Library of Congress, Prints and Photographs Division.

Brazilian buskers. Photograph by Genevieve Naylor. Courtesy of the Library of Congress, Prints and Photographs Division.

stand in long breadlines, and in another three child beggars sit on a rough-hewn wooden bench. The latter image is especially moving because Naylor photographs the children from behind; by emphasizing their ragged condition and diminutive size instead of their faces, she creates the feeling of unrecognized people and a powerfully emblematic portrait of child poverty. The shot is especially heart-rending because the children are so small—despite the lowness of the bench, their tiny bare feet dangle above the ground.

Brazilian schoolchildren. Photograph by Genevieve Naylor. Courtesy of the Library of Congress.

Naylor's photographs show Vargas's portrait displayed in shops, cafés, and even a samba school. Her picture of a local photographer's window display shows small-framed portraits of men, women, and children reverently assembled in front of a large picture of Vargas in presidential attire. Here Vargas resembles a patriarch presiding over his family, a role that many Brazilians associated with the leader. Interestingly, a slightly smaller portrait of Vargas sits above and to the right of this reverential display, as if the dictator were carefully overseeing his own adoration as *pater familias*. This is the kind of photograph the DIP might have approved of—perhaps without recognizing its panoptic implications.

Naylor's sizable work, a portion of which was lost during her travels in Brazil, makes an interesting comparison to Orson Welles's incomplete film about Latin America. Both Levine and Benamou have noted that Naylor helped Welles identify film locations in Rio for *It's All True*.[43] Like Welles, Naylor was intrigued by samba and carnival and had to work under the watchful eye of the DIP. But Naylor was less scrutinized than Welles, who naturally drew attention and pub-

licity because of his celebrity, movie cameras, and crew. A feature-length documentary by a world-famous director was far more important to the government
than individual pictures taken by a little-known woman with a portable still
camera. As we know, Welles's filming of black Brazilians celebrating carnival
and the reenactment of a trip made by four dark-skinned northern Brazilian
fishermen seeking economic justice were anathema to the DIP's desired image of Brazil. As described earlier, Welles's project incurred the displeasure of
not only Vargas but also RKO studio executives and Rockefeller, whose idea of
Good Neighbor Brazil included colorful tropical settings and figures such as Zé
Carioca and Carmen Miranda.

Anticipating Welles and quite unlike Disney, Naylor did not refrain from
portraying Rio as a racially mixed society, but her photodocumentary was

Getúlio Vargas as *pater familias* in a window display. Photograph by Genevieve Naylor.
Courtesy of the Library of Congress, Prints and Photographs Division.

more wide-ranging and eclectic. Her pictures of Brazil's relatively integrated population prominently feature trolley cars, trains, luxurious beachfront hotels, and high-rise buildings—symbols of modernity. Group shots of mainly working-class black, brown, and white children at play and in school arguably supported Brazil's much-touted image of itself as a "racial democracy"; and her focus on youth tied in well with the CIAA's emphasis on children as future hemispheric leaders. At the same time, her pictures of beggars, bread lines, and black poverty contradicted the idea of a racially egalitarian society. A seemingly innocuous shot of more than one hundred uniformed schoolgirls performing in an outdoor civic pageant conveys an image of a progressive Brazil that the government was eager to show, but it also reveals that all but a few of the girls were white.

Naylor's work from Minas Gerais and the Northeast is filled with images of churches and religious worship—an important aspect of Latin American life that prompted the CIAA to promote, especially in its documentaries, U.S. families at Sunday worship. But Naylor's images are far more interesting in their display of the multitudes gathered for outdoor religious processions or the extreme penitence of those who knelt on cobblestone streets in prayer. Her photographs of Minas Gerais are culturally informative, showing colonial towns with beautiful baroque architecture and the life-size statuary carved by Brazil's famous seventeenth-century artist Aleijadinho. Poverty is everywhere evident here and in photographs of the Northeast, but with few exceptions her focus is on family, community, faith, and work—elements that were to become central to the CIAA's image of an ethos uniting the American republics. Naylor captures the solemnity and dignity of people in poverty as well as the merriment of carnival revelers, street musicians, and children playing toy musical instruments. Her picture of a northeastern *sanfonista* (accordion player) could easily have been the model for the blind ballad singer in Glauber Rocha's famous revolutionary film, *Deus e o diabo na terra do sol* (1963, *Black God, White Devil*). Catherine L. Benamou is correct when she points out that Naylor's photographs of northeastern cowboys, families, and rural towns anticipate the dramatic style and radical substance of the 1960s films about the Northeast that came to be known as Cinema Novo.[44]

On January 27, 1943, just before her return to New York, a small exhibit of fifty of Naylor's photographs, titled *Faces and Places in Brazil*, opened at MoMA. According to a MoMA document, the photographs focused on seven areas: schoolchildren, Copacabana Beach, types of people in the interior, Rio de Janeiro, religious festivals, the São Francisco River, and carnival.[45] *New York*

Times columnist Edward Alden Jewell's favorable review mentioned that other, out-of-town reviewers were impressed by the exhibit. The Pittsburgh *Sun Telegraph* ran Naylor's photograph of a passenger-laden Rio trolley car and in a caption added a bit of humor while acknowledging the importance of Brazil to the Allied effort: "Ticket please. You think Pittsburgh's trolleys and businesses are overcrowded? Here's a trolley at rush time in Rio, Brazil, another country where Roosevelt stopped on his return from Casablanca."[46] In 1944 a Naylor exhibit containing more than a hundred photographs traveled to Boston, Rochester, Colorado Springs, San Francisco, and Seattle.

But Naylor's debut at MoMA was modest compared to the CIAA-cosponsored *Brazil Builds* exhibit, which occupied most of the museum's ground floor.[47] U.S. interest in Brazilian architecture had grown as a result of the widely acclaimed Brazilian Pavilion designed by Oscar Niemeyer and Lúcio Costa for the 1939 New York World's Fair. To build on MoMA's reputation in modern art, its Latin American collection, and the enthusiasm generated by the pavilion, Philip L. Goodwin, MoMA trustee and chairman of the museum's Department of Architecture, traveled to Brazil for the purposes of preparing a photo exhibit of the country's old and new architecture. His was an artistic and fact-finding mission that entailed studying how architects dealt with tropical heat and light in modernist structures with large glass surfaces (Deckker, 114–115). Photographer and architect G. E. Kidder-Smith accompanied Goodwin on the trip, and, like Naylor, they traveled to Rio, São Paulo, and Minas Gerais as well as the Amazon and Northeast. By the end of their spring 1942 tour, they had amassed nearly a thousand photographs in addition to a large collection of pictures and other materials that had been given to them by Costa, Niemeyer, Roberto Burle-Marx, and others.[48]

The MoMA exhibit ran from January 13 until February 24, 1943. Attendance was good, although New York reviews were uneven. Reviews elsewhere were favorable if not enthusiastic. A smaller version of the exhibit toured U.S. schools and universities, and the CIAA arranged a special showing in Brazil to inaugurate the official opening of the much-touted Ministry of Education and Health in Rio. Other tours encompassed Mexico City and London.[49]

The CIAA distributed two thousand copies of the catalogue *Brazil Builds* in Portuguese and English to architects, diplomats, writers, artists, and other professionals in Brazil and presented hand-bound copies to Vargas and Minister of Education and Public Health Gustavo Capanema. According to the publication proposal, two complete sets of duplicate prints were donated to the Brazilian Institute of Architects.[50] The estimated cost for the publication with

prints was $6,850. Justification for the publication was based on the U.S. need
to court Latin American countries like Brazil that sought recognition as modern, progressive nations:

> It is a common complaint of the nations of the other American Republics, that the
> United States fails to appreciate their contributions to contemporary thought and
> modern living, and that we only stress those picturesque aspects of their coun-
> tries that are in their own minds associated with their remote past or with their
> more backward regions. This complaint is constantly used by Axis sympathizers
> as evidence of their accusation that the U.S. does not wish to consider these na-
> tions as equals. The modern architecture of Brazil is an achievement in terms of
> the most advanced thought of the twentieth century that is without parallel in this
> hemisphere.[51]

Like *Faces and Places in Brazil*, *Brazil Builds* contributed to the CIAA's efforts
to draw attention to a region that was strategically vital to winning the war.
The project received the support of DIP officials, and the book's bilingual commentary promoting Brazil's historic-preservation efforts particularly gratified
the Vargas regime. If there were any question about the modernity of Brazil's
"face," *Brazil Builds* demonstrated that Rio and São Paulo were in the architectural vanguard. Among the exhibit's many Brazilian supporters was the distinguished writer Mário de Andrade, who wrote an ecstatic review essay. A mulatto, Andrade used the U.S. recognition to encourage Brazilians to take pride
in their mixed-race heritage:

> I believe that *Brazil Builds* is one of the most fruitful gestures that the United States
> has ever shown in relation to Brazilians. Because it will regenerate, it has already
> regenerated, confidence in ourselves as it has diminished the disastrous inferiority
> complex that we have as mestizos and that hurts us so much. . . . The United States'
> gesture of discovering us in *Brazil Builds* should renew us. It is not racial capability
> that we lack; this is ridiculous. (Andrade, 180–181; my translation)

As Zilah Deckker has noted in her book *Brazil Built*, architectural digests
of the day nearly swooned with excitement over *Brazil Builds*, and some, like
Architectural Review and the French *L'Architecture d'aujord'hui*, even featured
images of Brazil on their covers. Among the many ultramodern structures, the
Ministry of Education and Health building was singled out for pictorials in
journals, magazines, and newspapers. Appearing in the September 1943 issue
of *California Arts and Architecture*, a Ray Eames collage juxtaposed images of
the building and an Eames desk alongside those of a World War II helmet, an
airplane, a Willys Jeep, and Picasso's *Guernica*. Fashion magazines capitalized
on the building's grandiosity by using it as a backdrop in photo ads for what

Modernist Brazil. Photograph by G. E. Kidder-Smith. Courtesy of the Library of Congress, Prints and Photographs Division.

the sophisticated and up-to-date woman should wear (Deckker, 154–156). But unlike the fashion ads, Eames's collage has a political edge that suggests the proximity between not only the arts, architecture, and industry but also modernist design and the business of war.

The text and photographs in *Brazil Builds* bear a certain resemblance to the CIAA's travelogue-style documentaries, whose architectural images were regularly accompanied by exuberant voice-overs about Brazil's rich colonial heritage and modern urban landscape. That aspect was not appreciated by some New York reviewers, who were less appreciative of the juxtaposition of old and new and felt the exhibit lacked originality, simply recycling Good Neighbor postcard views. Writing for *The Nation*, Latin American art specialist Elizabeth Wilder recognized the show's merits but also described the urgent need for Brazilian architects to serve the welfare of the poor:

> It is only to balance this enthusiasm by the observation that most of Brazil is badly housed, that most of the country is without schools or hospitals of any sort, and

that outside the few cities represented here functionalism has hardly been heard of. In short, the architects are ahead of social planners; they ought to be set to work on small hospitals for provincial towns, day nurseries, community centers, and subsistence housing for the poor who now live between banana thatch and bamboo floor. Brazil needs all these things desperately, needs them more than casinos and hotels. (In Deckker, 150)

Translations

Although some CIAA-sponsored publication activities, including translating titles into Spanish and Portuguese, did not have the extensive public reach of films, newspaper articles, photographic exhibits, or radio programs, they transmitted a broad range of U.S. literary talent and scientific information to the Latin American region. The translations were a logical extension of CIAA educational initiatives that involved establishing American libraries and supporting library science training in Latin America. A June 9, 1942, memo from Robert Spiers Benjamin in the Publication Division to Jamieson summarizes important projects under way at the time.[52] Perhaps no one task was as demanding as the division's role as factotum literary agent for procuring titles and rights for editors and authors in the United States and Latin America. One of the largest projects, earmarked at $80,000, was to support translations of State Department–approved U.S. literary and scientific materials by Latin American publishers.

The CIAA helped publishers by purchasing and distributing, through the American Council of Learned Societies, a minimum of five hundred copies of each book. These negotiations were based on a report by the Library of Congress and Hispanic Foundation's Lewis Hanke, who visited Latin American publishers in fall 1941.[53] Victor Publishing in New York translated a few of its own works into English for a Good Neighbor Collection in tandem with its Rio company, Livraria Victor. The first title was Danton Jobim's questionable comparison, *Two Revolutions: F.D.R. and Getúlio Vargas* (from the original *A experiência Roosevelt e a revolução brasileira*), which appeared in English in March 1941 and by June was in its fourth printing.[54]

A status report for February 1944 lists dozens of Spanish and Portuguese translations with details of purchase arrangements for advance copies by the ACLS and estimated costs.[55] Books selected for publication varied according to the publisher. The Buenos Aires Editorial Losada published translations of Walt Whitman's "Song of Myself," Thomas Dewey's *Experience and Education* and *The Science of Education*, Edgar Lee Masters's *The Living Thoughts of Emer-*

son, Archibald MacLeish's *A Time to Speak*, and Ralph Waldo Emerson's *Representative Men and Other Essays*, while Guillermo Kraft issued, among others, Leland H. Hinsie's *Concepts and Problems of Psychotherapy*, Oliver L. Reiser's *A New Earth and a New Humanity*, Francis L. Wellman's *Success in Court*, and Frank Luther Mott's *History of American Journalism*. Benjamin's report refers to special subsidies for anthologies; one of these was the CIAA's contribution of $4,350 toward *An Anthology of Contemporary North American Literature* by Editorial Nascimento in Santiago, Chile.[56]

According to the same 1944 report, publishers such as São Paulo's Livraria Martins and certain government agencies, including the Serviço de Informação Agrícola in the Ministry of Agriculture in Rio, received most of the translation subventions, followed by Argentina, Mexico, Chile, and Haiti. The report lists some of the Latin American titles published in English after 1942. These included New Directions' *An Anthology of Latin American Poetry* (subsidized at $2,900) and *Five Young American Poets*; Macmillan's *Germans in the Conquest of America* by Colombian Minister of Education Germán Arciniegas and *Chile: A Geographic Extravaganza* by Benjamín Subercaseaux; the Knopf anthology *The Green Continent* and *Peruvian Traditions* by Ricardo Palma; Houghton Mifflin's *Anthology of Latin American Literature* (subsidized at $3,000); and the University of Chicago's *Rebellion in the Backlands* by Euclides da Cunha.

According to Benjamin's 1941 memo to Jamieson, the CIAA provided small grants of $600 to $700 to U.S. publishers to help with translation expenses, and the Press and Publication Division helped promote books in newspapers and magazines. In the cases of Brazil, Mexico, and most likely other countries, a local committee recommended titles. In 1942 the Brazilian committee had numerous judges including artist Cândido Portinari, literary critic Augusto Meyer, and writers Raul d'Éça, Luís Jardim, and Gilka Machado. In Mexico, writers Alfonso Reyes, Antonio Castro Leal, and Francisco de Monterde made the selections.

There is insufficient space to list all the Brazilian titles recommended for translation. Novelists dominated the list. Among these were Jorge Amado (*Jubiabá, Mar morto* [*Sea of the Dead*], and *Cacau*), Amando Fontes (*Os Corumbas*), and Machado de Assis (*Dom Casmurro* and *Memórias póstumas de Brás Cubas* [*Epitaph of a Small Winner*]), who was described in a note as the "best 19th-century writer[,] mother a negress."[57] Other authors suggested were Vianna Moog (*O rio imita o Reno* [The River Imitates the Rhine]), Rachel de Queiroz (*Caminho de pedras* [Path of Stones], *João Miguel, As três Marias* [*The Three Marias*] and *O quinze* [The Year 1915]), Octávio de Faria (*Os caminhos da vida*

[Byways of Life]), Érico Veríssimo (*Caminhos cruzados* [*Crossroads*], *Clarissa*, and *Olhai os lírios do campo* [*Consider the Lilies of the Field*]), and Graciliano Ramos (*Vidas secas* [*Barren Lives*], *Angústia* [*Anguish*], and *São Bernardo*).

The emphasis on the socially committed northeastern novels by Amado, Queiroz, and Ramos and southern "regional" writers such as Moog and Veríssimo is not surprising, given their popularity at home and the radical and left-liberal sentiments of the era. Suggested authors who were actually translated at the time were Jorge Amado (*Terras do sem fim* [*The Violent Land*, 1945]); a fragment of *Sea of the Dead* in the Latin American literature anthology *Fiesta in November* (1942), organized by Eduardo Mallea; Érico Veríssimo (*Crossroads*, 1943; *Consider the Lilies of the Field*, 1947, and *O resto é silêncio* [*The Rest Is Silence*, 1946]), and Graciliano Ramos (*Anguish*, 1946). Other authors translated to English included northeastern novelist José Lins do Rego (*Pureza*, 1947) and the nineteenth-century regionalist writer Visconde d'Taunay (*Inocência*, 1945).

Short commentaries often accompanied the committee's list of recommendations. Lúcio Cardoso, who was beginning to make a name as a novelist, was described as "a young author who writes somewhat in the style of Julian Green." Committee members felt that Luís Jardim's *O tatu e o macaco* (The Armadillo and the Monkey) "should delight both children and adults in the U.S." and that Monteiro Lobato's "tales about a half-breed of the hinterland of São Paulo" (*Jeca Tatu*) was another worthy selection. Monteiro's story "The Funny Man Who Repented" appeared in the 1947 anthology *A World of Great Stories*. The committee suggested republishing Graça Aranha's *Canaan* (Boston: Four Seas, 1920), which did not reappear until the 1970s, and translating Euclides da Cunha's *Os sertões* (*Rebellion in the Backlands*), whose English translation by Samuel Putnam was published to wide acclaim in 1944 by the University of Chicago Press and is a canonical work still in print today.[58]

One of the particularly interesting features of the translation program is the high number of book recommendations that deal with race and slavery in Brazil—as if the committee were eager to point out similarities as well as differences in the histories of blacks in the United States and Brazil. Titles include Josué de Castro's *Alimentação e raça* (Alimentation and Race), João Dornas Filho's *A escravidão no Brasil* (Slavery in Brazil), Gilberto Freyre's *Casa grande e senzala* (*The Masters and the Slaves*, 1946) and *Sobrados e mucambos* (Mansions and the Shanties), Renato Mendonça's *A influência africana no português do Brasil* (African Influence in Brazilian Portuguese), abolitionist Joaquim Nabuco's *Minha formação* (My Education), Arthur Ramos's *As culturas negras no novo mundo* (Black Cultures in the New World) and *O negro brasileiro* (The

Black Brazilian), and Nina Rodrigues's *Os africanos no Brasil* (Africans in Brazil).[59] The committee's emphasis in this case departs sharply from the Vargas government's tendency to minimize or erase blackness in the construction and promotion of Brazil's image abroad.

Other CIAA translation activities around this time included $5,000 for best books in Latin America to be translated and published by Farrar and Rinehart. Peruvian Ciro Alegría's *Broad and Alien Is the World* (1941, *El mundo es ancho y ajeno*), translated by Harriet de Onís, won first prize; the competition generated enthusiasm and was continued. Two years later, Farrar and Rinehart published Alegría's earlier *The Golden Serpent* (*La serpiente de oro*, 1935), which, like *Broad and Alien*, portrayed poverty and class struggle, especially of indigenous peoples, in Peru. Historian Hubert Herring proposed translating magazine articles into Spanish, Portuguese, and English for inter-American consumption, a project that was funded by the Publications Division at $28,000.

Individual works deemed essential to U.S.-Latin American relations received special subsidies. A Portuguese translation of Morison and Commager's *The Growth of the American Republic* received $1,500; this U.S. history was published by Oxford University Press in partnership with the São Paulo–based Companhia Editorial Nacional. Seven hundred copies of *The Pharmacopoeia and the Physician* in Spanish translation were prepared for distribution to doctors and hospitals throughout the Americas. The division secured rights for the *Estado de São Paulo* newspaper to publish a collection of ten short stories by U.S. writers in Portuguese translation.

One of the U.S. publishers most actively engaged in the CIAA translation literary initiative was Knopf, and the person largely responsible for the Latin American selections was Blanche Knopf, a keen supporter of modern literature who brought major authors Jorge Amado, María Luisa Bombal, Graciliano Ramos, Eduardo Mallea, and Ricardo Palma, among others, to U.S. attention. On April 9, 1942, Sumner Welles took time to promote Knopf's Good Neighbor interests by writing to Claude Bowers about Blanche Knopf's forthcoming tour of South America "to establish contacts with authors and editors and to identify material for translation."[60]

Blanche Knopf's enthusiasm about what she discovered on her trip is apparent in her short essay "The Literary Roundup: An American Publisher Tours South America": "The chief impression I gained on my recent trip to South America was one of newness, of aliveness, of something being created virtually from the ground up by people who find joy and excitement in that creation, and a great hope for the future" (7). She concisely comments on the book-publishing world in Latin America and mentions her own company's author William Shirer (*Berlin Diary*, 1940) and John Gunther (*Inside Latin America*, 1941) as two of the best-selling contemporary U.S. writers in Spanish translation (8). Knopf was particularly impressed with Chilean writers and compared Gabriela Mistral's position in the Spanish-speaking world with that of Thomas Mann in pre-Hitler Germany. She praised historian and geographer Benjamín Subercaseux as "brilliant" and described Bombal as a "first-rate young novelist" whose work would soon appear in English by Knopf (9).

While most writers were eager for U.S. recognition, not every author was happy or completely well served. Bombal was so distressed by the translation of her experimental novella *The Shrouded Woman* (*La amortajada*, 1938) that she asked a friend to buy the remaining copies from Knopf and then proceeded to retranslate the work herself, which she published with Farrar and Rinehart in 1948 (Rostagno, 32).[61] Samuel Putnam's translation of Amado's *Terras do sem fim* (*The Violent Land*), about nineteenth-century cacao plantation society, eliminates the steamy sex that was to become a trademark of Amado's work. The bowdlerization was possibly the result of interracial sex scenes that were anathema to Brazil's preferred racially white image; ironically, those very kinds of scenes were the chief selling point for later Knopf translations, such as Amado's *Gabriela, Clove and Cinnamon* and *Dona Flor and Her Two Husbands*. These and other novels by the Brazilian writer were frequently reprinted and sold widely for classroom use, resulting in Amado's rise to become the most widely known and read Latin American author in the 1960s and 1970s in the United States.[62]

Doubleday was another company that published Latin American translations. The writer Waldo Frank worked for Doubleday and was responsible for many of its Latin American titles. A few CIAA documents refer to Frank as a Good Neighbor traveling ambassador. He was a Latin American literature enthusiast and was very popular in the region in the 1920s and 1930s for hemispheric-style commentary in works like *South of Us* (1930), which anticipated the Good Neighbor policy and inter-American cultural relations efforts by several years. In 1943 he published *South American Journey*, a cultural history and travelogue that touts "Our Island Hemisphere: Three Americas, One America."[63]

Among the division's many other, nonliterary projects was the publication of the first comprehensive travel guide to Latin America, organized by Earl P. Hanson and released in 1943 by Duell, Sloan, and Pearce in three volumes, titled *New World Guides to the Latin American Republics*. The division supported magazine and journal publication. A good example was the purchase of 1,250 yearly subscriptions of *The Hispanic American Historical Review* at $3,000. These and other subscriptions were routinely distributed to coordination committees throughout the region as well as to other targeted groups. Benjamin's aforementioned 1944 report refers to the division's role as informal book-purchasing agent for other CIAA divisions: "[W]e will purchase for Mr. Prendergast's section, with his advice, books of interest to Catholic readers in the other Americas; we will send one or two books of research material to some of the magazines and newspapers at the request of Mr. Hall; and, with the advice of Dr. Bressman of the Department of Agriculture, will send books on agriculture to magazines and newspapers."[64]

With the Book Publishers Bureau of New York, the Publications Division arranged visits to the United States by Latin American publishers. The division worked with the American Institute of Graphic Arts on an exhibit of U.S. book production and design that opened at the Pan American Union and went on to tour Latin America, with a first stop at the Biblioteca Benjamín Franklin in Mexico City. In 1943 it launched a bibliographic series, the first two titles of which were *A Preliminary Bibliography of Colombia* and *A Preliminary Bibliography of Paraguay* that contained 781 and 370 items, respectively, and were part of a CIAA's project titled Strategic Index of the Americas (Hanke, 45). In conjunction with the National Geographic Society the division produced a number of maps as well as an *Index to the Millionth Map of Hispanic America*. Another kind of publication was a comprehensive list of all the libraries in Latin America—a list that helped in the CIAA's dissemination of materials as well as its more ambitious plans for building libraries abroad, a subject to be treated in the next chapter.

Chapter Five

IN MUSEUMS, IN LIBRARIES, AND ON THE HOME FRONT

The Divisions of Cultural Relations and Inter-American Affairs in the United States

> It pays best to bring *people* north to the United States; it pays best to send *things* south to Latin America.
>
> John M. Clark to the Policy Committee on Cultural Relations Activities, December 11, 1941

Overlapping and competing interests between the State Department's Division of Cultural Relations and the CIAA's Division of Cultural Relations (1940–1943), which was charged with activities in music, art, literary publications, and scholarships, resulted in an April 22, 1941, presidential order that Rockefeller submit all CIAA Division projects for State Department approval through a special committee. Its membership included representatives from the CIAA and the State Department as well as from the American Council of Learned Societies, which frequently worked with the CIAA (Rowland, 91). By 1942 some CIAA cultural relations activities were reassigned to its Science and Education Division; others came under the supervision of the CIAA's newly created U.S. Inter-American Activities Division or were picked up by its Press and Publication Division. In September 1943 a Department of Special Services was created to combine the Cultural Relations and Inter-American Activities Divisions (*Federal Records*, 242–243).[1]

Special Services became an umbrella unit for three other divisions: Services and Field Coordination, Labor Relations, and Education and Teacher Aids. Most of the projects undertaken by these divisions can be characterized as working toward long-range influence in promoting hemispheric understanding and cooperation (Rowland, 92). For the purposes of simplifying the bureaucratic maze of reorganization and renaming of units, my discussion will employ the early divisional descriptors—Cultural Relations and Inter-American Activities in the United States—and will be organized chiefly in terms of subject headings that cut across the various offices.[2]

The Arts

On November 7, 1940, just months after the CIAA's inception, Robert G. Caldwell and Wallace K. Harrison, chairman and director, respectively, of the Cultural Relations Division, received written approval for twenty-six special projects at a cost of nearly one-half million dollars.[3] The most expensive, at $150,000, was an inter-American exhibit of art and culture under the direction of MoMA, to be held simultaneously with parallel exhibits in capital cities throughout the Americas.[4] Two hundred fifty-five U.S. paintings were curated by MoMA in conjunction with other major museums, and in April 1941 these were previewed at the Metropolitan Museum of Art in New York.[5] Portions of the large exhibit then toured eight South American republics, Mexico, and Cuba for close to a year, beginning with an exposition at Mexico City's Palacio de Bellas Artes in June. The emphasis was on modern art and included paintings by Georgia O'Keeffe, Thomas Hart Benton, Edward Hopper, Stuart Davis, Loren MacIver, Eugene Speicher, Peter Hurd, and Robert Henri, among others. A file in the MoMA archive has valuations of all the paintings at the time, the highest being George Bellows's *Dempsey and Firpo* and Georgia O'Keeffe's *The White Flower* at $25,000 each. Edward Hopper's watercolor *Box Factory, Gloucester* was valued at $400 and Arthur Dove's *Electric Peach Orchard* at $250.[6]

U.S. specialists accompanied the various tours: MoMA's Stanton Caitlin went to Mexico City, Quito, Lima, and Santiago; New Orleans artist Caroline Durieux, who had lived in Mexico and worked with Rivera and other muralists there, oversaw exhibits in Buenos Aires, Rio, and Montevideo; and Lewis A. Riley, who had studied art and archaeology and lived in Central America for nearly a decade, traveled to Havana, Caracas, and Bogotá. The ambitious project was successful in introducing a little-known aspect of U.S. culture to the other American republics. Durieux was enthusiastic about the South American reception, stating in a newspaper interview that more than sixty thousand people attended the three capital city exhibits. In Good Neighbor fashion, she emphasized fundamental similarities among the Americas that should outweigh any differences, but she seemed to put emphasis on race: "There is a definite kinship between North and South Americans who, after all, have sprung from the same European stock, and there is no reason why misunderstandings should exist between them." She was particularly pleased that Latin Americans "were learning that there is more to the United States than business"—a recurring slogan in cultural relations.[7]

The CIAA project entailed the publication and distribution of 35,000 trilingual exhibit catalogues titled *Contemporary Painting in the U.S.* with a preface by novelist Waldo Frank, who was a major proponent of Latin American literature and culture in the United States. A donation of ten sets of fifty-three U.S. art books each went to major institutions in the ten exhibiting capital cities. Total attendance for the exhibitions abroad was 218,089.[8] Press reaction was positive and widespread, and included reviews in the November 12, 1941, issue of Rio's *A Manhã* newspaper by two of Brazil's most celebrated writers, novelist José Lins do Rego and poet Manuel Bandeira.[9] Meanwhile, an amusing anecdote about the exhibit appeared in U.S. newspapers. Among the paintings on display was Eugene Speicher's portrait of Broadway star Katharine Cornell in the role of Bernard Shaw's Candida—a painting that Cornell had donated to MoMA. According to Leonard Lyons's syndicated column, "Broadway Medley," Cornell suddenly began receiving fan mail from South Americans who had seen the exhibit and praised her extraordinary beauty. Intrigued by this outpouring, she obtained a catalogue of the show and discovered that two of the artwork titles had been switched: "Cornell as Candida" had been transposed to one of Speicher's voluptuous nudes.[10]

The second part of the inter-American art project involved an exhibition of Latin American works to be loaned by various U.S. art museums, private companies, and institutions, among them MoMA, the Art Institute of Chicago, the Pan American Union, IBM, the Philadelphia Museum of Art, and the Taylor Museum in Colorado Springs.[11] The San Francisco Museum of Modern Art (SFMoMA) was one of the most heavily invested, with a contribution of contemporary Latin American paintings, drawings, and photographs valued at $10,000. Among the artists selected by SFMoMA director Grace McCann Morley were Mexicans Rufino Tamayo, Diego Rivera, José Clemente Orozco, David Alfaro Siqueiros, and Fermín Revueltas; Brazilian Cândido Portinari; Colombian Luis Alberto Acuña; Peruvian Julia Codesido; and Cubans Wifredo Lam and Amelia Pelaez. In addition to items from SFMoMA's permanent collection, the tour package was supplemented by works on special loan by artists whom Morley had met during a three-month Latin American tour in 1941 for the CIAA initiative.[12]

An April 20, 1942, document from SFMoMA to MoMA lists titles and artists as well as photographs of artwork loaned for the exhibition. The photograph-

Grace McCann Morley, c. 1940.
Photograph by Brett Weston.
Courtesy of the Brett Weston
Archive and the San Francisco
Museum of Modern Art.

ic record gives an idea of the museum's Latin American collection as well as
subjects that appealed to Morley during her tour of the region. Overall, there
is stylistic variety, but there are also recurring images and motifs. Unlike the
parallel exhibit of U.S. modern art, the overwhelming focus of the Latin American exhibit is on representations of indigenous peasant culture, with images of
women and children as primary subjects. Most of the women appear as wives,
mothers, or statuesque models. Antonio Sotomayor's *Chola* depicts a Bolivian
"mestiza" dressed in traditional high-rounded hat and colorful garb. Religious
motifs appear in several works, such as Ecuadorian Eduardo Kingman's *Pro-
cession* and Acuña's woodcut-style drawing titled *The Annunciation as Visu-
alized by the American Indian*, in which a fleshy, barefoot Indian woman sits
cross-legged in a desert landscape. Like *The Annunciation*, Acuña's *Wild Boy*
harks back to a tradition of colonial woodcuts that display indigenous subjects
for a white European gaze. In this case, a lush, tropical setting serves as backdrop for a naked boy with a bow in his hand and an anteater at his feet.

Most landscapes in the exhibit were rural images depicting mountainous
terrains; the Argentine Onofrio Pacenza's *Marine* is the only painting of a sea-
shore. Tamayo's surrealistic *The Window* is perhaps the most artistically dar-

ing and unusual of the canvases: a serene, moonlit setting is framed by an open window, on the ledge of which lies a large, menacing revolver. An unidentified Argentine painting of factory workers and smokestacks is one of the few to depict the urban working class or to evoke social-realist aesthetics. In fact, the SFMoMA selections did very little to suggest to North American viewers that Latin America was modern except in regard to certain stylistic approaches. The CIAA was preoccupied with this phenomenon and therefore added modernistic poster art to the exhibit. It contracted art photographers to produce images of urban architecture, city centers, and the Latin American middle class; among these were selections from Julien Bryan's photographic series People of Pan America.[13]

One of the dividends from the inter-American art project was an exhibit at the Toledo Museum of Art in March 1942 that was publicized as the first major show of Chilean art in North America. The exhibit was a goodwill gesture arranged by the Chilean government in appreciation for the U.S. show and the visit by Toledo Museum of Art's Blake-More Godwin, who was sent by the CIAA to report on the status of contemporary Chilean art. It featured artists Camilo Mori, Samuel Roman, Totila Albert, Héctor Cáceres, and others. A news story dated April 16, 1942, reported that over twelve thousand people had seen the more than 150 artworks displayed during the first two weeks and that the exhibit would tour the United States with a final stop at the Metropolitan Museum of Art.[14] (The tour continued into Canada under the auspices of the Canadian government.) The story made much of the idea that with the Americas cut off from Europe by the war, the twenty-one republics were now in the process of discovering one another through art museum exhibitions. In a letter to John Abbott, Stanton Caitlin mentioned that Chilean artists were eager to sell as well as to show their works in the United States.[15]

Museums were not the only venue for Good Neighbor art. Several South American countries loaned artworks to Macy's department store in New York, and they were later displayed in other stores in the United States. The size of the Macy's exhibit was impressive, with a loan of forty-three paintings and thirteen sculptures from Colombia alone.[16] Railroad stations, libraries, and city halls were used for "informational exhibits" like the Americas Cooperate, a large photographic display in which vital wartime materials from Latin America such as copper, manganese, and mercury were artfully displayed.[17]

As a result of CIAA initiatives, certain Latin American artists quickly came to the attention of critics, and markets for their works grew in the United States. Already in late 1940, Cândido Portinari was on the rise in art circles as a result of his larger-than-life, modernist murals of northeastern Brazilian *jangadeiros* (fishermen on rough-hewn rafts with sails) and baianas, as well as gauchos. His murals were displayed in Lúcio Costa and Oscar Niemeyer's acclaimed Brazilian Pavilion at New York's 1939 World's Fair.[18] During his U.S. stay for the exposition, Portinari was commissioned to paint portraits of Florence Horn (who wrote the catalogue description for his 1940 one-man MoMA show) and Brazilian poet Adalgisa Nery (wife of Brazilian DIP head Lourival Fontes) as well as a self-portrait for Nelson Rockefeller. He painted four portraits of Arthur Rubenstein family members. In November 1940 Archibald MacLeish invited Portinari to paint a set of murals for the Library of Congress's Hispanic Reading Room. As a Good Neighbor gesture, the Brazilian government paid for Portinari's return to the United States, and the CIAA matched Brazil's funds to support the artist's work. Once sketches were completed, Portinari began painting the reading room murals in October 1941 and finished two months later.[19]

Like other muralists at the time, Portinari was drawn to the rural poor and urban working class as inspiration for his work. His World's Fair murals also depicted Brazil's three races through modernist-style figures of men and women. While the Vargas government wanted to promote the country's modernity and put limits on images of Brazil as poor, black, or mixed-race, Portinari continued to celebrate the nation's racial heritage in his floor-to-ceiling paintings for the Library of Congress. His murals depict four important moments in colonial Brazilian history involving the encounter of the three races: the founding of the land, the exploration of the interior, the conversion of the Indian, and the discovery of gold and diamonds in Minas Gerais.

The murals focus on the most humble social types: Portuguese sailors on a ship bound for Brazil; mixed-race São Paulo frontiersmen, or *bandeirantes*, pushing into the interior to seize land for the crown and capture fugitive Indian slaves; Portuguese Jesuits converting Indian women and children; and African slaves being transported during the eighteenth-century gold rush to the Minas Gerais interior. In each of the murals the adult human body is large and misshapen, with oversized, muscular arms and large feet. Cultural historian Daryle Williams describes in detail some of the unfavorable critical reaction in Brazil to Portinari's "ugly" human forms, which, for many, were considered deplorable because of his emphasis on poor and largely dark-skinned figures (225–226). The Library of Congress murals were nevertheless well received at the official opening on January 12, 1942, at which a specially produced publication, *The Portinari Murals*, was released to celebrate the artwork as a step forward in U.S.-Brazil cultural relations.

In spring 1942 Brazil's minister of education Gustavo Capanema reciprocated the MacLeish-CIAA commission to Portinari by inviting U.S. artist George Biddle to teach a course at the newly created Escola Técnica in Rio. Biddle had been heavily influenced by Diego Rivera and the Mexican muralist tradition and was a central proponent of the Federal Arts Project under FDR, his first mural having appeared in the 1933 Chicago World's Fair. Brother of Francis Biddle, U.S. attorney general under FDR, George Biddle chaired the U.S. War Department's Art Advisory Committee (1942–1944) and wrote *Artist at War* (1944) about his experiences as art war correspondent for *Life* in North Africa and Sicily.[20]

Capanema invited Biddle and his wife, sculptor Hèléne Sardeau, to create two murals in fresco and bas-relief for the capital's Biblioteca Nacional.[21] Bid-

Preparatory study for *Entry into the Forest* mural by Cândido Portinari. Courtesy of the Library of Congress, Hispanic Digital Collections.

Preparatory study for the *Discovery of the Land* mural by Cândido Portinari. Courtesy of the Library of Congress, Hispanic Digital Collections.

dle wrote enthusiastically to Henry Allen Moe, who chaired the CIAA's educational activities section of the division:

> I feel very happy now the way things have turned out. The two large murals are in as fine a building as any in Rio, on the main avenue of the City; and the themes which I intend to use have, I believe, great significance: (1) Not hatred, Destruction and Death over America, but (2) Intelligence and Humanity Shall Rule Our World. As far I know, it is the first time that two artists from the States have been invited by a South American Government to execute an important mural commission.[22]

The completed artwork has a dramatic, somewhat gothic quality. The first mural's central figure, presumably representing hatred and death, is a skeleton

head atop a body of white, emaciated flesh, riding an equally white and emaciated horse that breathes fire and flies over a tranquil landscape, bringing destruction to an Edenic group of men, women, and one child who appear at the bottom of the painting, their eyes closed or cast down in despair. Carrying a fiery
torch in one hand and a bloodied knife in the other, the skeleton is made all the
more frightening by virtue of a cavernous grin and pointy, blood-red toenails.

The Edenic figures appear again at the bottom of the second mural, looking up toward a fleshy woman with fire-red hair and large breasts who reaches
out to them from the sky as if to catch them up in an embrace. The themes of
knowledge and science are allegorically conveyed by two other figures, a woman reading a book to a child and a nude man holding a microscope in his lap.
There is an anachronistic quality to the male figure, who is shown covering
his genitals with a scientific instrument that looks rather like a metallic phal-
lus. Sardeau's bas-relief for the murals reconciles Biddle's opposing images of
destruction and humanity by giving humanity, in the form of the woman, a
greater emphasis.[23] It contains three figures—two males, one of whom is dying and cradled by the other in the image of the Pietà. The female figure offers
comfort, holding on to the dying man's outstretched arm.

Two years later, at Diego Rivera's urging, the Mexican government invited
Biddle and Sardeau to Mexico City, where they painted murals and bas-relief
for the library entryway in the Supreme Court building. In the central panel,
titled "The Cannibalism of War," Biddle reproduced the skeletal horse and
rider figures, which here are surrounded by monstrous winged creatures, most
of them shown consuming one another like cannibals. In the painting's lower-
left corner, a giant sci-fi-style lizard attempts to devour a dog that is being held
in the horse's mouth; in the lower-right corner a hippopotamus, jaws opened
wide, looks up as if anticipating a meal of the ravenous winged prey. Meanwhile
Sardeau's bas-relief shows naked figures, two of them hanging upside down,
reminiscent of Dante's agonizing souls in their suffering and tortured poses.

Biddle's social activism and horror of war, wedded with his various experiences as a teacher and artist in Brazil, led him to draft a document (dated
December 23, 1942) advising the CIAA to convene a congress of Latin American and U.S. artists and writers in the United States. He compared Western Europe's long-standing program of cultural relations with Latin America to the
United States' historic and lamentable indifference to cultural exchange:

> Over and over again in a year's stay in Brazil I saw tragic evidence of the lack of
> such a program. Commenting on this situation a Brazilian publisher and editor
> said to me: "You are thirty years late at the start. But for these next few months you

George Biddle mural in the Biblioteca Nacional, Rio de Janeiro.

Hélène Sardeau sculpture in the Biblioteca Nacional, Rio de Janeiro.
Courtesy of the Library of Congress.

are without competition. For God's sake do something NOW. After the war it may be too late. At any rate you will no longer be in a position where you can shape an intelligent cultural program for an eager and friendly audience of 120,000,000.[24]

Having resided in Brazil for a year, Biddle was possibly unaware of CIAA efforts to promote art exhibits and literary translations—areas he specifically targeted in his proposal. On July 22, 1942, Rockefeller had written to Biddle: "If you ask Dr. Aranha to recommend the ten books he feels are most appropriate, we will make a special effort to have them published under this project."[25] On February 19, 1943, Rockefeller authorized the Brazilian division to negotiate, at $500 each, Portuguese translations of U.S. publications that Biddle recommended.[26] Among them were Charles A. Beard and Mary Beard's *The Rise of American Civilization* (1927), Van Wyck Brooks's *The Flowering of New England* (1936), and Samuel Eliot Morison and Henry Steel Commager's *The Growth of the American Republic* (1930). Biddle recommended broader, more comprehensive actions as well, such as binational discussions over copyright laws to protect artists and writers; federal programs to support the arts, literature, and theater; laws to preserve historical monuments and art objects; and ways to address common educational problems and goals.

His most detailed recommendation involved CIAA sponsorship of a U.S. visit by fifty Latin American artists and writers at an estimated cost of $70,000—a figure he deemed a bargain in terms of goodwill and intellectual dividends and a scant amount compared to the *New York Times* (December 10, 1942) report of the $46 billion that had been spent to date on the war effort. Written shortly before his departure from Rio, Biddle's proposal had the support of U.S. ambassador to Brazil Jefferson Caffery and top-level officials in the Brazilian government. Ultimately no congress of this kind was convened, but the CIAA did invite numerous Latin American writers and artists to the States, and, as will be discussed later, the agency worked to augment pedagogical assistance and exchange.

There were disappointments and difficulties to address in the arts venture. Just weeks before Biddle's proposal was written, San Francisco Museum's Grace McCann Morley wrote worriedly to René d'Harnoncourt about CIAA exhibition delays, a lack of coordination between the agency and museums locally and abroad, and her anxieties about an exhibit planned for visiting Argentine artist Emilio Pettoruti:

Pettoruti will be terribly disappointed if no exhibition is forthcoming. He is restive now at not hearing sooner. . . . You have no idea what a bad name the cultural side of the Coordinator's office is beginning to get in this country [the United States]. I hear it—the gossip and innuendo—from all sides when it isn't definite complaint. I am sorry; I had such faith in there being some sort of coordinated and continuous program here and abroad. I only hope that the field I hear most about, which seems to be the art and education one, is simply suffering most and is not an indication of what is happening elsewhere. If it were I should feel completely disillusioned.[27]

Ultimately in the letter her trooper-like demeanor seems to have won out over her concerns: "We shall keep on planning as many Latin American exhibitions as possible and building around them interests of different kinds." She ended the missive on a high note and commented on the success of the exhibit at that time of Argentine Florencio Molina Campos's popular gaucho caricatures—a few of which (along with the artist himself) had just debuted in Disney's *Saludos amigos*.

As if anticipating Morley's appraisal and concerns, CIAA researcher Tommy Cotter wrote Francis Alstock of the Motion Picture Division in March 1942 for information on the scope of the CIAA's cultural exchanges. The tone and content of his letter convey his urgency to curb or counter displeasure and complaints about the agency's performance in the cultural relations area: "The general over-all facts and figures we need will be on Art, Music, Science, Medicine, Jurisprudence, Literature, Education, etc.; how many people have been brought here from Latin America, let us say in the last two years—and why? And during the same period, how many people have we sent down there—and why?"[28] Cotter asked for specific details on exchanges involving celebrities, scholarship students, doctors, writers, and educators; and he requested film footage that might be used for a documentary on the subject. He asked for information on exchanges "gone sour" as well: "Have we brought somebody up here, only to have him go back and give us a black eye? There must have been more than one case—out of which we can take a lesson from our own mishandling of the job."[29]

In the meantime, the Cultural Relations Division was receiving numerous queries from individuals and institutions stateside and abroad about financial support, exhibition loans, and publication projects. Brazilian filmmaker Mário Peixoto cabled about possible CIAA interest in buying for $2,500 a copy of his now classic avant-garde film *Limite* (1930).[30] The National University of Colombia proposed a Spanish-English catalogue on the collection housed in the newly constructed Museum of Colonial Art in Bogotá.[31] A grant was provided to cover the costs of a U.S. edition of the *Revista de Arte*, a quarterly publication of the Universidad de Chile.[32] Among other projects funded by the CIAA were a twenty-eight-week Latin American tour by the American Ballet Caravan under the direction of Lincoln Kirstein, co-founder of the American Ballet; ten archeological expeditions to Mexico and countries in Central and South America; the preparation of bibliographies on Latin American music; and a South American tour by the Yale University Glee Club.

Along with the Latin American and U.S. art exhibits, the CIAA sponsored a South American tour by sculptor Jo Davidson, who was commissioned in spring 1941 to create bronze busts of ten Latin American presidents.[33] Davidson received especially long and favorable newspaper coverage while he was working in Montevideo (*El Día*, August 3, 1941) and Caracas (*Crítica*, May 14, 1941). In June 1942 the National Gallery of Art in Washington, D.C., hosted an exhibition of his works accompanied by a catalogue, *Presidents of the South American Republics*.

The CIAA's Good Neighbor agenda was forefront in the museum directors' priorities when Davidson's earlier busts of Roosevelt and Vice President Henry Wallace were placed among those of the Latin American leaders. No expense seems to have been spared: the CIAA gave the busts to the Latin American presidents and their families and dispatched hundreds of catalogues in Spanish and Portuguese for distribution through U.S. embassies in South America.[34] But Davidson's war efforts did not end there. He sculpted bronzes of other key leaders, including Charles de Gaulle and Madame Chiang Kai-Shek; arguably his most renowned bust was of a young British soldier who briefly appeared in David MacDonald's much-admired film, *Desert Victory* (1943), a British Ministry of Information documentary about the Allied battle for North Africa. The bust became a symbol of the Eighth Army that fought in Africa, and it accompanied the film's exhibition throughout England.

Davidson is just one example of an artist whose life was radically changed by his wartime assignments. Writing to Claude Bowers in August 1944, he reminisced about his South American tour and referred excitedly to his chairmanship of the high-profile Committee of Artists, Writers, and Scientists for the Re-election of FDR: "This is the very first time in my life where I have taken any active part in a political campaign—but I feel it so, that I simply had to do it."[35]

Books Abroad

As historian Héctor J. Maymí-Sugrañes has pointed out, because of government concerns about the political improprieties of a U.S. government agency funding a U.S. library on foreign soil, it was decided to filter CIAA monies through the American Library Association (ALA) for the creation of the Biblioteca Benjamín Franklin (BBF) in Mexico City in April 1942 (312). Gary E. Kraske

Sculptor Jo Davidson. Courtesy of the Library of Congress, Prints and
Photographs Division.

has discussed the project's history as a collaborative venture in his study *Missionaries of the Book*: the Mexican government donated the structure, the CIAA provided funding for staffing salaries, equipment, and central book collection, while the ALA offered technical support and advice on book buying and named as director former New York Public Library head Harry M. Lydenberg, a member of the CIAA Cultural Relations Division.[36]

Ostensibly an apolitical institution, the BBF was a powerful cultural vehicle that supported the CIAA's mission to influence and promote modernity in Latin America. Its influence was seen not only in the books selected for the collection but also in cultural activities such as film showings and instruction in English and Spanish. English classes easily outpaced Spanish classes in popularity; by the war's end, as many as two thousand students were enrolled each month in BBF classes (Kraske 73). The CIAA funded the American Council of Learned Societies (ACLS) for the Biblioteca Americana de Nicaragua in Managua (November 1942) and the Biblioteca Artigas–Washington in Montevideo (June 1943), both of which came under ALA administration in 1943 (Maymí-Sugrañes, 314). The CIAA gifted books to all three libraries as well as to other venues under the 1942 project Books for Latin America that was headed by ALA Latin American Committee member Rodolfo O. Rivera, whose *Preliminary Lists of Libraries in the Other American Republics* (1942) was fundamental to the dissemination of books by the CIAA.

The primary source for titles sent to Latin America was the ALA's annotated *Selected List of Books in English by U.S. Authors* (1942), which emphasized modern works on the U.S. "way of life." Among the suggested readings in literature were Norman Foerster's *American Poetry and Prose*, "an anthology based on the newer conception of American literature as something more than a division of general English: as the expression of a developing continent" (111), and Lucy Hazard's anthology *In Search of America*, recommended "less for literary value than for the light the selections shed on U.S. life" (111).

Surprisingly and impressively, the choice of titles tended to favor socially critical literature. The section on drama consists almost exclusively of left-liberal playwrights such as Maxwell Anderson (*Eleven Verse Plays*), Norman Corwin (*Thirteen by Corwin*), Lillian Hellman (*Four Plays*), Clifford Odets (*Six Plays*), and Thornton Wilder (*Our Town: A Play in Three Acts*).[37] Among the novelists were Stephen Crane (*The Red Badge of Courage*), Willa Cather (*My Antonia*), Erskine Caldwell (*God's Little Acre*), John dos Passos (*U.S.A.*), Theodore Dreiser (*An American Tragedy*), and William Faulkner (*Go Down, Moses and Other Stories*).

Alongside social plays and novels about social class, the ALA list featured books on race relations in the United States, among them Langston Hughes's *Not Without Laughter*, "a realistic story of a poor colored family in Kansas, told simply, with genuine sentiment, without bitterness" (122), and Richard Wright's *Native Son*, "a disturbing book, with revelations of Negro misery and degradation. A notable achievement in portraying a segment of America" (126). Class and race were represented in Erskine Caldwell and photographer Margaret Bourke-White's pictorial *Say, Is This the U.S.A.* (1941)—a frank and bleak portrait of inequality whose entry simply reads: "shows the diversity of American life" (62).

Maymí-Sugrañes argues that the Books for Latin America project was a form of cultural imperialism because the ALA selected the titles from which Latin American librarians could choose. There is no doubt that this kind of prese-lection shaped the way the United States would be perceived abroad, all the more so given that most Latin American libraries had very few books on the United States. A 1939 survey reported that the university and public libraries in São Paulo had a total of ten books on U.S. history in English (Kraske, 157). But the ALA's emphasis on works that laid bare U.S. racial and social class ten-sions clearly refutes Maymí-Sugrañes's claim that the organization only listed books that would "improve Latin America's conception of the United States and counter fascist propaganda" (325).

The desire to improve the U.S. image abroad by a kind of whitewashing be-came a greater issue in 1943 when the State Department replaced the CIAA as the central funding agent. As Maymí-Sugrañes notes, that year U.S. embassies began to function as middlemen in deciding how many and which books Latin American institutions were to receive—an intervention that dismayed the ALA administration (325). Perhaps not surprisingly, once the war was over and the chill of the cold war began to be felt, the State Department ended the ALA's involvement and assumed total control of the book project (Kraske, 164).

U.S. Cultural Institutes and Coordination Committees

According to Donald W. Rowland, building and strengthening U.S. cultural in-stitutes and libraries in the other American republics were among the Cultural Relations Division's highest priorities (94). Hundreds of thousands of dollars were invested in creating new institutes, supporting existing ones, and increas-ing reference collections. Institutes were an important part of the CIAA's out-reach through various cultural activities, especially English-language instruc-tion. However, far more important for the agency's purposes was a decision in spring 1941 to form a network of coordination committees in Latin America. Their primary mission was to disseminate information on CIAA activities, ar-range local support for cultural exhibits, and, as we have seen, provide feed-back on audience reactions to films and radio programs.[38] Committees were composed of U.S. citizens in residence, but business executives were the pre-ferred choice for membership.

In the case of the first committee, which was formed in Rio, the six-man membership was hand-picked by U.S. ambassador Jefferson Caffery, who ap-pointed General Electric regional chairman Earl C. Givens as the committee's chair (Rowland, 248). An unsigned memo dated September 10, 1942, from Rio spells out the relationship between the CIAA's special Brazilian division that directly reported to the CIAA and was headed by Berent Friele and the coordination committee that for diplomatic reasons worked in strict concert with the ambassador. Given the scope of CIAA operations, coordination subcommittees were set up to oversee press, motion pictures, radio, public opinion analysis, and cultural relations activities.[39] All communications were to be channeled to the CIAA through the State Department. By 1944 there were eighty-six committees in Latin America with approximately six hundred members.[40]

In a May 9, 1942, memo to Harry Frantz, Francis Jamieson suggested that press subcommittees carry out specific tasks to support the CIAA and Allied causes. Establishing friendly relations with newspaper editors, obtaining information on press circulation figures and general editorial trends, distributing *En Guardia/Em Guarda* and posters, keeping track of proposed U.S. visits by journalists, and providing monthly reports on the use and effectiveness of CIAA materials were among their duties.[41] Ultimately committees carried out these and many other assignments, greatly increasing awareness of U.S. culture and the Allied cause. Monthly reports turned into a weekly newsletter titled *Coordination Committee Activities* that carried news of regional committees and highlighted one special event per issue. The May 30 to June 6, 1944, issue (no. 120) featured the Bahia committee's months-long trip along the São Francisco River to project fifty 16mm films in towns where movies had never been shown before. Other news focused on local art exhibits and contests, radio broadcasts, materials for classroom teaching, analysis of U.S. news press coverage, motion picture showings, and short notes on committee personnel.

Given the corporate makeup of their memberships, it is not surprising that the committees were often conduits for information and ideas provided by visiting corporate executives. In an October 8, 1942, communication to Rockefeller, Mexico coordination committee executive secretary W. C. Longan forwarded a letter from Colgate-Palmolive executive J. C. Rebaza, who was traveling in Mexico and whose company was represented on the local radio subcommittee. Having visited several small towns where CIAA films were being shown, Rebaza wrote: "It is my impression that Mexico is a long way from being concious [sic] of the war danger [and] . . . that these movies could be improved upon somewhat."[42] Rebaza listed several nationalist and militaristic ideas for their improvement, such as opening and closing films with shots of the Mexican flag fluttering to the sound of Mexico's national anthem, filming Mexican military personnel in maneuvers, and showing actual combat scenes in Europe.

But the main purpose of Rebaza's letter was to inform the CIAA of his company's plans to support the U.S. and Allied cause and instill "hatred of Japs and Nazis" locally by transforming its sixty sales representatives in Mexico into a "Colgate-Palmolive Legion": "Every salesman is supplied with a gold star and on merit they will become corporals, sergeants, lieutenants, second lieutenants, up to colonels. . . . The principal idea here is to inject the military idea into them and to make them really patriotic." (The only thing missing was a uniform, perhaps with a hood.) Other plans outlined in the letter involved company press ads with the Mexican flag, radio ads with the slogan "En la Unión es la Fuerza y en la Fuerza el Triunfo" (In Union Is Force and in Force Triumph), and offers to project CIAA movies in Mexico with the Palmolive sound truck and distribute CIAA pamphlets.

There is no documentation to indicate whether Rockefeller or any CIAA official replied to Rebaza's plan of action. It was one thing for businesses to support the Allied cause through advertising or trade; it was quite another for a U.S. corporate sales force to assume a proactive role in a federal agency's overseas propaganda activities. In Longan's brief cover letter to Rockefeller he indicated his uneasiness with Rebaza's correspondence: "The Committee is retaining no copy of this letter for its file." Perhaps out of concern for the committee itself or out of some loyalty to Rockefeller, Longan sent Rebaza's letter directly to the coordinator instead of channeling it through the Mexican embassy and the State Department—probably not the first or last time that a circumvention of this sort occurred.[43]

A more common example of how corporate interests and the work of the coordination committees intersected was the request by MGM's Latin American executive S. N. Burger for the Rio committee's promotion of the film *Mrs. Miniver*: "The propaganda value and the message carried by the picture is such as to elevate it beyond the value and importance of an ordinary motion picture. . . . We are going to extraordinary expense in order to convince the Brazilian public of the unusual value of MRS. MINIVER. The entire proceeds of the opening night revert to the 'Legião Brasileira de Assistencia' and the performance will be sponsored by Mme. Darcy Vargas [wife of the president]."[44]

The CIAA Motion Picture Division's general enthusiasm over the film and its potential to increase popular support for the Allied cause alone would have moved the Rio committee to help in its publicity. It probably also did not hurt that David L. Lewis, an MGM executive stationed in Rio, sat on the local motion picture subcommittee. But Burger expressed the need to declare further that MGM was not using the committee to make money—even though it likely did profit: "Whilst it may inevitably be said that in [making this request], Metro

Goldwyn Mayer are merely trying to further their commercial interests, we wish to take this opportunity to state this is merely a superficial and erroneous impression."[45] In reality, there was simply no way to uncouple corporate capitalism from agencies like the CIAA, which depended directly or indirectly on big business for numerous projects. The only military factor was the country's united concern about the war and the socially committed climate during FDR's administration that together may have tempered some corporate moneymaking schemes.

The propaganda effectiveness of Hollywood films was of special concern to Rockefeller, who in July 1943 wrote to the Motion Picture Division of the Mexican coordination committee to ask its help in assessing local audience reaction. Exhibition and analysis of audience reception of CIAA 16mm films were among the main functions of the coordination committees, although the analysis often had comments on strengths and weaknesses of feature films. The Mexican unit's response to Rockefeller in August was both conscientious and thorough. It was the members' belief that a true cross-section of public reaction required surveys of theatergoers at the neighborhood theaters as well as the second- and third-run houses. The division staff felt a larger pool would provide a truer picture of public opinion.[46] One month later, on September 14, the division carried out its first evaluation with mixed success. Overall, the 382 individuals surveyed were cooperative, but the survey elicited responses that seemed too vague—perhaps because the films viewed—among them *Spitfire* (1942, Leslie Howard), *The Moon Is Down* (1943, Irving Pichel), and *In Which We Serve* (1942, Noel Coward)—were too fresh in their minds. The survey did yield some basic information: of the 382 surveyed, 239 selected the plot as the most important feature of the films, 126 chose actors, and the rest were divided among photography (78), sound (39), and dialogue (3).

A second, door-to-door survey of 386 people was taken to assess their reactions to fourteen features released in 1942 with similar distribution. Individuals were asked to identify which films they liked, which ones effectively presented their propaganda messages, and which ones had memorable scenes. All the films had Spanish subtitles. The least popular was the low-budget *Sherlock Holmes in Washington* (Universal), with tallies of 22, 29, and 27 percent, respectively.[47]

The degree to which studies of this kind benefited the agency was a concern of the CIAA's Philip Reisman, who was visiting Mexico in September and informed the local coordination committee that perhaps the movie studios should conduct and pay for their own surveys. The coordination committees in Ecuador, Colombia, and Bolivia were asked for opinions about feature films, although their approach was primarily to comment on the films themselves. There was consensus in an October 1, 1943, document that the Spanish dubbing of *The Battle of Midway* (John Ford, 1942) was very poor; that *Remember Pearl Harbor* (Joseph Santley, 1942) was "decidedly poor, filled with improbable and illogical occurrences"; that *Sergeant York* (Howard Hawks, 1941) was a crowd-pleaser; and that *Public Deb No. 1* (Gregory Ratoff, 1940) was "too anti-communist."[48]

An undated report on 1941 movies drafted by the coordination committee in Brazil (prior to the country's declaration of war) provided general assessments and recommendations for individual studios. In the case of Warner Brothers, the report emphasized the importance of avoiding too many black Brazilians and images of poverty on screen—a recommendation that was taken to heart by the CIAA in general:

> In making scenes of Brazil not more than 20 percent of people appearing in the scenes should be colored—if South Brazil, the percentage should be even smaller. Jungle characters are seen on the streets as often as we see American feathered Indians on Broadway . . . [DIP] Censorship board more concerned with politics both

Table 5.1 Latin American Viewers' Responses to Six U.S. Films

Film title	Liked it (%)	Accepted propaganda (%)	Remembered sequences (%)
Mrs. Miniver (MGM)	88	59	65
Casablanca (Warner)	75	68	65
Mister "V" (United Artists)	53	49	42
Commandos Strike at Dawn (Columbia)	51	34	27
The Young Mr. Pitt (20th Century Fox)	51	42	28
This above All (20th Century Fox)	46	40	40

Source: CIAA Motion Picture Division
Courtesy of the National Archives and Records Administration, College Park, Maryland

local and international than with morals in a picture, [and] will not stand having poverty of the country shown.[49]

RKO was advised that "women (and not all of them, naturally) only wear the [Carmen Miranda] 'Bahiana' costume during Carnival." The report twice recommended that studios avoid disparaging reference to Brazilian products, especially coffee.[50]

By 1945 the number and size of committees had expanded considerably. In addition to a nine-member central Rio committee, regional subcommittees were established in thirteen major cities from Porto Alegre in the south to Belém in the north and as far as Manaus in the interior. Subcommittees had two to six members each from corporations such as Singer Sewing Machine, Kodak, GE, and Atlantic Refining who were assigned to oversee operations in radio, cultural relations, personal relations, sports, the press, printers and publishers, motion pictures, and finances. Chile's central coordination committee was the largest in Latin America, with twenty-six members in addition to those on its regional subcommittees; Panama and Costa Rica had the smallest organizations, with a total of two and four members, respectively. Monies for the motion picture subcommittees in the various countries doubled from $240,000 in 1944 to $475,000 in 1945.[51] According to the coordination committee reports, of the more than six hundred coordination committee members in 1944, only fourteen, or 0.02 percent, were women, four of them in Honduras. One was the daughter-in-law of the committee's chair, another the wife of a Honduran physician, a third taught English, and a fourth was listed as the chair of the subcommittee in La Ceiba. Other female members were connected to humanitarian and society organizations such as the Red Cross in Chile, the Baptist Hospital in Nicaragua, and the American Society in Peru.[52]

Making Good Neighbors at Home

Although there was no question of the need to promote Good Neighbor activities in the United States, the CIAA was slow to establish the U.S. program. It was finally announced by Wallace K. Harrison in a February 4, 1942, memo to the CIAA executive staff.[53] Three weeks later, a decision was made to change the title to the Division of Inter-American Activities in the United States. Its official authorization was delayed until March 23, 1942. In reality the division's director, University of Chicago political scientist Walter H.C. Laves, had been on the job prior to his official appointment on December 8, 1941, when he traveled to Washington to work under Harrison.[54] In his unofficial capacity Laves surveyed faculty colleagues in Illinois and Indiana about their interests and activities in relation to Latin America. Indiana University professor of govern-ment John E. Stoner wrote to Laves on December 4, 1941, that Indiana's presi-dent Herman B. Wells had just returned from a South American tour and had insisted that courses in Latin American history be added to the curriculum: "[Wells] is much concerned about the Nazi power down there. He said on one occasion something to the effect that Hitler could take South America by a tele-phone call."[55]

Suggestions from Laves's other academic correspondents called for sub-sidizing Latin American tours for individuals appointed to lead community discussion groups, producing better graphic materials on U.S.–Latin Ameri-can–Canadian relations, transmitting twenty-four-hour radio programs to the United States from various South American countries, commissioning artists to sculpt and paint Latin American heroes and historical events, developing ways to increase the political consciousness of South American women, and translating books from Spanish and Portuguese into English.[56] Laves wrote to state and national agencies such as the Economic Policy Committee in Des Moines, Iowa, to ask about ways to build public opinion in the Midwest favor-able to inter-American relations. Committee secretary Harry E. Terrell wrote from Iowa that Laves should tread cautiously when it came to "the less thickly populated states . . . where the people are very suspicious of federal agencies."[57] But he also remarked that films on Latin America and follow-up discussions there had been constructive in building a better-informed public.

A hand-drawn diagram by Laves of the yet-to-be-established division il-lustrates his early thinking about connections among the media, print, and cultural relations divisions as well as its tie-in with other federal information agencies such as the Office of Facts and Figures, the Office of Civilian De-fense, and the Coordinator of Information.[58] On December 16, 1941, he wrote: "It was my understanding in undertaking this preliminary survey, that I was brought to the Coordinator's Office for the express purpose of directing the United States Program." He was quite specific about the chains of command: "Those agencies concerned partly with the United States and partly with Latin America . . . should clear their United States activities with the United States Program." He added: "To insure the maximum utilization of the technicalities of communication [film, radio, print, and so on], either one person should be assigned in the United States Program section to act as liaison, or someone in each of the technical agencies should be designated as responsible liaison with the United States Section."[59]

His memo divides individuals in terms of specific target groups under the following classifications: organized formal education (public school and higher education), formal agencies of adult education, informal civic agencies of adult education (women's organizations, community projects, for example), government agencies of adult education (Army, Navy, and conscientious objector camp), intergovernmental agencies (Pan American Union), and public and private libraries. He identified the media, print, and cultural relations divisions as the primary conduits to reaching these groups through the use of film, radio, exhibitions, posters, pamphlets, and other materials. A more detailed memo on January 6, 1942, lists his meetings with staff and directors of various CIAA Divisions as well as a representative of the Pan American Centers; these centers' main responsibility was to coordinate activities carried out by various hospitality groups and institutions.[60]

Laves was eager to move forward with the division's work, but his first meeting with Rockefeller did not occur until January 8, 1942. With Harrison in attendance, Laves set out his ideas for the program and suggested that he report directly to Rockefeller—a suggestion that was tabled and ultimately not approved. According to his notes on the meeting, he asked Harrison to inform the CIAA staff of the program and his directorship, and Harrison complied,

Walter H.C. Laves. Courtesy of the Lilly Library, Bloomington, Indiana.

although only after a delay of nearly a month. In his diaries for January and February 1942 Laves noted his ongoing work but also complained about the agency's disorganization and Rockefeller's "attempt early in the game to see everyone sent by senators—even stenographers . . . !" There is an indication that Archibald MacLeish, then head of the OFF, expected Laves to clear everything with his office after a February 16 meeting between Harrison and Laves on the subject.[61] Laves was able to proceed with filling a few positions to work with religious and patriotic organizations and service clubs, as well as in the hospitality sector. But the division still had no permanent office space, a source of frustration until March 4, when he wrote in his diary: "All set at last in new office overlooking Pennsylvania Av." Later that same day he wrote: "Word that we move again . . . Monday we will know if we can find ourselves!!"[62]

The division reached out to numerous entities in its mission to develop an informed U.S. public. The key to its success was coordinating its own many inter-American initiatives with those of outside agencies and groups. Because hospitality for visiting Latin Americans was a major concern, Marian Christie was transferred internally to head the division's hospitality section, which formerly operated out of the Cultural Relations Division. To support the work of this unit, an inter-American reception center was approved for Miami, the principal port of entry for visiting Latin American officials in the United States. The State Department collaborated on this center as well as a second one in Washington so that official visitors could be properly received (Rowland, 106). A third center, called the Pacific House, was established in San Francisco to accommodate visitors on the West Coast. Plans were made to locate U.S. citizens who had recently traveled to Latin America and solicit their opinions and active support for the division's speakers bureau and inter-American centers.

Like the coordination committees in Latin America, inter-American centers were grassroots or volunteer organizations created to distribute CIAA materials. They hosted guest lectures, educational film showings, and art exhibits. By the end of 1942 there were eight centers nationwide, five of them strategically placed in the Midwest. A year later the number had more than doubled, to eighteen centers, with ten in the Midwest and four in the Great Lakes region alone. A CIAA pamphlet titled *Some Specific Suggestions for Inter-American Programs* (in its third edition, printed in 1945) provided eighteen recommendations for activities that private organizations and community groups might sponsor. Celebrating Latin American independence days, Pan-American Day, and Flag Day, showing slides and films, organizing concerts and music competitions, and offering classes in Spanish and Portuguese were among the educational and cultural activities recommended. Publications on the order of *Pan-American Day: An Anthology of the Best Prose and Verse on Pan Americanism and the Good Neighbor Policy* (1943) provided CIAA and other materials that could be used in commemorating the day. Prominently featured were selected speeches by FDR, Secretary of State Cordell Hull, and Nobel Peace Prize recipient Elihu Root, plays about pan-American ideals and the life of Bolívar, and "A Dialogue on Pan-Americanism by Mrs. Franklin Roosevelt and Nelson Rockefeller" based on a 1941 radio broadcast.

Local merchant groups were encouraged to place Latin American goods in window displays. Culture and commercial interests coalesced in fiesta celebrations held in each of the forty-eight states, the first of which was organized by a women's club in Greenfield, Iowa.[63] A monthly CIAA *Speakers Bureau Bulletin* apprised organizations of current topics of inter-American interest and a list of approved speakers arranged according to their expertise and locations for public lectures.[64] The Pan American Union published a ten-volume *Good Neighbor Tour* (1943) that provided clubs with a treasure trove of information for "an imaginary visit to the republics of Latin America," replete with sources for films, speakers, books, and recipes, as well as advice on obtaining passports, steamship tickets, and maps.

Prior to the establishment of the Inter-American Activities Division, the Cultural Relations Division under Erskine Caldwell engaged in discussions about the possible roles that U.S. institutions of higher education might play in the CIAA mission. This discussion led Rockefeller to write to various university presidents for their input, and that resulted in the formation of faculty committees on U.S.–Latin America relations. The University of Chicago played a key role because of its strong social sciences and Latin American specialists and its vice president and Rockefeller adviser William Benton. But there was an impetus in colleges and universities nationwide to do their part by way of inter-American institutes, conferences, and faculty and student exchanges—all of which led to the emergence of Latin American and inter-American studies as fields for teaching and research.

On April 1941 Caldwell wrote a letter in support of a $37,500 grant for Latin American studies research at the University of Texas in Austin.[65] That recommendation was partly based on the university's fourteen-page report on inter-American cultural relations and ideas for projects that might produce quick results for the CIAA.[66] One of these ideas was the creation of regional centers at the universities of Texas, Chicago, California, and Harvard that would conduct conferences on implementing inter-American cultural relations topics into adult and community education, higher education, and teacher education. Prior to the CIAA's inception, the State Department's Division of Cultural Relations and private foundations had sponsored exchanges and occasional conferences—such as the spring 1940 Inter-American Educational and Cultural Conference at the University of Florida and the summer 1940 conference on inter-American cultural relations in Mexico City, where Diego Rivera appeared on the roster of guest speakers. By 1942 the University of Texas had added an executive board for an Institute of Latin American Studies; the institute sponsored an April 1942 conference predominantly for Southwest U.S. scholars on Cultural Bases of Hemispheric Understanding.[67] Held during Pan-American Day celebrations, the conference featured speakers on art in the Americas, Latin American literature, the politics of pan-americanism, and Hispanic culture in the U.S. Southwest.

Several inter-American educational activities were sponsored by the Division of Science and Education prior to the creation of the Inter-American Activities Division. One of the most successful was a public-speaking competition titled the National Discussion Contest on Inter-American Affairs for College and Universities. The 1941 contest, devoted to the Good Neighbor policy, attracted more than twenty thousand undergraduate students from 352 institutions. The success of this event led to a second contest in 1942 on How the American Republics are Cooperating in Winning the War, and a third in 1943 on the Bases of Permanent Cooperation among the American Republics. Winners of regional competitions received $500 for study in Mexico and proceeded to the national finals in Washington or New York, where their speeches were broadcast on radio.[68] Other national contests included an essay competition on "What Inter-American Cooperation Means to My Country" that was open to high school students in both the United States and Latin America. Regional winners received $100 each, and the first-place winners, one from Latin America and the other from the United States, each received four-year scholarships to the university of his or her choice anywhere in the Western Hemisphere.[69]

Adult education was of special interest to the Inter-American Activities Division, and its staff devised projects to increase awareness of the other Americas through regional organizations such as the Texas Junior Chamber of Commerce, the Rhode Island World Affairs Council, the Pan-American Council in Chicago, and the Pan-American Society of Massachusetts. Materials on Latin America and inter-American relations were often scarce and at a premium; the division attempted to address Midwestern needs by investing in the collection and facilities of the Library of International Relations, a free public reference library founded in Chicago in 1932.[70] That project dovetailed with another division plan to stimulate public interest in books on the other Americas that was to be carried out in conjunction with the Library of International Relations. Under the Press Division, twelve feature articles on inter-American affairs would be published during a four-month period in 326 communities in the Midwest. Local librarians would track the demand and circulation of inter-American materials at specific intervals and report the findings through the Library of International Relations.

The division played a key role in distributing CIAA 16mm films through the support of forty-seven university depositories created for that purpose, one of the most important being at Indiana University, which was involved in both production and distribution. A March 1943 report by Indiana University professor Agapito Rey provided circulation feedback via Indiana University President Herman B. Wells to Laves (and his interim successor, Raymond T. Rich) on Indiana's Bureau of Audio-Visual Aids (BAV) as well as suggestions for improved viewing. According to Rey, the BAV's main problem was the imbalance between supply and demand for the more than four hundred groups it served locally and in neighboring states: "[W]e are refusing many requests for films on Latin-America because our available prints are completely booked several months in advance."[71] Based on figures from September 1942 to March 1943, Rey reported that the BAV's seven prints of Julien Bryan's *Americans All* were in constant use, with 109 bookings, 325 showings, and an estimated audience of 37,714. The one or at most two copies of the other eighteen CIAA films in the depository were also in demand, with 398 bookings, 1,313 showings, and an estimated audience of 135,320 during the same period. Rey argued that film showings alone were insufficient to create an informed audience, and he recommended that discussion guides be produced and distributed as part of a packet of CIAA materials to accompany each film.[72]

The Spanish-Speaking Minorities in the United States

On March 6, 1942, the Division of Inter-American Affairs was given the responsibility of addressing an array of issues associated with "resident Latin Americans" in the United States. The division contacted the coordination committee in Mexico for information and assistance as well as the OFF, which expressed interest in the project but had no funds to support initiatives. Other agencies contacted were the Committee on Information and the Office of Civilian Defense (OCD). On April 3, 1942, CIAA staff member David J. Saposs filed a report for Laves titled "Resident Latin American Problems and Recommended

Program."[73] At the time, the division's concerns were to inform U.S. Spanish-speaking minorities about the importance of inter-American relations to ensure their support of the Allied war effort. The division focused on discrimination and inequities that could work to the advantage of Axis propaganda and trouble the other American republics. Saposs's report was a devastating commentary on the status of Mexican American and other Spanish-speaking communities in Texas, New Mexico, Arizona, California, Colorado, and Illinois. Unemployment, extensive illiteracy, slum housing, and malnutrition were only a few of the economic and social realities documented in the report. Civic injustices ranged from discrimination in schools to denial of admission to public parks and restaurants.[74]

Three populations were studied in detail: urban slum communities, migratory workers, and subsistence farmers. Saposs argued that the division's intervention on behalf of these communities, whose total population in the United States was an estimated 3.5 million, would counteract possible enemy propaganda efforts, increase the U.S. labor supply for wartime industries, and create "intermediaries" to promote hemispheric solidarity.[75] His recommendations included funding of support centers such as the Barelas Community Center in New Mexico; the Taos County, New Mexico Project; and Chicago's Hull House. Saposs noted the need to educate non-Hispanic citizens against racist attitudes and practices, especially in areas with large Spanish-speaking populations.

Laves brought together the heads of several CIAA divisions to discuss the Saposs report. There was consensus that CIAA officials would attend a League of United Latin Americans convention to be held in mid-June 1942 and that Rockefeller should make an appearance. Laves's April 14, 1942, memorandum shows the division heads in agreement with Saposs's recommendation for public and private minority-center support. They suggested a scholarship fund for promising Hispanic high school students to attend colleges and universities in the United States. Laves followed his memorandum with a project authorization request for a Program for Cooperation with Spanish Speaking Minorities in the United States with an annual budget of $105,000.[76] The list of recommended initiatives encompassed smaller ones as well, such as assistance for the Tucson Alianza para Victoria celebration, community centers, and special radio news broadcasts and newsletters in Spanish.

In May, Saposs contacted the War Manpower Board headed by Paul V. McNutt to study minority employment issues. Alan Cranston from the OFF (later the OWI) requested weekly broadcasts for Southwest populations, funds for local radio transcriptions, and an in-house adviser for Latin American resident affairs. These initiatives were especially critical after Saposs reported on court filings of discriminatory acts against Hispanics in public restaurants, parks, and movie theaters in Texas, Arizona, and California. Saposs recommended that local civic and business leaders and members of the Mexican coordination committee close to the border form goodwill missions to support the Spanish-speaking communities and educate the general public in the U.S. Southwest. An appendix to his report had suggestions for a presidential statement in support of the Spanish-speaking people of the Southwest.[77]

The week of May 29, Laves traveled to Chicago to work on a plan for a cooperative to serve the 30,000 to 40,000 Hispanics living there. But just as the division's efforts were getting under way, the Bureau of the Budget, in accordance with a plan to establish the OWI, decided that the CIAA should not operate in the United States "except as a prodding or stimulating agency, and then only under the direction of the OWI."[78] Funds for minority activities were cut, and staff positions for the Division were temporarily frozen. On July 22 Laves wrote that if the program were reestablished, the 1943 budget should be $150,000. After several months and some reflection, the OWI agreed in mid-September that the CIAA and other agencies should continue their work with minority communities. That change of mind was undoubtedly influenced by the events described below.

On August 2, 1942, a little over a week after Laves's July budget memo, what became known as the Sleepy Lagoon murder was reported in southeastern Los Angeles. The body of a young Mexican, José Díaz, was found in an area close to a reservoir (dubbed "Sleepy Lagoon" by the media, after a popular song) that was a favorite swimming area for Hispanics, who were regularly denied public pool access. Prior to the body's discovery, two groups of Mexican American youths had confronted one another in the area, and Díaz's death from blunt force trauma was attributed by police to the fight. Numerous books and articles have been written about the case, which was the focus of a media frenzy about the violent nature of young Mexican American "zoot suiters," also called *pachucos*.[79] Twenty-two of these young people were arrested and tried, and seventeen were found guilty in January 13, 1943, by an all-white jury on charges ranging from assault to first-degree murder. Sentences ran from time served to life in prison. Due process was denied the defendants, who were tried together in *The People v. Zammora et al.* Separated from their lawyers in the courtroom, they had no access to legal counsel. They were denied clean clothes and haircuts. Several young women associated with the defendants were arrested and illegally detained for months in the Ventura School for Girls, a reformatory for "wayward girls."

Frank P. Barajas has described the thirteen-week trial and the community, civic, political, and labor groups that came together to mount a defense of the young men, whose convictions were overturned on appeal in October 1944. However, the court remained firm that racial prejudice had not been a factor in the original trial proceedings. In its preparations for the appeal, the defense committee elicited broad public support by arguing that the trial and convictions were part of a Fifth Column plot to undermine both a unified U.S. wartime community and inter-American Good Neighbor relations—arguments that echoed Saposs's earlier assessment of the damage potential of right-wing Mexican Sinarquistas within the Latino community. In his study Barajas quotes from an April 29, 1943, defense committee circular on the link between the convictions and enemy infiltration and propaganda:

> Hitler, too, began his attack against the people of Germany by first attacking the minorities. It wasn't long after his success in whipping up disunity among the various groups that he was able to destroy them all. We have seen Hitler work too often in too many places not to recognize the fascist rattle when we hear it in our own

Headline in the Los Angeles *Daily News* of June 9, 1943. Courtesy of the Franklin D. Roosevelt Library, Hyde Park, New York.

midst. Nor, indeed, was it just by chance that the axis radio harped on the outcome of this trial for days on end as an example of "democratic justice" and our "Good Neighbor Policy."[80]

At the same time the defense committee was building its case, and within weeks of this circular's distribution, fighting broke out in Los Angeles between Mexican American youths and white U.S. sailors and Marines who were stationed in the area. Called the Zoot Suit Riots, the attacks grew from fighting between small groups to a vigilante-style movement in which thousands of servicemen and civilians set out to track down, beat, and disrobe Mexican American youths as well as African Americans and people of other ethnicities who adopted the distinctive pancake hat and draped suits. City police were complicit in these storm-trooper tactics to rid the streets of the pachuco presence, and attacks spread to other heavily populated Latino and African American areas in Texas, New York, and the Midwest. The *Los Angeles Times* used inflammatory rhetoric in headlines such as "Freak Suits" and "Zooters Taught a Lesson." To quell the rioting, local military officials declared Los Angeles off limits for Navy, Marine, and Coast Guard personnel. According to the *Times* article "Zoot Suiters to Lose One of Hangouts," the Los Angeles County Planning Commission approved a plan to convert Sleepy Lagoon into a privately run recreational area—thus eliminating the popular socializing spot for Latinos.[81]

Civic and local government replies to inquiries from the Mexican embassy in Washington and the Mexican consul in Los Angeles asserted that the violence was not the result of race discrimination. Both the OWI and CIAA were reported to have had "lively interest" in the situation because of the grave consequences for inter-American wartime relations.[82] As clashes diminished, California Governor Earl Warren appointed a committee composed of local civic and religious leaders and the actor Leo Carrillo; it issued a report that violent acts would be punished regardless of the uniforms or suits worn. In the meantime, the federal government attempted to ban zoot suits as unpatriotic at a time of wartime clothing shortages. A Watts pastor, Reverend Francisco Quintanilla, charged that Mexican American youths were encouraged to commit crimes by enemy agents—an argument that reiterated Saposs's fears and the Sleepy Lagoon defense committee position.[83]

At a press conference on June 17, 1943, Eleanor Roosevelt argued that the Los Angeles confrontations could be attributed to long-standing discrimination against Mexicans in the Southwest: "For a long time I've worried about the attitude toward Mexicans in California and the States along the border."[84] The following day, headlines in the *Los Angeles Times* and other conservative newspapers and public statements by officials such as Los Angeles Chamber of Commerce president Preston Hotchkis charged Mrs. Roosevelt with blindly provoking racial tensions. Members of the Sinarquista movement blamed the fighting on the lack of education and discipline in Hispanic homes; they charged that communists contributed to the rioting by characterizing the Sinarquistas as enemy Axis agents. Labor unions and communist leaders argued that race was unquestionably a determining factor in the riots, along with irresponsible media.

A conference held from July 12 to 14, 1943, on U.S. Spanish-speaking minorities in the Southwest reiterated the CIAA division's early recommendations for scholarships and educational improvements, as well as textbook revisions to address incorrect and/or discriminatory content. It suggested that the War Department recognize Mexican Americans for their patriotic service, that the classification of "Mexican" be eliminated from all records, and that organizations such as the Red Cross and the USO encourage Latino/a participation.[85]

Most of the above information is part of the published record. Less well known are details of the CIAA's activities during and after the Sleepy Lagoon trial. On September 1, 1942, Rockefeller received a letter from Harry F. Henderson of the Los Angles County grand jury asking his agency's assistance in the preparation for public hearings on the Sleepy Lagoon case.[86] Henderson requested that the agency send an official to attend the session. Laves contended that no other federal agency would step in to help and that the CIAA's presence was vital.[87] He pointed out the international implications of the hearings and the need for a "forthright statement" by the CIAA, adding that "proper handling of these hearings can be a first step toward a fundamental solution of a serious condition affecting our relations with the other American republics."

The grand jury was scheduled to convene on October 8, 1942. As the CIAA official representative to the hearings, Laves drafted a statement to be read at the session. Among the papers in Laves's archive is a copy of a statement from the Office of Los Angeles County Sheriff Eugene W. Biscailuz that was sent to the jury's foreman, E. W. Oliver. (Published sources cite Lieutenant Ed Duran Ayres of the Foreign Relations Bureau in the Los Angeles County Sheriff's Office, who read the statement, as the author of the text.)[88] The statement initially acknowledged educational disadvantages, poverty, and discrimination as contributors to minority social unrest. But the bulk of the lengthy testimony focused on Mexican Americans' inherently violent nature attributable to their bloodthirsty Aztec ancestors, who practiced human sacrifice. The testimony noted that while whites tended to use their fists to engage in nonlethal fights,

Mexican Americans were inherently drawn to knives and deadly acts. The sheriff's office was explicitly racist in delivering its own fatal blows to the Hispanic defense: "Basically it [their violence] is biological—one cannot change the spots of a leopard. . . . As to the negro, we also have a biological aspect to which the contributing factors are the same as in respect to the Mexican, which only aggravates the condition as to the two races."

Laves's own statement was built around studies and information shared in his division's weekly meetings, whose main agenda item in 1942 was the Spanish-speaking minority. The minutes for the weeks of August 7 and August 21 describe the division staff's anxiety about the Sleepy Lagoon case and Laves's frustration with the OWI's lack of interest in the various proposals for minority support. Laves was in Chicago when he submitted his grand jury statement to the CIAA for approval. Passing through various hands, his 1,800-word testimony was reduced to 400, and even that abbreviated version failed to be approved. Finally, the day before the hearings, Laves received a telegram from Wallace Harrison with the CIAA's authorized statement:

> The OCIAA welcomes this opportunity to have an observer present at this hearing in response to the request of the Los Angeles County Jury. In my opinion, the result of this hearing will be of great significance—a significance that cannot be overemphasized. The American Republics are in varying degrees aligned against the Axis Powers. The wartime collaboration of the Americans rests fundamentally on a community of interest which has had its peaceful expression in the Good Neighbor policy. This policy is essentially one of understanding and respect, of trust, and of confidence. As you all know one of the functions of the OCIAA is to further this understanding among the peoples of the hemisphere. For this reason we are grateful to be able to follow this hearing with you.

The cable ended with instructions to Laves: "You are instructed to make no further statement nor to grant any interviews with newspapers, except to reply in answer to their questions that you are present at the hearing only as an observer."

Laves argued that his attendance as an observer would breach the commitment made to the grand jury, and finally he received CIAA approval to read parts of his earlier statement in a private half-hour grand jury session. He argued that the case jeopardized the inter-American alliance necessary to winning the war:

> Every effort is made by [the] enemy to exploit to its maximum any incident or action which may serve to weaken the [Allied] united front. . . . [This includes] cleav-

ages between groups of people. . . . While the alleged violations of law are clearly a matter of local jurisdiction, the trial will have a very important bearing upon the relation between Mexico and the United States, and upon hemisphere solidarity.

In the days and weeks that passed as the case went to trial, Laves received letters from various individuals about the case; one from Eleanor Roosevelt expressed her concern about the trial's outcome. In the meantime, the Hearst-run *Los Angeles Examiner* ran a story on October 16 that claimed Laves said the hearings cleared the air and Southern California was a source of pan-American friendship—untruths that rankled him and the CIAA community.

During the week of October 30, Laves convened a meeting with officials from the OWI, the OCD, Defense Health and Welfare Services, and the War Man-power Commission to discuss the Los Angeles situation. Everyone agreed that the newspapers were hysterical and impressionistic in their coverage, and that was only increasing the tensions in the Los Angeles area and fueling trouble in other parts of the country. OWI representative Alan Cranston agreed to travel to the West Coast to urge newspaper editors to rein in the media hysteria. On November 28 Cranston wrote to OWI director Elmer Davis that the newspa-pers agreed to stop using the word "Mexican" and would run positive stories about Mexican Americans' distinguished service records. He met with the Los Angeles district attorney John F. Dockweiler about the wartime propaganda implications of charging all twenty-two youths with first-degree murder—the first time in U.S. history that so many individuals had been charged with one person's death. Cranston wrote that Dockweiler might narrow the first-degree case to two youths (three were charged) and that he would inform the judge about the dangerous consequences of a "too stiff verdict." During his coast-al visit, Cranston asked Walt Disney to conduct a poster contest for Mexican Americans in the United States. He ended his report stating optimistically if not naively that "the critical situation has been overcome completely."

In the interim, Laves consulted with the Civil Liberties Division of the De-partment of Justice on the mass arrests and charges of police brutality during the riots. The division was sending out its information on minority issues to agencies everywhere. Saposs was appointed to head a labor groups section in the division that was specifically created to help the Spanish-speaking popu-lation. That appointment enabled Laves to send a reassuring note to Eleanor Roosevelt, who wrote to him on December 5 about the urgent need to address problems between Mexican Americans and non-Hispanics in the workplace. In her letter she acknowledged his trip to California and appearance before the grand jury. But by the end of the year Laves decided to resign his post and was named chief of special operations in the OCD. Rockefeller appointed Victor Borella, a close associate and former Dartmouth classmate, to replace Laves. According to Rowland, Rockefeller released Laves and most of his staff to work in the OCD (107). In 1943 Rockefeller raised the division to a department classification, and the following year he renamed it the Department of Special Services. The unit continued to work with inter-American centers and the Spanish-speaking minority, but its mission was increasingly focused on teacher aids, speakers, and labor relations.

Postscript

While Walt Disney was being contacted to sponsor a poster contest to help ease tensions in Los Angeles, Orson Welles, who continued to speak out on Good Neighbor matters, became a prominent voice in the work of the Citizens' Committee for the Defense of Mexican-American Youths, later renamed the Sleepy Lagoon Defense Committee. On November 30, 1942, Welles chaired a forum in Hollywood to provide information and bring attention to troubling details of the case. That meeting drew together various left-leaning constituencies, Hollywood celebrities, and militant labor organizer Harry Bridges. An FBI agent attended and filed a report on the proceedings that was added to Orson Welles's FBI file.[89]

Following the verdict and in support of the youths' appeal, ten thousand copies of a five-cent pamphlet titled *The Sleepy Lagoon Case* was "prepared by the Citizens' Committee for the Defense of Mexican-American Youth." It was published in June 1943 with a foreword by Orson Welles. A second, revised edition of twenty thousand copies was released by the Sleepy Lagoon Defense Committee in September 1943. The printing firm for both editions was listed as the Mercury Printing Company based in Hollywood, California. This was undoubtedly a Welles operation, and there is little question that Welles authored the pamphlet's main text as well as the foreword.

The attributed foreword is pure Orson Welles in the dramatic mode. He describes a chance encounter with a Pete Vasquez at an induction center who knew some of Welles's black jazz musician friends, had listened to Welles's *Hello Americans* broadcasts, and knew he was interested in the Los Angeles trial. As in the Welles radio shows, the stage is given over to a dramatic character, Pete in this pamphlet, who describes the difficulties of being Mexican American in Los Angeles and is happy to be signing up with the Army. "I'm glad to be going. Things'll be better in the Army, and I'm glad of the chance to fight.

The
SLEEPY
LAGOON
Case

WITH A FOREWORD BY
Orson Welles

5c

Pamphlet prepared by the Citizens' Committee for the Defense of Mexican-American Youth and published by the Sleepy Lagoon Defense Committee. Courtesy of the Lilly Library, Bloomington, Indiana.

It makes it hard, though, for a lot of our fellas to see things that way. They want to fight for their country, all right—but they want to feel like it's their country." The foreword ends there and is signed "Orson Welles."[90]

The unsigned text that follows, the work of an unnamed narrator, is a compelling account of the history and importance of the Good Neighbor policy and relations, prefaced by an illustration of newspaper headlines in large, bold lettering about "Baby Gangsters" and the "Hoodlum Roundup." The piece describes the facts of the case and the verdict and points out the irony that the verdict came at the same time as the U.S. importation of Mexican workers to help with the local food supply. The narrator introduces the damaging statement by the Los Angeles Sheriff's Office. After an italicized word-for-word quote of the disparaging and racist remarks about the bloodthirsty urgings of Aztec-descended Mexican Americans, the narrator interjects an aside that is redolent of Welles as radio showman: "[We pause for station identification. This is not Radio Berlin. It is the 'Foreign Relations Department' of the Sheriff of Los Angeles speaking.]" The sheriff's office text is then resumed and quoted in full. The remainder of the text describes the Citizens' Committee and the arguments supporting the appeal, and calls on all Americans to join the struggle to free those convicted. The inside back cover uses the popular patriotic image of war bonds and slogan "For Victory Buy U.S. Savings Bonds and Stamps" alongside a wartime public appeal to destroy fascism and spare the innocent: "You can help to crush the Axis fifth column in our midst by helping to free the 17 boys convicted in the Sleepy Lagoon Case."

Although there were attempts by Jack B. Tenney's Los Angeles–based Fact-Finding Committee on Un-American Activities to challenge and discredit the left-wing defense committee, its fifth-column argument and patriotic rhetoric proved more effective than Tenney's red-baiting. In part because of the efforts by Welles and other figures on the left, the defendants' appeal was finally heard, and in October 1944 their convictions were overturned by the U.S. District Court of Appeals for lack of evidence.[91]

AFTERMATH

It seems unlikely to me that there could be any other region of the earth in which nature and human behavior could have combined to produce a more unhappy and hopeless background for the conduct of human life than in Latin America.
George F. Kennan, Counselor to the State Department, March 29, 1950

If that's art, then I'm a Hottentot.
President Harry S. Truman, *Washington Post*, February 18, 1947

Despite the many surveys, questionnaires, and interviews conducted by the CIAA during the Good Neighbor years, despite all the reviews, commentaries, and letters by Latin American intellectuals or political figures who witnessed the effects of the program, and despite the extraordinarily ambitious range of cultural and educational events that the program either sponsored or influenced, we have no way of producing a neat balance sheet of the CIAA's accomplishments and failings and no way to scientifically measure the impact of specific films, radio broadcasts, news magazines, literary translations, museum exhibits, and educational initiatives. Here at the conclusion of our story, however, it might be useful to compare the diplomacy I have been describing in detail in the previous chapters with a few generalizations about the broad outline of U.S. foreign policy that emerged after the war. This will at least show what was lost when the CIAA closed its operation and what happened to some of its key players. In my own view it cannot help but make reasonable people feel a certain nostalgia for Good Neighbor policies.

In November 1944, as World War II was drawing to a close, FDR nominated Nelson Rockefeller to be assistant secretary of state for Latin American affairs; and after a bumpy Senate confirmation involving Rockefeller and five other nominees for cabinet seats, including Archibald MacLeish as assistant secretary for public and cultural affairs, Rockefeller assumed the new post. Writing for *Political Science Review*, Walter Laves, who, as we have seen, was an important observer at the Sleepy Lagoon trial and became a consultant to the Bureau of the Budget, together with his co-author, Francis Wilcox, applauded the creation of the Latin American and cultural affairs positions, noting that FDR was giving inter-American relations a uniquely high priority (313).

In December, Rockefeller appointed Wallace K. Harrison as deputy coordinator of inter-American affairs and granted him full power to exercise the duties and functions carried out by the coordinator.[1] On March 23, 1945, FDR changed the name of the CIAA to the Office of Inter-American Affairs (OIAA) and appointed Harrison as its director. But soon after FDR's death and one month after the bombing of Hiroshima and Nagasaki, with the Japanese surrender all but official, the new president, Harry S. Truman, submitted an order for the transfer of all OIAA and OWI informational functions performed abroad to an Interim International Information Service in the State Department. Less than a year after his cabinet appointment, Rockefeller resigned and temporarily returned to public life. On April 10, 1946, Truman signed the order to close the former CIAA, and the agency officially ended operations on May 20, 1946.[2]

The U.S. focus on "universal" or "international" as opposed to "regional" interests—meaning the Marshall Plan for rebuilding Europe and the cold war policies designed to contain the spread of international communism—now overshadowed Good Neighbor diplomatic relations. The United States remained sufficiently interested in economic relations with Latin America to ensure the continued flow of vital resources, but its major "regional" concern was Soviet influence. As historian R. A. Humphreys has noted, by mid-1946, three-quarters of Latin America's nations had established diplomatic relations with the Soviet Union, a situation that increasingly preoccupied the U.S. government and ultimately transformed what had been a friendly attitude into one of oscillating indifference and aggression (229).

In the 1946 elections the Republicans took control of the U.S. Congress, and the political climate changed. Despite having departed the State Department, Rockefeller encouraged Truman to fund the Point Four Program, which would continue the work of the Institute for Inter-American Affairs—the only CIAA-related program to survive the immediate postwar period. A CIAA subsidiary, the institute promoted health education in Latin America through investments in medical facilities, technical training, and personnel exchanges as well as providing support for agricultural development. Truman supported the Point Four Program as part of a "Third World" aid package, although Congress allocated far fewer funds than requested for the president's plan.[3]

Ironically, while the U.S. government was funding Point Four to develop public health initiatives in Latin America, the U.S. Public Health Service was conducting a different kind of program that exposed mental patients, prisoners,
prostitutes, and soldiers in Guatemala to venereal disease. These human ex-
periments on the spread and treatment of the disease were conducted for two
years, from 1946 to 1948, without the knowledge, let alone consent, of those
infected with the diseases.[4]

Unlike the years prior to and during the war, hemispheric conferences in the
immediate postwar period were regularly postponed and frequently dispiriting to Latin American leaders, who had hoped for a U.S. Marshall Plan to support their own exports and industrial growth.[5] Orson Welles, who was briefly
a columnist for the *New York Post*, used his public platform to encourage the
continuation of New Deal reforms and criticized the 1945 Pan-American War
and Peace Conference held in Mexico City, organized by Welles's old patron
Rockefeller, as simply a forum for big business interests. He observed that the
dictatorial rulers of some of the Latin American countries would never have
achieved power "without the help of a couple of North American countries you
could name," and he charged that "State Department millionaires" were making deals with Latin millionaires. A proponent of world democracy, he wrote
that the complacent U.S. attitude toward Spain's Franco regime was especially
hypocritical given the Latin American wartime propaganda program waged
against fascism.[6]

Historian Roger R. Trask suggests that the Charter for the Organization of
American States (OAS), drafted in 1948, was more a means for the United States
to ensure military and political solidarity in the face of communist threats
than a Good Neighbor initiative. Ultimately the OAS enabled the U.S. government to intervene whenever it deemed left-wing movements or leaderships as
posing a threat ("Impact of the Cold War," 279–280). Following his first tour
of Latin America, George F. Kennan wrote a 1950 memorandum on U.S.–Latin
American relations that is a paean to U.S. imperialism and provides a basis for
the U.S. policy of "neglect" that followed the heady courtship of neighbors to
the south during wartime:[7]

> It is important for us to keep before ourselves and the Latin American peoples at
> all times the reality of the thesis that we are a great power; that we are by and large
> much less in need of them than they are in need of us; that we are entirely prepared
> to leave to themselves those who evince no particular desire for the forms of col-
> laboration that we have to offer; that the danger of a failure to exhaust the possi-
> bilities of our mutual relationship is always greater to them than to us; that we can

afford to wait, patiently and good-naturedly; and that we are more concerned to be respected than to be liked or understood. (In Trask, "George F. Kennan's Report," 310)

Not surprisingly, the transfer of U.S. foreign-policy interests and large economic aid packages to areas other than Latin America seriously impacted investment in CIAA-style cultural programs. Once the war was won, such programs were deemed by many in Congress to be wasteful and unnecessary. Cultural diplomacy in general was under scrutiny because of its association with the liberalism of FDR's New Deal, or, as labeled by Spruille Baden (who succeeded Rockefeller as assistant secretary for Latin American affairs), "do-gooders and one-worlders" and "communist-fellow-travelers"—the latter term intended as a specific reference to the CIAA (in Erb, 267). Cultural programs were now the purview of the State Department, which in 1950 was attacked by Joseph McCarthy as having been infiltrated by communists.

Among those being investigated by McCarthy, the House Un-American Activities Committee (HUAC) and/or the FBI were Archibald MacLeish, Orson Welles, and former Rockefeller and CIAA adviser William Benton, who had served as assistant secretary for public and cultural affairs after MacLeish and was now a U.S. senator from Connecticut. MacLeish was singled out by McCarthy and J. Edgar Hoover for his communist associations; his bemused response was that "no one would be more shocked to learn I am a Communist than the Communists themselves" (in Donaldson, 296). Welles was secretly and officially listed by the FBI as "a threat to the internal security" of the United States; during the period of the Hollywood blacklist he was given few opportunities and as a result became a European exile for nearly a decade (Naremore, *Magic World*, 22). Benton's criticism of McCarthy's vituperative and unsubstantiated attacks against State Department officials and his formal call for McCarthy's expulsion from the Senate resulted in similar attacks against him and U.S. cultural programs in general.

According to historian Frank Ninkovich, the remaining monies that had been appropriated for the CIAA (OIAA) and the OWI needed to be disbursed prior to June 30, 1946. An early postwar arrangement between the State Department and the National Gallery of Art that gave the gallery authority over the government's art program came to an end because of the department's dissatisfaction with exhibitions that failed to promote U.S. art abroad. To respond to the overseas demand for cultural materials, the department's J. Leroy Davidson used the unspent funds to purchase seventy-nine contemporary oil paintings by such figures as Georgia O'Keeffe, Stuart Davis, Walter Gropper, and Marsden Hartley at the extraordinarily low price of $49,000—which, as Ninkovich points out ("Currents," 226), was the result of negotiations with artists who agreed to sell under market value as a patriotic gesture. Like the CIAA's earliest touring exhibits on U.S. and Latin American art, the department's emphasis was on modern art and its association with progress and modernity. The purchase was in keeping with the idea of offering cultural media (as opposed to informational media) directed specifically at the upper and ruling class.

The paintings were displayed in New York under the exhibition title Advancing American Art, already a sign of changing attitudes: formerly used to describe the Good Neighbor community of twenty-one republics, "American" now was being used to describe only the United States.[8] After a favorable reception in New York, Advancing American Art was shipped to a UNESCO international art exhibit in October 1946 in Paris, where it received glowing reviews and, in Ninkovich's words, "provide[d] an excellent stimulus to further intercultural relations."[9] The collection was later split into two touring exhibits, one for Europe and the other for Latin America. But a cultural backlash began when the February 18, 1947, issue of Look magazine featured an illustrated article on the collection with the headline "Your Money Bought These Pictures." Denunciations from Hearst-owned newspapers and Republican Party leaders soon followed, accusing the State Department of pushing a left-wing agenda through the purchase and display of art that subverted the "American [U.S.] way of life."

Truman agreed with this view—as his "Hottentot" reference in this chapter's epigraph made clear—and he stood with political conservatives who considered representational art to be the only acceptable form for U.S. cultural exchange. Yasuo Kuniyoshi's Circus Girl Resting was the specific source of Truman's reaction and one of the paintings most virulently attacked. Benton, who was assistant secretary at the time and approved the purchase of the paintings, received a special drubbing. Reaction was even fiercer when HUAC declared that some of the artists in question had communist affiliations. As John Merryman, Albert Edsen, and Stephen Urice have noted in their book Law, Ethics, and the Visual Arts (647), the populist hue and cry against the paintings was not so terribly different in style from the 1937 Nazi condemnation of modernism as degenerate art (or, one might add, the Stalinist program of social realism in the arts).

Ultimately the traveling exhibits were cancelled, Davidson's job was eliminated at the State Department, and the entire collection of paintings was put

on the block and auctioned off as "war surplus" by the War Assets Administration for less than $6,000.[10] Benton was personally pursued by McCarthy in
the early 1950s for his role in the purchase of the collection and for the "un-
American" act of printing his *Encyclopedia Britannica* in England instead of
the United States.[11] In 1952, at the height of the Red Scare, Benton lost reelection to the U.S. Senate. U.S. cultural diplomacy was scrutinized as never before
and became increasingly tethered to U.S. cold war interests.

Looking back on the CIAA today, its policies seem, at least in comparison
to what followed, a remarkably enlightened example of the government's enthusiastic prioritization of modern and relatively progressive forms of public
culture as a powerful mediating force for political and economic interests. It is
doubtful that Good Neighbor relations would have yielded the same degree of
mutuality or cooperation without the cultural agency and its broad-based program of public information and education through radio, print media, and the
visual arts. Of course, as a wartime propaganda agency, the CIAA used its resources to sway attitudes, build friendships abroad, and promote an economic
agenda that was abundantly favorable to the United States. In this sense, the
CIAA was more than the sum of its parts and played a crucial role in what is
sometimes called U.S. cultural imperialism.

But while acknowledging the agency's self-interested character, we should
not lose sight of the fact that it helped change, even if only in the short term and
to a degree we cannot precisely calculate, the way the U.S. public and policy
makers viewed Latin America and the way Latin Americans viewed the United
States. Most scholars and students of U.S.–Latin American relations would
agree, I believe, that relations among Western Hemisphere nations were never
as good as during the period when FDR was in office. Some of the recognition
for this Good Neighbor closeness belongs to the United States' wartime belief and investment in culture and in its creation of an agency whose mission
was, for whatever mixed reasons, aimed at engaging, negotiating, and making
friends with neighbors.

Notes

Introduction

1. Public diplomacy scholar Nicholas J. Cull makes the following distinction between cultural (or public) diplomacy and soft power: "PD [Public diplomacy] can be the *mechanism* to deploy soft power, but it is not the same thing as soft power, any more than the army and hard power are the same thing. . . . The advantage of the term 'Soft Power' is that it has moved the conversation around PD into the realm of national security and provided a language for arguing that attention be paid to PD. The disadvantage is that Nye has presented it [as] a mechanism for 'getting what one wants.'" Cull contrasts this "negative" soft power to the more "attractive" form, which involves "listening and being open to being changed by an encounter." *Public Diplomacy*, 15.

2. See http://www.life.com/image/50551080/in-gallery/26762/jackie-kennedy-at-her-most-elegant. The reference to "loveliest" might rankle some today, but attention was being drawn to Jacqueline Kennedy's rising success as an international relations figure at a time when U.S. diplomacy was perceived as an exclusively male domain. The perception of the diplomatic role as a male undertaking has not entirely disappeared. In a recent series of enlightening lectures at Indiana University by a renowned former diplomat, the pronoun "he" was repeatedly used when referring to the individual training for diplomatic service. At least a third of the audience was female, and I wondered how the speaker, a seasoned and accomplished statesman, could make such a gaff. But it is interesting to consider the role of gender in diplomacy and whether women's increasing presence in the field has had any general or distinctive impact.

3. "Case for Cultural Diplomacy," 20. Nye's essay "The Decline of America's 'Soft Power'" appeared one year later in the same journal.

4. In his essay "The Purposes and Cross-Purposes of American Public Diplomacy," U.S. senior diplomat John Brown refers to Under Secretary for Public Diplomacy and Public Affairs Charlotte Beer in stating that public diplomacy was the use of education, culture, and information for international purposes, while the area of public affairs denoted outreach at home. The CIAA made no such distinction and was preoccupied with both audiences.

5. "Smart power" is used by Nye in his book *Soft Power: The Means to Success in*

World Politics (2004) to signify the combination of soft and hard powers in international relations.

6. The CIAA was created by Executive Order 8840. It is sometimes referred to by historians and in archives as the OIAA or OCIAA.

7. For discussion of the word "mutuality," see Cull's *Cold War*, xviii, and Kathy R. Fitzpatrick's *U.S. Public Diplomacy's Neglected Domestic Mandate*, 14. In a lecture broadcast from Harvard to the Institute of Cultural Diplomacy in Berlin, Nye listed culture, values, and policies as the three principal components of soft power. The lecture can be seen on the institute's website at http://www.culturaldiplomacy.org.

8. *Compact Oxford English Dictionary*, 1971, 1:622.

9. Ibid., 1:734.

10. The quotation is from the title of Creel's book, *How We Advertised America: The First Telling of the Amazing Story of the Committee on Public Information that Carried the Gospel of Americanism to Every Corner of the Globe* (1920). The word "Americanism" was strictly associated with the U.S. way of life.

11. For more information on the use of media by presidents prior to FDR, see Richard W. Steele's initial chapter in *Propaganda in an Open Society*, 3–31.

12. Nye comments on the generally slow process of building soft power that, he contends, is one of the main reasons for its underuse by politicians. Consult his "Case for Cultural Diplomacy." The CIAA was unusual in its fast-track approach to forging stronger inter-American cultural ties.

13. See Frank D. McCann, *The Brazilian-American Alliance, 1937–1945*, for an in-depth discussion of this period in U.S.-Brazilian relations. In a July 19, 2011, email McCann describes the reluctance of Latin American countries to declare war because of their poorly equipped militaries. Prior to the summer of 1942, the United States was not equipped to send them arms.

14. See, for example, studies by Gerald Haines (diplomatic history), Catherine L. Benamou (film), Frank D. McCann (history), Irene Rostagno (literature), Héctor Maymí-Sugrañes (library science), Pennee Bender (documentary newsreels), and Fred Fejes (radio). Gersão Moura's and Antônio Pedro Tota's works are among those broader in scope. The fullest official account is Donald W. Rowland's History of the Office of the Coordinator of Inter-American Affairs. See my bibliography for other sources.

Chapter 1

1. For more information on the CPI, see George Creel, *How We Advertised America*, and Nicholas Cull, *The Cold War and the United States Information Agency*, especially 6–9.

2. Chief among hemispheric publications at the time was Lewis Hanke's *Handbook of Latin American Studies* (1936–) in the Library of Congress. Three years later, it was published under the auspices of the newly created Hispanic Division in the LOC.

3. The Division of the American Republics was one of four units devoted to area affairs. It and the Division of Cultural Relations worked under the Adviser on Political Relations, who reported to the offices of the assistant secretary of state. See 1941 State

Department diagram, Lilly Library (hereinafter LL), Walter H.C. Laves manuscript (hereinafter Laves mss.), box 1.

4. Nicholas J. Cull refers to the British "Strategy of Truth" approach that influenced how the United States shaped its wartime propaganda program. *Cold War*, 14.

5. Roosevelt's first choice for the coordinator job was James V. Forrestal, who recommended Rockefeller. Forrestal became FDR's secretary of the Navy.

6. As an undergraduate at Dartmouth College, Rockefeller transformed a dull student-run arts program into a campus success by inviting celebrated writers to lecture on campus. The list included Edna St. Vincent Millay, Sinclair Lewis, and Bertrand Russell. He was equally successful with his innovative redesigning of *The Pictorial*, the college yearbook. See Reich, 66–69.

7. Years earlier, in 1914, his father, John D. Rockefeller Jr., negotiated a grievance plan for striking workers in the family's Colorado Fuel and Iron Company in Ludlow following a massacre of striking miners and thirty-two women and children. For a detailed discussion of Rockefeller's idea of "progressive capitalism" in Venezuela, see Darlene Rivas's *Missionary Capitalist*.

8. In his book *The First Resort of Kings*, Richard T. Arndt critiques Rockefeller's plan, stating that it showed his ignorance or dismissal of the context of a "burgeoning cultural exchange with Latin America" at the time—not to mention the much earlier efforts by individuals such as Under Secretary of State Sumner Welles to initiate a program of inter-American cultural relations (78).

9. The Division of Cultural Relations had two main objectives: to provide travel grants for inter-American intellectual exchange and to produce and distribute educational films to be shown throughout the Americas.

10. British authors worked to influence U.S. public opinion during World War I as well. For more on the subject, see Susan A. Brewer, *To Win the Peace*, and Robert Calder, *Beware the Serpent*. Germany deployed its own propaganda program to sway public opinion, especially among U.S. citizens of German descent, at the start of both world wars.

11. Quoted in Salina Hastings, *The Secret Lives of Somerset Maugham*, 456. For an in-depth study of British propaganda toward the United States, see Nicholas J. Cull, *Selling War*.

12. For example, the November 12, 1940, policy committee minutes discussed work by Karl Bickel (former head of United Press and chair of Scripps-Howard Radio), who was overseeing the translation and distribution of the Spanish version of *Reader's Digest*. William Benton Papers, University of Chicago archives (hereinafter WB), box 371, folder 3. In addition to Caldwell and Rockefeller, the policy committee members were John E. Abbott (director, MoMA Film Library), William B. Benton (advertising executive and part-time vice president of the University of Chicago), Francis A. Jamieson (Pulitzer prize–winning journalist and CIAA press division director), Henry R. Luce (communications magnate and founder of *Time*, *Fortune*, and *Life* magazines), Harry Lydenberg (director, New York Public Library), Carleton Sprague Smith (head of the New York Public Library music division), David H. Stevens (director, Humanities Di-

vision, Rockefeller Foundation), Monroe Wheeler (director, MoMA exhibitions), and James W. Young (head, J. Walter Thompson Advertising Agency). The committee was disbanded in February 1941, although most of the members continued to advise informally or work directly for the CIAA. William Benton, a close friend and adviser of Rockefeller's, was appointed CIEE "consultant" effective March 27, 1943. Letter from Rockefeller to Benton, WB, box 371, folder 19.

13. WB, box 371, folder 17.

14. In the letter Rockefeller states that he also had written to the presidents of the University of California, University of Texas, and Harvard University for similar assistance. WB, box 371, folder 17.

15. WB, box 371, folder 9.

16. Rippy memo, n.d. WB, box 371, folder 3. Another document indicates that there was a group of Chicago scholars who were exchanging views on the subject of cultural relations, among them Rippy, Quincy Wright, political scientist Walter H.C. Laves (who later worked with the CIAA), economist Jacob Viner, geographer Robert S. Platt, and microbiologist William Hay Taliaferro.

17. Rippy memo. Ultimately assessments of this kind fell to individuals like Leonard W. Doob, a propaganda and public-opinion expert recruited early on by the CIAA whose work I discuss later in this chapter.

18. Rippy memo.

19. Ibid.

20. This approach was in direct contrast with that of the director of the CIAA's Cultural Relations Division, Wallace K. Harrison, who said the masses should be the main focus of cultural initiatives.

21. Rippy memo.

22. His undated report was sent directly to Caldwell. WB, box 317, folder 9. All citations and references to the document are from this source.

23. He authored *Propaganda Techniques in the World War* (1927) and *World Revolutionary Propaganda: A Chicago Study* (1939), both published by Alfred A. Knopf.

24. Lasswell discussed the desirability of safeguarding native cultures and at the same time adapting Indians to the needs of modern production.

25. The Reich ministry was responsible for information and propaganda locally and abroad. It produced films, radio programs, music, and newsletters; organized art exhibits; and translated books from German into other languages. All of these activities were ultimately undertaken by the CIAA. For more on this topic, see Frye, 20–21. The CPI offered another possible organizational template for the CIAA.

26. Donald Marquand Dozer has estimated that a half-million Germans were living in southern Brazil and that the German immigrant populations were even larger in Argentina and southeastern Chile (74). Frye describes the use of special German correspondents sent abroad to cultivate personal relations with employees of the non-German press in order to bolster the Reich's propaganda efforts (24–25).

27. The document, "The Proclaimed List of Certain Blocked Nationals," was issued as Proclamation 2497 on July 17, 1941. Among those blacklisted were Brazilian affili-

ates and subsidiaries of German and Italian companies like Bayer, Fiat, and Olivetti along with German and Italian banking firms. See also Max Paul Friedman, "There Goes the Neighborhood." This proclamation affected all aspects of cultural life in Latin America and created greater opportunities for U.S. exports there, especially Hollywood movies. For further information on its impact in Brazil, consult Tania Quintaneiro, "Cinema e guerra."

28. Iversen arrived in Berlin in 1938 and began working for German state radio in 1939. By February 1942 he had four different time slots on Spanish-language shortwave transmissions from Berlin. National Archives and Records Administration II, Record Group 229 (hereinafter NARAII, RG229), CIAA, Radio Division, box 244. "He proved to be an accomplished journalist and broadcaster; to listeners in Latin America, he projected Germany as an enlightened and progressive country . . . His objective was to alienate Latin America from Washington by ridiculing the Pan-American ideal as an "instrument of U.S. expansionist policy." Comment in an August 19, 2010, email from Gisela Cramer, who cites Lotz and Bergmeier, *Hitler's Airwaves*, 41.

29. NARAII, RG229, CIAA, Radio Division, box 1461. Claude Bowers, U.S. ambassador to Chile during the war, was constantly concerned about German propaganda there. In a December 31, 1940, letter to Columbia University president Nicholas Murray Butler he wrote: "The propaganda against us here is tremendous and heavily financed. The German embassy is spending close to 2,000,000 pesos a month on propaganda." LL, Bowers mss. II, correspondence 1939–1942, box 5. In this letter Bowers discusses his idea of sending top Chilean journalists to work with U.S. newspapers for a two-month period as a way to foster good relations with the local press. His idea turned into a reality in 1941 for seven Chileans, who were the first of numerous journalistic delegations from Latin America to tour the United States at the CIAA's invitation.

30. In a personal note dated October 13, 1941, Doob wrote: "Suddenly summoned to Nelson's office. . . . In the meantime I had sent on Sat. my memo on Hemisphere Enlightenment . . . and [Wallace K.] Harrison made head of Propaganda." From Doob's archive of personal papers made available to me by his son, Anthony N. Doob, professor of criminology at the University of Toronto. ("Propaganda" was a short-lived title ultimately replaced by "Information.")

31. Similar to other CIAA reports, the document does not list the author. Rockefeller Archive Center (hereinafter RAC), Nelson A. Rockefeller (NAR), RG III, 40, CIAA, box 8, folder 61.

32. MacLeish's reference in this chapter's epigraph to cultural relations as a dangerous enterprise was based, in part, on his concern that power would be wielded by "self-appointed groups of culturalists with careers to make, or creeds to propagate, or fads to follow" (172)—a possible critique of Rockefeller and the New York group, which anticipated the CIAA credo campaign. But by 1941, the year MacLeish became head of the Office of Facts and Figures (OFF), he and Rockefeller were close allies in building U.S. public awareness of wartime matters. For more on this agency, see Ramon Girona and Jordi Xifra, "The Office of Facts and Information."

33. An undated but early hand-drawn diagram of the CIAA organization lists the various media sectors under an umbrella department titled Psychological Warfare. LL, Laves mss., box 13, Manuscripts Department. A December 1, 1942, CIAA report, "The Inter-American Movement: An Outline," contains an entire section devoted to what the individual can do to encourage inter-American understanding and cooperation. It lists ten activities for U.S. citizens to consider, including showing films in the inter-American field; studying the languages, history, and cultures of Latin American countries; and welcoming and entertaining visitors from the other American republics to U.S. communities (14). This document is from the Benson Latin American Collection, University of Texas.

34. The CPI was reluctant to use the word "propaganda" in World War I as well. Creel stated: "We did not call it propaganda, for that word, in German hands, had come to be associated with deceit and corruption. Our effort was educational and informative throughout, for we had such confidence in our case as to feel that no other argument was needed than the simple straightforward presentation of facts" (4–5). The factual basis of CPI materials, like most propaganda, is open to interpretation.

35. Doob, *Public Opinion*, 232–233. According to Doob, the single exception was the "unimportant and publicity-shunning Propaganda Branch of Military Intelligence in Washington, D.C." (232).

36. My book focuses on CIAA cultural activities specifically, although the other divisions had obvious implications for strengthening inter-American political and economic relations.

37. NARAII RG229, CIAA, Records of the Department of Press and Propaganda, box 1467.

38. An August 19, 1943, document in the MPSA archive, Francis Alstock file, at the Margaret Herrick Library in Los Angeles (hereinafter MHL) lists CIAA funding for 1943–1944 at $50,000. A CIAA project authorization dated April 1, 1941, designated $54,000 for the year to the MPSA. Yearly renewals followed. NARAII, RG229, Records of the Department of Press and Propaganda, box 942.

39. The Breen Office in Hollywood was already censoring movies that challenged the Motion Picture Production Code, although there was nothing in that code specifically to prevent negative stereotypes of Latin Americans.

40. NARAII, RG229, Motion Picture Division, box 942.

41. MHL, MPSA collection, Francis Alstock file.

42. See Catherine L. Benamou for a detailed study of *It's All True*, Welles's aborted CIAA film project on Latin America.

43. According to the 1943 *Film Daily Yearbook*, RKO was also distributing Disney's films (221). Rockefeller's father, John Jr., gave his son a letter of credit that stated he would personally guarantee any loans given by the family bank, Chase Bank, to support business with the CIAA. To shore up his business dealings, Nelson Rockefeller convinced Joseph Rovensky to leave his position as head of Chase Bank's foreign department and take charge of the CIAA trade and finance division in Washington. See

Reich, 190. RKO was proactive in importing Latin American stars for its movies; these included Aurora Miranda (Carmen's sister) for *Tell It to a Star* and Corinna Mura for the Cantinflas feature *Magnificent Tramp*. Aurora Miranda is perhaps best remembered for her role in Disney's *Three Caballeros*.

44. Letter dated August 13, 1942. Centro de Pesquisa e Documentação de História Contemporânea do Brasil/Fundação Getúlio Vargas (hereinafter CPDOC/FGV), OA (Oswaldo Aranha), cp 1942.08.13/2, reel 19, photo 230.

45. According to Buñuel's memoir, he resigned from the MoMA because the State Department pressured the museum to fire him following the publication of a book review in the *Motion Picture Herald* that quotes Salvador Dalí, the book's author, who described Buñuel as an atheist. Buñuel wrote: "In his book, *The Secret Life of Salvador Dalí*, I was described as an atheist, an accusation that at the time was worse than being called a Communist. . . . I felt I had suddenly been sentenced to the electric chair. . . . After my resignation, I made an appointment to meet Dalí at the Sherry Netherland bar, and I was beside myself with rage. He was a bastard, I told him, a *salaud*; his book had ruined my career. 'The book has nothing to do with you,' he replied. 'I wrote it to make *myself* a star. You've only got a supporting role'" (182–183).

46. The size of the country and its thousands of movie theaters were important cultural and commercial considerations.

47. South American movie preferences, MHL, MPSA, MPAA (Motion Picture Association of America), Breen Office files.

48. Ibid.

49. Samuel N. Burger, MGM general supervisor for Latin America, wrote to E. C. Givens, chair of the CIAA coordinating committee in the Chamber of Commerce in Rio, to request his help in getting the U.S. community in Rio to support *Mrs. Miniver*: "The propaganda value and the message carried by the picture is such as to elevate it beyond the value and importance of an ordinary motion picture. . . . We are going to extraordinary expense in order to convince the Brazilian public of [its] unusual value. The entire proceeds of the opening night revert to the 'Legião Brasileira de Assistência' and the performance will be sponsored by Mme. Darcy Vargas [wife of the president of Brazil]." NARAII, RG229, Motion Picture Division, box 226.

50. According to Neal Gabler, Disney made between 150 and 300 hours of government movies in four years (412). Brazilian newspapers gave extensive coverage to Orson Welles's visit, and there was considerable dismay and disappointment expressed by the press when the RKO fiasco brought his filming to a halt.

51. NARAII, RG229, Motion Picture Division, box 226. A major challenge for the CIAA was finding announcers who could speak Portuguese and Spanish.

52. NARAII, RG229, Radio Division, box 1461.

53. All domestic programming had to be approved by the OFF and, after its dismantlement in 1942, by the OWI. Overseas broadcasts were cleared by the State Department as well as censors of the various Latin American governments, such as Brazil's Departamento de Imprensa e Propaganda (DIP).

54. Confidential report to the Department of State on the Activities of the Radio Division from the Coordinator of Inter-American Affairs. NARAII, RG229, Radio Division, box 240.

55. A September 1945 Radio Division "Resume of Operations" by Rockefeller adviser William Benton provides statistics on the number of surveys done between 1941 and 1944, many of which were door-to-door. The report summarizes a typical survey in Argentina (October 1944) as follows: "4,800 interviews were made among 2,400 women and 2,400 men in 10 cities." The list begins with Buenos Aires, where 1,000 interviews were conducted. The report reproduced the survey with questions about favorite programs, listening hours, foreign broadcasts received, and magazines and newspapers often read. This final question helped the CIAA to determine where to place ads for program schedules, which resulted in regular listings in the Spanish and Portuguese versions of *Reader's Digest*. The Benton report can be found in NARAII, RG229, Radio Division, box 963.

56. American Social Surveys was a nonprofit organization created by the CIAA and based at Princeton University. George Gallup was president, and Henry Cantril was vice president (Rowland, 84).

57. From the personal papers of Leonard W. Doob.

58. The report added that the poor, elderly, and uneducated mentioned radio more frequently as a news source than did respondents in the middle and upper classes.

59. According to Rowland, Doob assisted Cantril in public opinion surveys prior to becoming a CIAA member (83).

60. August 31, 1942, report to Harry Frantz and Walter H. C. Laves, Doob personal papers.

61. Jamieson was the head of the Department of Information, and Frantz worked under him as Press Division director. In 1944 the various information print units became the Press and Publication Division with Jamieson as its head.

62. September 3, 1942. NARAII, RG229, Press and Publication Division, box 1470.

63. "Press Objectives: Outline of Editorial Policy," NARAII, RG229, Press and Publication Division, box 1470.

64. See Rowland, 183, for a transcription of Roosevelt's April 22, 1941, letter to Rockefeller.

65. Advice contained in a December 11, 1941, memorandum from John M. Clark to the Policy Committee on Cultural Relations. In Rowland, 92n7.

66. NARAII, RG229, Press and Publication Division, box 1462.

67. Letter from Frantz to Jamieson dated May 9, 1942, NARAII, RG229, Press and Publication Division, box 1467.

68. NARAII, RG229, Press and Publication Division, box 1467.

69. LL, Bowers mss. II, correspondence 1939–1942, box 5.

70. LL, Bowers mss. II, correspondence 1939–1942, box 5. Fairbanks' visit to Chile went equally well, as did his visit to Brazil. U.S. ambassador to Brazil Jefferson Caffery wrote to Armour on May 5, 1941, that the actor was "pleasant" and that "the people in general find him 'simpatico.'" The Brazilian press was more enthusiastic about Fair-

banks, who was accessible, humorous, and eager to learn about Brazil—as reported in a front-page article, "Douglas Fairbanks no [in] Itamarati," in Rio's *A Noite* of April 26, 1941. Caffery's letter and the 1941 article on Fairbanks's visit to the government offices in Rio are in the University of Louisiana Archive Special Collections Department, Jefferson Caffery Collection 45, box 47, folder 1, and news clippings box 2 (1940–June 1941).

Fairbanks was less than enthusiastic about Caffery in his May 20, 1941, letter to Sumner Welles: "I hope you will keep this in the strictest confidence, but it was my untrained opinion that Mr. Caffray [*sic*], respected and able though he may be, is a little too aware of his position." FDR Library, Sumner Welles Papers, Office Correspondence, 1920–1943. This archive contains a large file of correspondence between Fairbanks and Welles. Concerned about the impact of Axis propaganda, Fairbanks wrote detailed, perceptive, and well-crafted dispatches on each Latin American country that he visited.

An epistolary friendship grew between Bowers and Fairbanks after the actor's departure from South America. The Bowers archive contains several long letters from Fairbanks to Bowers. Among personal and wartime news, Fairbanks informs Bowers on October 4, 1941, that Brazilian President Getúlio Vargas was making Fairbanks an officer of the Brazilian Order of the Southern Cross.

71. In a July 12, 1941, letter to Bowers, Fairbanks wrote that he had spent considerable time with Hull and Welles in Washington following his return from Latin America. He confided that "the new announcement of propaganda activities by the Rockefeller group is in part a result of my final report." LL, Bowers mss. II, box 5.

Chapter 2

The epigraph source is in RAC, RG4, box 262, folder 2627.

1. NARAII, RG229, Motion Picture Division, box 214.

2. For further discussion on this topic, see Adams as well as O'Neill.

3. For more information on this topic, see Joanne Hershfield's "Dolores Del Río, Uncomfortably Real."

4. For additional information, see Tania Quintaneiro, "Cinema e guerra." A similar but more broadly international tactic was used by the Creel Committee on Public Information during World War I to ensure that "no American pictures of any kind would be sold to houses where any sort of German film was being used"; in Creel, 276.

5. Both quotes are from a file on censorship in the MPSA collection at the MHL. According to the CIAA report "The Inter-American Movement: An Outline," Axis propaganda emphasized the figures of gangsters as well as strikers, the unemployed, and Bolsheviks in its portrayal of the United States (8).

6. Memo from Warner to Robert T. Miller, September 23, 1941. NARAII, RG229, Motion Picture Division, box 213.

7. March 26, 1941, report by Bruno Cheli. NARAII, RG229, Motion Picture Division, box 214.

8. According to Richards, the sailor scene was inserted to make use of visiting Bra-

zilian seamen whom the MPSA was honoring with a goodwill banquet (xxxiii). But Assis de Figueiredo felt the representation was inauthentic; and as O'Neill notes, the sailors were changed from Brazilian to Portuguese (376).

9. In *Andy Hardy's Private Secretary* (1941), the judge helps a talented linguist and father of one of Andy's Hispanic friends find a job in the Brazilian consulate.

10. For a commentary on Carmen Miranda and *Springtime in the Rockies*, see the chapter titled "Good Neighbor Brazil" and notes in my *Brazil Imagined: 1500 to the Present*, 209–233 and 323–327.

11. NARAII, RG229 DV contains 136 stills of Dutra on this trip, which involved meetings with Rockefeller, U.S. military heads, and Brazilian soldiers who were training in the United States, as well as visits to military sites. The MHL Breen Office file titled "The Story of the Motion Picture Society for the Americas" has a fifteen-page list of other individuals and groups who were feted by the MPSA.

12. The report is from RAC III, 40, Washington, CIAA, box 7, folder 56.

13. "Prencinradio, Inc.," RAC, NAR III, 40, box 8, folder 64.

14. February 10, 1942, memo from A. W. Ellis, chair of the American Association in Mexico, to Rockefeller. NARAII, RG229, Motion Picture Division, box 214. Ellis's comments were shown to be true, and the CIAA greatly benefited from its investments in the Mexican film industry.

15. For a detailed discussion of the CIAA financial intervention in the Mexican film industry, see Seth Fein, "Hollywood, U.S.-Mexican Relations."

16. See "Nazi Propaganda Pix Real War Weapons Hollywood Learns," in *Daily Variety* (January 27, 1943), n.p. Clipping found in NARAII, RG 229, Motion Picture Division, box 214. The MoMA work began in 1941 and by 1943 385 German films had been reviewed by Library head Iris Barry and her staff. The authorization for this project can be found in NARAII, RG 229, Motion Picture Division, box 208. The hundreds of MoMA reviews of the German films are located in box 213.

17. NARAII, RG229, Motion Picture Division, box 214.

18. Contracts with Pathé and News of the Day can be found in NARAII, RG229, Motion Picture Division, box 942.

19. NARAII, RG229, CIAA, Motion Picture Division, box 214.

20. Data provided in "Report of Production of the Museum of Modern Art Film Project for the Office of the Coordinator of Inter-American Affairs." RAC collection III, 40, series title Washington, subsection CIAA, box 6, folder 43.

21. In addition to cartoons and comics, Disney characters were featured in a miniature book series published in Buenos Aires by Editorial Abril in 1941. Titles included *El Pato Donald pierde su paciencia* (Donald Duck Loses His Patience) and *El ratón Mickey y los siete fantasmas* (Mickey Mouse and the Seven Ghosts). A few of these booklets can be found in the Nettie Lee Benson Collection, University of Texas at Austin.

22. NARAII, RG229, Motion Picture Division, box 215.

23. For a discussion of *La guerra gaucha*, see Paula Félix-Didier and André Levinson's "The Building of a Nation."

24. Appearing on U.S. publicity for the movie, the word "jitterbird" was directed

at U.S. audiences to make Zé seem more familiar. Zé performs samba steps but at no point does he "jitterbug."

25. In his book on film noir, *More than Night*, James Naremore discusses how Hollywood used a playground image of Latin America as foil to the stoic, tough-guy character: "No matter how the Latin world is represented, however, it is nearly always associated with a frustrated desire for romance and freedom; again and again, it holds out the elusive, ironic promise of a warmth and color that will countervail the dark mis-en-scène and the taut, restricted coolness of the average noir protagonist" (230).

26. Schale notes that the turnout in Latin America was so great that the practice of showing double features was suspended in certain areas so the film could be repeatedly shown without interruption (48).

27. In 2009 Ted Thomas, son of Disney animator Frank Thomas, made a 35mm feature-length documentary that revisits the Latin American trip by "El grupo," which was how Disney's staff referred to themselves during the tour.

28. NARAII, RG229, Motion Picture Division, box 216.

29. See, for example, articles by Burton-Carvajal and José Piedra and Eric Smoodin's *Animating Culture*. Piedra errs in his critique when he refers to Bahia as Zé Carioca's birthplace. Zé is not a Bahian but a Carioca, the Portuguese word for a citizen from Rio de Janeiro. For a discussion of Disney's animated and live-action or hybrid approach in *The Three Caballeros*, see J. P. Telotte, "Crossing Borders and Opening Boxes."

30. For further discussion of queer Donald, see Piedra's essay.

31. Unlike the colonization of the United States, women did not accompany the early expeditions to Latin America.

32. *Victory through Air Power* is a powerful argument for the development of long-range airplanes and a separate Air Force division. It is an intelligent film whose power is largely a result of Disney's effective use of real and animated maps.

33. For information on Disney health films, see Cartwright and Goldfarb's "Cultural Contagion."

34. The only Latin American reference in *The Pelican and the Snipe* is found in the names given to the birds: Monte and Video.

35. Disney's DVD titled *At the Front* contains many of the CIAA-sponsored shorts in addition to the feature *Victory through Air Power*.

36. In his autobiography, *My Last Sigh*, Buñuel wrote that while working for MoMA he was asked to cut down Leni Rienfenstahl's *The Triumph of the Will* and another Nazi film on the conquest of Poland for their public exhibition. He stated: "René Clair and Charlie Chaplin rushed to see them and had totally different reactions. 'Never show them!' Clair said, horrified by their power. 'If you do, we're lost!' Chaplin, on the other hand, laughed, once so hard he actually fell off his chair. Was he so amused because of *The Great Dictator*?" (180).

37. "Report of Production of The Museum of Modern Art Film Project for The Office of the Coordinator of Inter-American Affairs," RAC, NAR III, 40, box 6, folder 43. See also Iris Barry's note titled "Latin America" in the *Bulletin of the Museum of Modern*

Art. A list of contracts with independent filmmakers and Hollywood studios can be found in NARAII, RG229, Motion Picture Division, box 956.

38. The article and pictures focus on six steps for preparing available films: 1) films are reviewed and discussed; 2) new commentaries are written; 3) new musical accompaniments are arranged; 4) the films are re-edited and recut; 5) the foreign language narration is recorded on the new versions of the film; and 6) the films leave for South America.

39. "Motion Picture Division," 1942 report, RAC, NAR III, 40, box 9, folder 72. Curator Iris Barry loaned MoMA footage to March of Time and negotiated to make Spanish and Portuguese versions of its films. Barry was active in promoting the Film Library in South America through articles such as "Un museo de películas" (A Film Museum) that appeared in the Buenos Aires newspaper *La Nación*, April 13, 1941, section 2, pp.1–4. She also lectured widely in the United States on topics such as "The War as Shown to the German People: Excerpts from Nazi Propaganda Films," which she presented at The New School for Social Research on February 11, 1943. (This talk was probably based on the eleven-reel nontheatrical subject, "German Propaganda Films, 1934–1940," which the MoMA showed to twenty-five government agencies to analyze and combat Axis propaganda. See *Bulletin of the Museum of Modern Art* 10, 1 [October-November 1942].) In July 1944 Barry proposed to her husband, John Abbott, the creation of a Commission for the Presentation, Protection, and Salvage of Artistic and Historic Monuments. One of its main objectives was to find and preserve films found in war-torn Europe. See Film Library, Iris Barry, Department of Film, 02.10–02.12. MoMA Archives.

40. RAC, NAR III 40, box 9, folder 72.

41. Letter dated November 22, 1941. WB, box 371, folder 8. There are five letters from Brooks to Benton that detail how both men anticipated the increased role of 16mm educational films as a result of the war. In his first letter, of November 22, Brooks criticized ERPI, which was to come under Benton's control in 1943 as head of Encyclopedia Britannica, for charging the CIAA and State Department excessively for prints of fourteen of its films. Brooks described ERPI (bankrolled by AT&T) as a "bottle-neck" in the production of educational films and proposed a cooperative among colleges and universities for making and distributing such films. He wrote in his December 14, 1941, letter: "My hope for the cooperative distribution of educational films is to break the present too-high print cost, which limits the market. School films should be available at a price nearer the $8.00 per reel that is charged by the Office of Education than the current price charged by ERPI and others. Too many inconsequential films are being sold at $50 per copy." In his third letter, dated March 28, 1942, he promised to send Benton a print of Julien Bryan's first CIAA film, *Americans All*, as part of the CIAA's university film distribution program. Brooks's April 16, 1942, letter included a copy of a form to be completed by borrowers of CIAA 16mm movies. Among the topics were audience totals (broken down by age groups and sex), location and number of showings, audience reaction, and the brand of sound projector used. On May 20,

1942, Brooks informed Benton that CIAA films would be distributed to forty-seven university libraries.

42. In a July 27, 1943, letter to Rockefeller, Abbott argued that the proposed $5,000 per reel was insufficient for a "first-class product," which he estimated would cost between $10,000 and $15,000. He suggested that the contract be changed to "produce 6 to 8 films for $100,000." Department of Film/LOC contracts, file 5-B, OEM, cr 320, 1. The Museum of Modern Art Archives, New York (MoMA Archives).

43. Department of Film/LOC contracts, file 5-I, OEM, cr, Film Production, 19, MoMA Archives. In a telegram sent on February 11, 1944, Abbott tells Nesbitt that he likes the *Art Discovers America* idea and not to worry about OWI duplication. Department of Film/LOC contracts, file 5-I OEM, cr, Film Production, 20. MoMA Archives.

44. According to Miller and Rowe, "Subjects had to be timely and available for distribution as quickly as possible. . . They should be inexpensive—the cost of producing one reel of 16-mm film has been estimated at from $4,500 to $6,000" (7). To help the wartime cause, Hollywood allowed some of its 35mm shorts to be copied on 16mm and shown nontheatrically here and abroad.

45. Fillers-in tended to favor sports, such as *Art of Skiing*, *Super Athletes*, *Olympic Champions*, and *How to Fish*; Miller and Rowe, 9.

46. For example, racial mixing was prevalent in Latin American countries because of the absence of European women in the early colonization process. In fact, the coupling of white men and Indian women in Brazil was encouraged by the crown as a way to populate the territory with faithful subjects.

47. Department of Film/LOC contracts, file 6-G OEM, cr 364, 77. MoMA Archives. Bryan's work deeply impressed Canadian-born industrialist and philanthropist David B. Mills. His Davella Mills Foundation awarded the filmmaker $300,000 to establish his International Film Foundation, which presently is administered by Bryan's son, Sam.

48. June 15, 1942, contract signed by Whitney and Alstock. RAC, NAR III, 40, box 7, folder 56.

49. In an article on wartime Mexican public relations, Melissa A. Johnson notes that Mexico paid a Los Angeles firm to produce and distribute films about the country. Although she does not mention the source, the likelihood is that it involved the MPSA and the CIAA.

50. Coca-Cola was introduced into Mexico in 1926, and Hollywood actress Lupe Vélez ("the Mexican Spitfire") appeared on Mexican adverting posters in 1935. In 1940 Coca-Cola's first coin-operated vending machines were installed there. For further information on Coca Cola and Latin America, see "100 Years of Coca-Cola" at http://www .thecoca-colacompany.com/citizenship/pdf/Timeline_Coca-Cola_Latin_America _English.pdf. For an analysis of U.S.-Mexican business relations during this period, see Julio E. Moreno.

51. The recurring image of Latin America as a haven for sexual relations with women (and more recently children) has given Brazil a reputation similar to that of Southeast Asian nations such as Thailand.

52. Mexico was also the focus of numerous James A. FitzPatrick travelogue shorts produced by MGM in the tradition of his earlier *Traveltalks* and *Voice of the Globe* series. These included *Glimpses of Mexico*, *Land of Orizaba*, *Mexican Police on Parade*, and *Modern Mexico City*. Although the CIAA invested in this series, in a 1945 memo Rockefeller complained to Alstock about FitzPatrick's off-screen narration with its poor pronunciation of Spanish names and places. RAC, NAR III, 40, box 7, folder 7.

53. In 2005 I interviewed Brazilian producer Herbert Richers, who met Disney in Rio during World War II and was sent to Fordlândia and the Tapajós region for six months in 1943 and 1944 to film footage for CIAA films. I suspect that some of the live-action footage in *The Amazon Awakens* was shot by Richers. He became a major figure in the Brazilian film industry. He started a company that dubbed U.S. and other films into Portuguese, a lucrative enterprise that he attributed to advice given to him by Disney.

54. "U.S. to Make Films Illustrating Brazilian-U.S. War Cooperation," NARAII, RG229, Motion Picture Division, box 953. There is no signature on the document, although it refers to William Murray, who went to Latin America in 1942 for the CIAA to make a few films and train cameramen. An August 3, 1943, memo indicates that the mission was planning to film two shorts, one on Brazilian folk and popular music and another about learning the samba. The CIAA expressed concern that such topics, while desirable as educational and theatrical possibilities, were outside the CIAA-OSS agreement and that the State Department would not be pleased. NARAII, RG229, Motion Picture Division, box 226.

55. NARAII, RG229, Motion Picture Division, box 226. See also LL, John Ford mss., for Ford's itinerary and letters to his wife written from his Rio base at the Hotel Glória.

56. Engel made this suggestion in a letter dated July 28, 1943, to support the CIAA's Health and Sanitation Division in Brazil. He wrote that the idea for the educational short was based on the 1934 Fox film *White Parade* with Loretta Young and John Boles that proved to be a boon for nurses' training throughout the United States. NARAII, RG229, Motion Picture Division, box 226.

57. Engel to Toland, NARAII, RG229, Motion Picture Division, box 953. See Francis Alstock's letter of January 12, 1944, to B. E. Cunningham about CIAA funding of the mission. NARAII, RG229, Motion Picture Division, box 953.

58. Toland to Engel, NARAII, RG229, Motion Picture Division, box 953.

59. Ibid.

60. Ibid. Toland was clearly referring to the written authorization that stated: "The DIP selected the material, writes the scripts, photographs and cuts the negative, and forwards the original negatives for editing and distribution to the Motion Picture Division"; NARAII, RG229, Motion Picture Division, box 226.

61. Pierce to Francisco, NARAII, RG229, Motion Picture Division, box 953.

62. Toland to Alstock, NARAII, RG229, Motion Picture Division, box 953. The document contains what appears to be Alstock's handwritten notations in the margins. Several comments indicate his frustration with Toland's explanations for why certain projects were still incomplete or should be abandoned.

63. Toland to Ford, NARAII, RG229, Motion Picture Division, box 953.

64. Quoted in a May 30, 1944, communiqué from Arnold Tschudy (chairman of the São Paulo CIAA office) to Francis Alstock. NARA II RG229, Motion Picture Division, box 953. In his report Tschudy stated that most São Paulo newspapers covered the film showing and wrote appreciatively.

65. Review dated May 28, 1944, NARAII, RG229, Motion Picture Division, box 226.

66. In this sense it is very different from the MoMA volume by author Goodwin and photographer Kidder-Smith titled *Brazil Builds* (1942), a Good Neighbor project that gave equal emphasis to the old and the new. See chapter 4 for a discussion of CIAA photographers.

67. The words "Order and Progress" appear on the nation's flag and derive from nineteenth-century Positivist thought.

68. The Japanese were allowed entry in the early twentieth century to work coffee plantations in São Paulo and Rio. Justifications were that the Japanese were experienced agricultural workers with a strong work ethic.

69. NARAII, RG229, Motion Picture Division, box 953.

70. NARAII, RG229, Motion Picture Division, box 953. The six films were *São Paulo*, *Belo Horizonte*, *Wings over Brazil*, *Brazil Today*, *Rio de Janeiro*, and *Southern Brazil*.

71. NARAII, RG229, Motion Picture Division, box 953.

72. LL, John Ford mss., Photographs, Miscellaneous, Brazil, 1943–1944.

73. Letter from Brazilian member Berent Friele to Jefferson Caffery, March 24, 1944. Jefferson Caffery Papers, Rio de Janeiro, 1937–1944, Correspondence F, Collection 47, folder 6, University Archives and Arcadiana Manuscripts Collection, Edith Garland Dupré Library, University of Louisiana at Lafayette.

74. The cartoon is posted at http://www.loc.gov/pictures/item/acd1996005059/pp.

75. CIAA footage of Brazil and Latin America in general was meant to be shared.

76. I want to thank Martha Harsanyi, media librarian at Indiana University, who called my attention to the existence of CIAA guides in the IU collection. I found no other guides in the government or private archives consulted.

77. Herman B. Wells Library, Audio-Visual File GS-190, Indiana University–Bloomington.

78. In fact CIAA films continued to be shown throughout the 1950s and the 1960s, and the miles of footage shot in Latin America were used as background for feature films and other documentaries.

79. The guide was published by *Time*, *Life*, and *Fortune* magazines.

80. RAC, NAR III 40, box 7, folder 56.

81. RAC, NAR III 4L, box 65, folder 623.

82. Philip Dunne and Robert Vogel report, MHL, MPSA collection. Vogel and Dunne were members of the MPSA. Dunne later took a job as head of documentary filmmaking at the OWI. NARAII, RG229 Motion Picture Division files contain numerous references to CIAA and MPSA-Mexico working relations, including a May 10, 1943, commentary on cinematographer Gabriel Figueroa's work on CIAA projects and a March 23, 1944, approval for a tour by Mexican actor Arturo de Córdova, who was working in

Hollywood, to talk about his experiences and the war work being done by U.S. Latinos. See boxes 207 and 953. Hollywood technicians were sent to Mexico to train locals to use state-of-the-art movie cameras and equipment purchased through Prencinradio.

Chapter 3

The epigraph source is in NARAII, RG229, Radio Division, box 241.

1. April 16, 1942, memo from Frederick A. Long to Walter H. C. Laves, LL, Laves mss., Manuscripts Department, box 5.

2. Doob's personal papers. The confidential report was sent to Doob via Rockefeller's Assistant Coordinator Wallace K. Harrison and was produced by the Military Intelligence Service's Psychological Warfare Branch. The date of receipt by Doob is incomplete on the cover sheet: August 13, 194[?].

3. William Paley of CBS was the first to sign up affiliates as a result of his November 1940 tour of Latin America. John Royal of NBC followed suit and was equally successful in attracting affiliates.

4. These surveys are located in NARAII, RG229, Radio Division, boxes 968–972. They had spaces for writing the listener's name, town, and country of residence, radio stations listened to (including the BBC and USSR, German, and Italian broadcasts), likes and dislikes, and personal observations.

5. NARAII, RG229, Radio Division, box 62.

6. A novelist of considerable renown, Lessa worked with NBC during the war. NARAII, RG229, box 239, contains a long memo dated November 23, 1942, from Lessa to the Radio Division's William Hillpot about problems with an officious DIP censor who had changed the wording of a *Rádio Teatro* script to suggest that Poland and other occupied countries were avenging themselves against the Axis powers as opposed to being avenged against. When corrected by Brazilian announcer Pompeu de Sousa, the censor stalked out of the station but not before banning Sousa from participating in future radio shows. Lessa assured Hillpot that the censor would not dare report to Brazil on the incident because of his less-than-solid DIP backing and possible counter-charges about his error and arrogance.

7. John W.G. Ogilvie, "The Potentialities of Inter-American Radio," 19. The joint lease signed on November 1, 1942, gave the CIAA one-third of the shortwave broadcast time at one-third the cost. The OWI received the other two-thirds at two-thirds the cost.

8. For more on negotiations between the CIAA and local stations and networks, see Fejes, 115–164. Ogilvie notes that in addition to the original fourteen shortwave transmitters leased by the CIAA and OWI, the agencies built another twenty-two that provided multifrequency coverage throughout the Americas and the rest of the world (21).

9. See Maxwell, 74–75, for more specifics on this report.

10. William Benton report, NARAII, RG229, Radio Division, box 963.

11. Authorization, "Screen and Radio Stars for Radio Programs." NARAII, RG229, Radio Division, box 244.

12. Consult James Spiller for a detailed commentary on the series.

13. NARAII, RG229, Radio Division, box 244.

14. Project authorization for radio stations in the U.S. Southwest and in northern Mexico to integrate 2.5 million Spanish-speaking citizens and residents into the war effort, NARAII, RG229, Radio Division, box 244.

15. NARAII, RG229, Radio Division, box 271. A "gold-star" mother was one who had lost a son or daughter in the war.

16. Script in Spanish, NARAII, RG229, Radio Division, box 289, and quoted in Spanish in Ortiz Garza, *La guerra de las ondas*, 132–133.

17. Project authorization, NARAII, RG229, Radio Division, box 258. The program was likely a response to a German radio show called *El cabaret político de Marquita e sus secuases* (The Political Cabaret of Marquita and Her Followers) that ridiculed British and U.S. war claims and mocked Allied leaders.

18. Memo from John White to Production Department, June 6, 1942, NARAII, RG229. Radio Division, box 241.

19. Report dated December 18, 1942. NARAII, RG229, Radio Division, box 271.

20. August 18, 1943, report from Alis de Sola to Wiff Roberts. NARAII, RG229, Radio Division, box 241.

21. Ibid. In 1943 several programs were cancelled because of the strong Allied advances in the war, including *La marca del Jaguar* and *Tributo a los héroes*. Similar to *Radioteatro, Hacia un mundo mejor*'s premise was broadened to encompass social and industrial developments that were of Latin American interest.

22. For a discussion of Brazilian music in the 1940s and Villa-Lobos's survey on the subject of foreign influences, see Bryan McCann, *Hello, Hello Brazil*.

23. More than four hundred songs were commissioned and transcribed by the Coca-Cola Company, and the CIAA had full and free access to them. NARAII, RG229, Radio Division, box 244.

24. From William A. Hillpot to John W. G. Ogilvie, NARAII, RG229, Radio Division, box 244.

25. The model for the *Inter-American University* was the CBS program *The American School of the Air*, which began in 1930 and was renamed *The School of the Americas* in 1941. Its target audience was public school students.

26. Library of Congress (hereinafter LOC), Recorded Sound Reference Center, RWA 3649 B2–3.

27. A full description of the series is in *"Land of the Free*: A Projected Curriculum of History and Government of the Nations of the Western Hemisphere," NARAII, RG229, Radio Division, box 244.

28. *Land of the Free* scripts, NARAII, RG229, Radio Division, box 244.

29. "Music of the Americas," outline. NARAII, RG229, Radio Division, box 244. The title was subsequently changed from "Americas" to "the New World."

30. From the preface by James Rowland Angell and Sterling Fisher to Muna Lee's handbook for the series titled *American Story*, 6.

31. Recording, "The American Story," LOC Recorded Sound Center, RWA 6211 B1–2.

32. The Papers of Archibald MacLeish in the LOC Manuscript Division contain an undated document with proposals by Muna Lee for the *Inter-American University of the Air* program. Among the topics suggested are freedom and democracy; Mexican critic Alfonso Reyes on similarities among the Americas; Don Carlos de Sigüenza y Góngora, the first Mexican newspaperman (seventeenth century); racial pride (the Chilean epic, *La Araucana*); and the Inconfidência Mineira, the failed eighteenth-century attempt in Brazil to overthrow the Portuguese monarchy. Container 43, radio broadcasts.

33. NARAII, RG229, Radio Division, box 245.

34. Monica Rankin discusses a Mexican-produced show, *Women's Magazine of the Air*, whose coverage of U.S. women's fashions in the workforce influenced Mexican women to wear slacks instead of skirts (179–180).

35. NARAII, RG229, Department of Information, Radio Division, box 13.

36. NARAII, RG229, Department of Information, Radio Division, box 18.

37. In 1944 Ramírez unexpectedly broke diplomatic ties with Germany and Japan and was immediately ousted by Colonel Juan Perón, who established his own dictatorship.

38. Memorandum from Francisco to Rockefeller, n.d. RAC, NAR RGIII, 40, box 9, folder 73.

39. Scripts of Sux program can be found in NARAII, RG229, Radio Division, boxes 1–5. One recording exists in NARAII, RG229, 13.

40. CBS reception reports and comments from the other Americas, NARAII, RG229, Radio Division, box 258.

41. Report on Mexico City radio, NARAII, RG229, Radio Division, box 244.

42. For additional information, see Ortiz Garza, "Propaganda," 11–12, and Rankin, 227–230.

43. Getúlio Vargas developed and ultimately controlled most aspects of media in Brazil, especially during the Estado Novo. For further information on radio in Brazil, consult Doris Fagundes Haussen, "Radio and Populism in Brazil."

44. On September 4, 1943, the DIP staff in association with Mutual Broadcasting in New York launched *Brazil Parade*, a radio program on Brazil for U.S. audiences. Speaking from Brazil, Eurico Dutra, minister of war, opened the program with a Good Neighbor address to fellow Americans in the United States. Jefferson Caffery, U.S. ambassador to Brazil, was on hand to celebrate the event and to present Dutra with a radio—a gift from Nelson Rockefeller.

45. NARAII, RG229, Radio Recordings, 229–13A.

46. CPDOC/FGV, OA, cp, 40.03. 11/2.

47. For a detailed discussion of these two broadcasts, see Sadlier, "Good Neighbor Brazil," *Brazil Imagined*, 209–233.

48. The series had a total of twelve shows, but two were fill-ins called "Ritmos de las Américas" that were put together quickly when Welles called in sick.

49. I discuss this program and a later *Hello Americans* show titled "The Bad-Will Ambassador" in *Brazil Imagined*.

50. Manuscript titled "[Alô Americanos], 1942." LL, Welles mss., box 12, folder 10.

51. *Ceiling Unlimited* was cancelled the same week as *Hello Americans*. Welles shines in the October 16, 1943, *People's Platform* roundtable discussion of "How Should the Movies Be Used Today?" The panel included studio head Walter Wanger, magazine editor Louie Delavey, screenwriter Dudley Nichols, and Groucho Marx, who was uncharacteristically quiet.

52. NARAII, RG229, Radio Division, box 241.

53. The serial became the inspiration for a comic book and a 1947 Hollywood movie starring Buster Crabbe.

54. "The Envelope" and other *Sea Hound* episodes can be found at http://www .archive.org.

55. NARAII, RG229, Radio Division, box 244.

56. No information is given in any document on how that proficiency was measured.

57. NARAII, RG229, Radio Division, box 244.

58. NARAII, RG229, Radio Division, box 245.

59. The reason given was that Welles and CBS could not agree on expenditures. NARAII, RG229, Radio Division, box 245. This conflict led to the cancellation of *Hello Americans*. In March 1943, after Welles left *Ceiling Unlimited*, Charles Boyer guest-hosted a program in the series dedicated to Brazilian aviator Alberto Santos Dumont.

60. NARAII, RG229, Radio Division, box 964.

61. For example, RG229, Radio Division, boxes 965, 968–972.

62. NARAII, RG229, Radio Division, box 965.

63. March 25, 1943, NARAII, RG229, Radio Division, box 256.

64. Ibid.

Chapter 4

1. Begun in 1940, *The Hemisphere: Confidential Newsweekly of the Americas* was a left-liberal weekly publication whose Brazilian coverage irritated Brazilian ambassador to the United States Carlos Martins and foreign relations minister Oswaldo Aranha. Its editor, Jack Bradley Fahy, fought in the Spanish Civil War and supposedly spied for the Soviet Union during World War II. The CIAA's control of U.S. Good Neighbor news and propaganda was considerable. In 1941 *The Hemisphere* stopped publication, and Fahy was brought into the Rockefeller organization for a short period before moving on to intelligence jobs in the federal government. CPDOC/FGV OA cp 40.03.11/2 has a November 6, 1940, letter from Fahy to Aranha acknowledging the Brazilian government's displeasure with the weekly and asking the minister to send *The Hemisphere* official publications for future guidance in the weekly's Brazil coverage. It should be noted that U.S. Brazilian agencies like the Brazilian Information Bureau in New York began publishing Good Neighbor material for U.S. consumption in the early 1940s. One example is *Brazil Today*, edited by Francisco Silva Jr. In a letter to Aranha, Silva pleaded for funds or subscription purchases for U.S. embassies and consulates to help keep the monthly publication afloat. CPDOC/FGV OA cp 40.03.11/2. In a document from February 1941 the Brazilian consul in Chicago urges Aranha to

provide the consulates with materials on Brazil that are increasingly in demand. CP-DOC/FGV OA cp 40.03.11/2.

2. The idea for a translation series was initially proposed by an early Policy Committee organized by Rockefeller shortly after the CIAA was founded in 1940. Among the projects discussed at the December 9, 1940, meeting was a "five-foot shelf" of U.S. titles that included "good literature, particularly from Whitman to the present, Popular Science and children's books." As for Latin American titles, translators "should be distinguished authors not only to insure the quality of the translation but also to add prestige to it." Among those suggested were John Dos Passos, who "had agreed to make at least one translation . . . and Sinclair Lewis, who is now on his way to Brazil, [and] might be glad to translate a well-known Portuguese book into English." A Portuguese-English dictionary was specifically recommended. WB, box 371, folder 3. The only dictionary to appear was a CIAA booklet titled *Glossary of Brazilian-Amazonian Terms* (1943).

3. NARAII, RG229, Records of the Department of Press and Publication Division, box 1460.

4. NARAII, RG229, Press and Publication Division, box 1462.

5. Frantz to Jamieson, memo, May 30, 1942, NARAII, RG229, Press and Publication Division, box 1463.

6. Ibid.

7. NARAII, RG229, Press and Publication Division, box 1461. Doob's diary of the period records his growing frustration with his job and the politics being played among CIAA officials. Ultimately, he moved to the OWI—a move that, according to Doob's son Anthony, Rockefeller never forgave.

8. NARAII, RG229, Press and Publication Division, box 1462.

9. According to a November 6, 1990, Oral History Interview with Professor Leonard Doob by Geoff Kabaservice, Cantril was a former Harvard psychologist and, like Doob, one of Rockefeller's Dartmouth classmates (7).

10. NARAII, RG229, Press and Publication Division, box 1461.

11. NARAII, RG229, Press and Publication Division, box 1471.

12. The CIAA placed a number of ads and articles in the *Boletín Linotípico*, which was received by all Latin American newspapers.

13. Frantz to Jamieson, June 18, 1942, NARAII, RG229, Press and Publication Division, box 1467.

14. Ibid.

15. NARAII, RG229, Press and Publication Division, box 1461.

16. NARAII, RG229, Press and Publication Division, box 1461.

17. NARAII, RG229, Press and Publication Division, box 1461.

18. The CIAA translation unit was used in consultation with George Kent, who was in charge of the magazine's Spanish and Portuguese editions. A May 15, 1942, document estimates circulation in Spanish at 750,000 and in Portuguese at 200,000. NARAII, RG229, Press and Publication Division, box 1468.

19. The character's name had a written accent in Spanish (Patoruzú), which *PM* de-

leted. In 1942 Quinterno made Argentina's first animated Technicolor short, titled *Upa en apuros* (Upa in Trouble). In the film Patoruzú's younger brother, Upa, is kidnapped by the villainous El Juaniyo and Patoruzú rescues him. Disney was so impressed with the cartoon's graphics that he invited Quinterno to work for him. More cautious than his compatriot Molina Campos, the famous gaucho caricaturist who worked briefly with Disney, Quinterno declined the offer.

20. NARAII, RG229, Press and Publication Division, box 1468.

21. NARAII, RG229, Press and Publication Division, confidential memorandum BD-2626, box 1461.

22. "Press Division Objectives: Outline of Editorial Policy," NARAII, RG229, Press and Publication Division, box 1462.

23. The CIAA's concern to reach both the masses and the upper class was perhaps unique in U.S. foreign diplomacy. Kathy R. Fitzpatrick notes in her discussion of U.S. public diplomacy: "The only question raised with regard to the publics of public diplomacy has been whether efforts should be directed to foreign 'masses' or to more narrowly targeted 'elites' or 'intellectuals'" (7).

24. "Office of the Coordinator of Inter-American Affairs: Summary of Activities," 7. RAC, NAR III, 40, box 15, folder 113.

25. NARAII, RG229, Press and Publication Division, box 1462. A *Reader's Digest* decision to publish Spanish- and Portuguese-language editions was a direct result of the war and CIAA efforts to build strong cultural relations with Latin America. George Kent, who worked with the CIAA's translation unit, oversaw their publication. *Selecciones*, the Spanish version, first appeared in 1941 and was followed a year later by *Seleções*.

26. See "Propagandas antigas" at http://propagandasantigas.blogspot.com/ for ads that appeared in 1942 issues.

27. NARAII, RG229, Press and Publication Division, box 1461.

28. N.p. *American Newsletter* file at the New York Public Library, hereinafter NYPL.

29. The *American Newsletter* file at NYPL has copies of a privately funded antiwar publication printed by American Peace Mobilization between April 5 and December 12, 1941, representing the different New York boroughs' mine, mill, and smelter workers. I cite it here as an example of just one of many groups and organizations that were against entering the war. The APM motif was "Johnny wants a job not a gun!" Among its leadership was Theodore Dreiser, who was listed as vice president.

30. "Office of the Coordinator of Inter-American Affairs: Summary of Activities," 5. RAC, NAR III, 40, box 15, folder 113.

31. "Philosophy and Organization of the Office of the Coordinator of Inter-American Affairs," 7. RAC, NAR III, 40, box 8, folder 61.

32. This information was provided in an email communication dated June 21, 2009, from Moacyr Scliar.

33. For more information on these films, see Lisa Cartwright and Brian Goldfarb's "Cultural Contagion."

34. The Portuguese title of Tota's book is *O imperialismo sedutor*.

35. NARAII, RG229, Press and Publication Division, box 1461.

36. Report on Ecuador committee feedback, n.d. NARAII, RG229, Press and Publication Division, box 1461.

37. Ibid.

38. Ibid.

39. "Best War Posters from All the Americas," *Life*, November 2, 1942, 13. An undated and unsigned CIAA report on the competition states that there were 874 Latin American entries and 337 from the United States (with no mention of Canada). An exhibition of both award-winning posters and those not selected for prizes toured the United States. NARAII, RG229, Press and Publication Division, box 367.

40. "The Museum and the War," *Bulletin of the Museum of Modern Art* 10, no. 1 (October-November 1942): n.p. The MoMA archive has a copy of the trilingual pamphlet *United Hemisphere Posters*, which features numerous poster images.

41. See Rankin, 188–197, for a discussion of Mexican caricaturist Antonio Arias Bernal, who worked with the CIAA and whose poster art defined the Mexican image in wartime propaganda.

42. There is a large collection of Naylor's photographs in the LOC. Levine's edition is a photographic tribute to her.

43. See Levine, especially 39, and Benamou's volume on *It's All True*, 153–154.

44. Benamou, review of the video *Brazilian Images*.

45. "Portraits of Genevieve Naylor," MoMA, Kirstein I. D., pamphlet.

46. *Sun Telegraph*, January 29, 1943. See Ana Maria Mauad's article "Genevieve Naylor, fotógrafa" for further information on Naylor in Brazil. Robert Levine made a documentary short on Naylor's photographic work titled *Brazilian Images: The 1940s Photographs of Genevieve Taylor* that is narrated by her and Mischa's son, Peter Reznikoff.

47. The CIAA helped fund the enterprise by purchasing copies of the 200-page *Brazil Builds* based on the MoMA exhibit. Deckker, 123.

48. The collection of three hundred photographs taken by Goodwin and Kidder Smith was donated by the CIAA to the LOC Archive of Hispanic Culture in 1943. *Annual Report of the Librarian of Congress: For the Fiscal Year Ended June 30, 1943* (Washington, D.C.: U.S. Government Printing Office, 1944), 211. In 1944 that archive was transferred from the Hispanic Foundation to the Prints and Photographs Division. Ibid., 24. I am grateful to Katherine D. McCann, who provided me with this information from the LOC reports.

49. *Bulletin of the Museum of Modern Art* 12, no. 2 (November 1944), n.p.

50. "Project Authorization: Purchase of 2000 copies of 'Brazil Builds': A volume on modern architecture of Brazil." René de Harnoncourt Papers II.27. The Museum of Modern Art Archives, New York (hereinafter RdH).

51. Ibid.

52. Early Museum History: Administrative Records, II.9. The Museum of Modern Art Archives, New York (hereinafter EMH).

53. In his October 1, 1941, report, Hanke suggested that the CIAA purchase one

thousand copies each of Nathaniel Wright Stephenson's book on Abraham Lincoln and Thomas Jefferson's autobiography. EMH, II.10.

54. June 3, 1941, letter to Oswaldo Aranha from Livraria Victor (sender's signature indecipherable), CPDOC/FGV, OA cp II43A. The CIAA was eager to sponsor visits by Latin American publishers to the United States. Having just returned from a Latin American tour in September 1941, Lewis Hanke proposed a visit by five Brazilian publishers: Freitas Bastos, José Olympio, "Senhor Martins" (Livraria Martins), Geraldo de Ulhoa Cintra (Editora Anchieta), and Orlando Rocha (Editora Universitária). NARAII, RG229, Press and Publication Division, box 62. An early Committee on Publications, whose September 1940 membership included the heads of Macmillan, Harper and Brother, and Simon and Schuster and poet Carl Van Doren, worked to reduce postal rates for Latin American publishers. The members suggested the creation of a Latin American Book of the Month Club. EMH, II.10.

55. NARAII, RG229, Press and Publication Division, box 1467.

56. EMH, II.9a, 2. A note to this and other anthologies financed by the Publication Division states: "All of these anthologies have necessitated a great deal of correspondence with the authors and publishers of the original material; purchase of translation rights to this material; correspondence with Latin American publishers and authors, etc."

57. RdH, II.27. Actually, Machado's father was a mulatto, while his mother, a Portuguese from the Azores, was white.

58. In a February 25, 1944, letter from University of Chicago Press advertising manager Mary Irwin to John M. Robey of the CIAA Press and Publication Division, she comments on the broad and enthusiastic coverage given to the translation by more than a dozen newspapers in and outside New York. She adds: "Our first printing was exhausted within three weeks after publication, and the second printing is being rushed through. You will be delighted to know that the Navy Department has just ordered 450 copies for navy libraries." WB, box 371, folder 5. However, not every notice was favorable. Claude Lévi-Strauss reviewed the book for the *American Anthropologist* (46 [1944]: 398–399) and was less than pleased with Putnam's translation.

59. Donald Pierson's *Negroes in Brazil* (1942) was written in conjunction with CIAA efforts to focus on the social sciences in Brazil, and a Portuguese version was contracted for 1944. According to a November 7, 1940, memo, Pierson, who taught at the Universidade de São Paulo, was tapped to edit a CIAA-funded series in Portuguese at an estimated cost of $2,000. RAC, NAR III, 40, CIAA box 5, folder 1.

60. LL, Bowers mss. II, folder 5.

61. Bombal was successful in suppressing the Knopf translation.

62. The Knopfs' dedication to Latin America would continue after the postwar years with the "discovery" of authors such as João Guimarães Rosa and Alejo Carpentier. But the case of the best-selling Amado was unique.

63. For more information on Frank's background and works, see Rostagno, 1–30.

64. EMH, II.9a, 3.

Chapter 5

The epigraph is quoted in Rowland, 92n7. Clark was a University of Chicago political economist who joined the CIAA and was the first Cultural Relations Division head prior to becoming director of the agency's Public Health and Welfare Division.

1. In 1943 the division's long-term projects in the arts, music, educational exchange, and American libraries were reassigned to the State Department's Division of Cultural Relations. Rowland, 92.

2. Perhaps conscious of agency overlaps, Harrison and Benton discussed changing the division's name from Cultural Relations to Advancement of Knowledge and Welfare. Letter from Harrison to Benton, December 11, 1941. WB, box 371, folder 11.

3. RAC, NAR III 40, CIAA, box 5, folder 1.

4. MoMA's John Abbott was a member of the CIAA Art Committee.

5. Abbott chaired the MoMA committee and Grace McCann Morley, San Francisco Museum of Art director, was a special consultant on Latin America. The CIAA covered the costs of putting the collection together, including insurance and travel expenses. The collection was split into three smaller exhibits that circulated throughout Latin America.

6. EMH, II.21a.

7. "New Orleans Painter Tells of Exhibit in South America," *Times-Picayune*, December 27, 1941. Apparently there was some tension between Durieux and U.S. ambassador to Brazil Jefferson Caffery that stemmed from a show of some of her own works in Rio. In a letter dated November 10, 1941, Caffery wrote to congratulate her on the exhibit but added: "I am sure that you will not take tragically what I said about not liking some of your pictures—I don't, but I will keep it to myself." However, his opinion was not kept to himself, and his letter was sent to MoMA's René d'Harnoncourt with an anonymous handwritten note attached: "This is from your Embassador [*sic*] Caffery. [I]t will amuse you—please tear it up afterwards." RdH, II.7.

8. EMH, II.11.

9. NARAII, RG229, Science and Educational Arts, box 365.

10. The column appeared in newspapers throughout the United States, among them the Chicago *Times*, the Miami *News*, and the Bridgeport, Connecticut, *Post* on April 8–10, 1942.

11. The *Bulletin of the Museum of Modern Art* often mentioned that MoMA had been exhibiting and collecting Latin American art prior to the war. Examples were found in the articles "Orozco 'Explains'" (August 1940) and "Portinari of Brazil" (October 1940). Florence Horn comments in her lead article on Portinari in the *Bulletin* that he was mostly known as a portrait painter in Rio and that "he paints negroes and mulattoes" (8).

12. Some of Morley's correspondence on this tour can be found in EMH, II.26.

13. In a September 9, 1942, letter, Charles W. Collier, special assistant to the ambassador at the U.S. embassy in La Paz, Bolivia, to MoMA's René d'Harnoncourt, acting

director of the CIAA art section, noted that "most people are ashamed of the fact that all the buildings in Bolivia are not 'modernistic,'" But he was also concerned about photographs of the "most atrocious types of 'modernistic' German-derived buildings" there and encouraged instead shots and exhibits of "modern adaptations of indigenous and colonial architecture." RdH, II.I.

14. RdH, II.8. The tour went to the Columbus (Ohio) Gallery of Fine Arts, Pasadena Art Institute, SFMoMA, National Gallery, Carnegie Institute, and Worcester Art Museum. A catalogue accompanied the exhibit.

15. Letter dated April 10, 1942. RdH, II.1.

16. April 10, 1942, letter from Stanton Caitlin to John Abbott. RdH, II.1.

17. EMH, II.11. A photo reproduction of this exhibit can be found in the Laves mss. at the Lilly Library.

18. For a discussion of Portinari's artwork of this period, see Daryle Williams, *Culture Wars in Brazil*.

19. See Robert C. Smith's commentary in *Murals by Cândido Portinari*.

20. Biddle convinced the government to allow a select group of artists to accompany U.S. troops to Italy to make a pictorial record of the war. His correspondence with John Steinbeck on this subject shows the latter's desire for writers to be included in that group. Library of Congress, Papers of the General Manuscript Division, George Biddle Correspondence.

21. According to a letter dated April 30, 1942, from Rio and addressed to Moe Thompson of MoMA, Biddle was given a choice of painting the murals in the Escola de Belas Artes, the Escola de Medicina, or the Biblioteca Nacional. Biddle's letter made clear that his work was being subsidized by the United States. RdH, II.4.

22. Ibid.

23. I am greatly indebted to colleagues K. David Jackson and Elizabeth Jackson, who photographed the Biddle and Sardeau works for me while they were in Rio.

24. RdH, II.1.

25. LOC, Papers of the General Manuscript Division, George Biddle, container 15. This container also holds a January 20, 1943, letter from Rockefeller to Brigadier General Frederick Osborn in which Rockefeller mentions that Biddle had painted a portrait of Aranha's mother.

26. LOC, Papers of the General Manuscript Division, George Biddle, container 15.

27. RdH, II.3. Agnes Morgan, director of the Fogg Museum of Art at Harvard, was also struggling. Her March 21, 1942, letter to Caitlin pleads for funds to help defray hospitality costs for the many visiting artists to come through Cambridge, among them Pettoruti. RdH, II.1. The CIAA inter-American centers would assume some of the hospitality costs and responsibilities.

28. Cotter to Alstock, March 1942, EMH, II.11.

29. Ibid.

30. RdH, II.7.

31. RdH, II.9.

32. RAC, NARA III, 40, CIAA, box 5 folder 1.

33. The countries represented were Argentina, Bolivia, Brazil, Chile, Colombia, Ecuador, Paraguay, Peru, Uruguay, and Venezuela.

34. Sumner Welles, in a November 3, 1942, letter to U.S. ambassador to Chile Claude Bowers, remarked on the bust and catalogues sent to Santiago. LL, Bowers mss. II, folder 6.

35. LL, Bowers mss. II, folder 6.

36. See Kraske, 64–76. For more on Lydenberg, consult Phyllis Dain's article "Harry M. Lydenberg and American Library Sources." Lydenberg left the NYPL directorship in 1941 to serve as director of the Biblioteca Benjamín Franklin in Mexico City until 1943.

37. Anderson and Corwin were just two of several writers listed who were directly or indirectly associated with the CIAA. Others were Archibald MacLeish (*Poems*, 1923–1933, and *A Time to Speak*), Stephen Vincent Benét (*Selected Works*, 2 volumes), Sherwood Anderson (*Winesburg, Ohio*), and Claude G. Bowers (*Jefferson and Hamilton: The Struggle for Democracy in America*).

38. According to Rowland (245–246), Edward H. Robbins, special assistant to Rockefeller and CIAA Liaison with the State Department, came up with the idea for the coordination committees while accompanying Douglas Fairbanks Jr. on his Latin American tour in April 1941.

39. NARAII, RG229, Motion Picture Division, box 226. The Brazilian Division served as liaison between the U.S. and Brazilian governments and helped negotiate agreements between the CIAA and the DIP that involved the information program. Subjects of negotiation were highly variable: U.S. agreements to provide Brazil with radio tubes, U.S. advertising in Brazilian newspapers, technical staff for radio training and photographing current events in Brazil, and more. Documents on the Brazilian Division and coordination committees are in NARAII, RG229, Motion Picture Division, boxes 226–228.

40. *Summary of Activities: Office of the Coordinator for Inter-American Affairs*, August 16, 1944. Papers of Herman B. Wells, University Archive, Indiana University.

41. NARAII, RG229, Motion Picture Division, box 226.

42. NARAII, RG229, Motion Pictures Division, box 235.

43. There were frequent tugs-of-war between the State Department and CIAA. A February 25, 1941, letter marked "personal and strictly confidential" from the State Department's Laurence Duggan to U.S. ambassador to Chile Claude Bowers shows his wariness about the CIAA's involvement with the coordination committee activities: "You no doubt recognize as well as anyone that the Coordinator's program contains a large potential for helpfulness or for confusion, depending on the extent to which it is guided into desirable channels." He adds: "[W]e have had somewhat of a problem because of the seemingly inevitable tendency on the part of many people in the Coordinator's Office to view the Coordination Committees as branches of their own organization, rather than to regard them as groups set up to assist the Chiefs of Mission in carrying out their function as representatives of the United States Government in

general, and the Coordinator's Office as a part of that Government." LL, Bowers mss. II, Correspondence 1939–1942, box 5.

44. Letter from Burger to E. C. Givens, November 11, 1942, NARAII, RG229, Motion Picture Division, box 226.

45. Ibid.

46. August 25, 1943, letter from R. T. Crump, director, and W. C. Longan, executive secretary to Rockefeller. NARAII, RG229, Motion Picture Division, box 235.

47. Ibid.

48. NARAII, RG229, Motion Picture Division, box 214.

49. Undated Brazil committee report, NARAII, RG229, Motion Picture Division, box 214.

50. Ibid.

51. NARAII, RG229, Motion Picture Division, box 214.

52. RAC, NARIII, 40, box 1, folder 7.

53. LL, Laves mss., Diaries 1941, box 5, Manuscript Department.

54. This timeline is based on Laves's December correspondence with Joseph Lohman, who was assuming some of Laves's teaching responsibilities at Chicago. On January 9, 1942, University of Chicago president Hutchins sent a reassuring cable to Laves in Washington: "Matter of your office will be handled in such a way as not to inconvenience you." LL, Laves mss., Biographical material, Correspondence 1927–1947, box 1, Manuscript Department.

55. LL, Laves mss., Correspondence, box 1.

56. LL, Laves mss., Correspondence, box 5.

57. LL, Laves mss., Correspondence, box 1.

58. LL, Laves mss., Diaries 1941, box 5.

59. Laves December 16, 1941, memo, LL, Laves mss., Diaries 1941, box 5.

60. Project Authorization for Pan American Centers, LL, Laves mss., box 130.

61. The Division of Inter-American Activities in the United States was the official title on March 23, 1942. The removal of the "in the United States" in December 1942 may be a result of complaints by MacLeish, who was in charge of the OFF in 1942. Laves wrote a shorthand note in his diary for March 13, 1942: "our activities in the US (incl. Press Radio movies) under fire by MacLeish. (WKH [Wallace K. Harrison] yesterday made me think I alone am under fire.)" A month earlier, Harrison wrote to Laves: "Everything requires clearance with MacLeish organization." LL, Laves mss., Diaries, LMC 3006, boxes 6 and 5, respectively.

62. LL, Laves mss., Diaries 1942, box 6. The diary is blank until August 24, 1942, when Laves was invited to head the Office of Civilian Defense (OCD).

63. Summary Report, October 1942, LL Laves mss., Diaries I, box 6.

64. Two of these bulletins (March 12 and October 4, 1943) are in the Papers of Herman B. Wells, U.S. Office of the Coordinator of Inter-American Affairs, 1943–1944, University Archive, Indiana University.

65. WB, folder 6.

66. WB, folder 22.

67. The executive board was composed of the faculty members who wrote the report for the CIAA: A. P. Brogan, Donald Coney, George C. M. Engerrand, J. Lloyd Mecham, George Sánchez, Jefferson Rea Spell, and Charles W. Hackett, who chaired the group. WB, folder 22.

68. The detailed rules and extensive inter-American bibliographies in the fourteen-page contest brochure, combined with FDR's opening letter of appreciation and support to Rockefeller, indicate the contest's level of academic seriousness and wartime importance. The 1943 brochure is located in Papers of Herman B. Wells, U.S. Office of the Coordinator of Inter-American Affairs, 1943–1944, University Archive, Indiana University. Other discussion can be found in the Presidential Official File, CIAA, box 2, file 4512, Franklin D. Roosevelt Library, Hyde Park, New York (hereinafter FDRL).

69. LL, Laves mss., box 13, folder 4, Manuscripts Department.

70. Founded by philanthropist and international trade specialist Eloise ReQua, this library became a United Nations depository. It is now part of the Illinois Institute of Technology in Chicago.

71. Papers of Herman B. Wells, Office of the Coordinator of Inter-American Affairs, 1943–1944, University Archive, Indiana University.

72. April 29, 1943, letter from Herman B. Wells to Raymond T. Rich. Papers of Herman B. Wells, U.S. Office of the Coordinator of Inter-American Affairs, 1943–1944, University Archive, Indiana University. The three study guides in the Indiana University media archives were for the films *Brazil* (March of Time), *Brazil: People of the Plantations* (ERPI), and the 1944 film *Americans All* (March of Time). Rey also produced five lecture and slide packets on Latin America for distribution. Later, Indiana and other depositories circulated sets of 1,500 Kodachrome slides prepared by the CIAA on Mexico, Honduras, and Peru. The CIAA requested the use of Indiana's own 16mm films for its inter-American program. In 1945 the agency contacted Indiana's Bureau of Audio-Visual Aids (BAV) for permission to make Spanish and Portuguese versions of a ten-minute 1944 film by Indiana professor of physiology K. G. Wakim. Recommended by the American College of Surgeons, the educational short on the effects of metallic ions on the heart was considered valuable as a teaching tool for students in the sciences.

73. NARAII, RG229, Records of the Department of Press and Publication, box 1460. Saposs joined Laves's staff subsequent to his report.

74. In her novel *Giant* (1952), Edna Ferber describes the systemic racism experienced by Mexican migrants in Texas. Her novel was the basis for George Stevens's 1956 epic film of the same title.

75. The Bracero program brought Mexican laborers to the United States primarily as agricultural workers to support the wartime food industry. Saposs's report refers indirectly to discrimination against Mexican Americans in wartime industries. His report refrains from mentioning the number of Mexican Americans who had enlisted to fight for their country. In his 2006 article, Frank Barajas remarks on industry discrimination practices against Mexican Americans.

76. LL, Laves mss., Diaries 1941, box 13, and Division of Inter-American Affairs in the United States, 1942, box 11, folder 2.

77. LL, Laves mss., Diaries 1942, box 5.

78. LL, Laves mss., Office of the Coordinator of Inter-American Affairs, 1941–1942, box 13, folder 1.

79. See, for example, Eduardo Obregón Pagán, *Murder at the Sleepy Lagoon*, and Kevin A. Leonard, *The Battle for Los Angeles*.

80. Letter from the Citizens' Committee for the Defense of Mexican-American Youths to all CIO locals, April 29, 1943, in Barajas, 45.

81. *Los Angeles Times*, June 9, 1943, 1, 4.

82. *Los Angeles Times*, June 10, 1943, A.

83. *Los Angeles Times*, June 11, 1943, A.

84. In *Los Angeles Times*, June 17, 1943, A.

85. Office of Production Management 4245g, FDRL.

86. Documents and correspondence relating to the chronology of the CIAA and Laves's interventions into the Sleepy Lagoon case are in LL, Laves mss., Diaries, December 1941–December 1942, boxes 5 and 6, and Division of Inter-American Activities in the United States, 1942, boxes 11 and 13.

87. Others who testified at the Sleepy Lagoon hearings were Carey McWilliams from the California Division of Immigration and Housing, UCLA anthropologist Harry Hoijer, the War Manpower Commission's Guy T. Nunn, Los Angeles Mexican consul Manuel Aguilar, community leader Eduardo Quevedo, and Congress of Industrial Organizations director Oscar R. Fuss. Leonard, 94.

88. Pagán, 73, and *Sleepy Lagoon Case*, 14.

89. The report is available at http://www.wellesnet.com/?p=184.

90. LL, 6-1301, *Sleepy Lagoon Case*, June 1943.

91. Shortly thereafter, March of Time released the 16mm documentary *Americans All*; similar to Julien Bryan's 1941 film of the same title, it was about friendly relations but in this case was focused on the United States. It used troubling headlines from the Zoot Suit Riots to exemplify racial prejudice that had to be fought and eliminated.

Aftermath

The Kennan epigraph is from a memorandum quoted in Roger R. Trask, "George F. Kennan's Report," 310.

1. For a discussion of the confirmation hearings, see Sarantakes. Rockefeller actually named Harrison as his deputy coordinator, and he functioned in that capacity from 1942. Rockefeller's memo is dated December 26, 1944, and quoted in Rowland, 282.

2. The Truman documents can be found in Rowland, 283–284.

3. For more information on the Point Four Program, see Erb.

4. For further information, see U.S. Department of Health and Human Services, Report on Findings from the U.S. Public Health Service Sexually Transmitted Disease Inoculation Study of 1946–1948, based on Review of Archived Papers of John Cutler, MD, at the University of Pittsburgh, at http://www.hhs.gov/1946inoculationstudy /cdc_rept-std_inoc_study.html. Wellesley professor Susan Reverby uncovered this information in June 2009.

5. Historian Stephen G. Rabe has commented on the reluctance of the United States to meet with Latin American nations in the early postwar period: "As early as September 1945, officials predicted that a bitter clash would erupt at an economic conference since the United States was unprepared to grant 'requests which they are likely to make.' Unwilling to 'reveal before the world' their fundamental disagreement with their Good Neighbors, United States diplomats chose postponement over confrontation" (291). Rabe cites the quote sources as *Foreign Relations of the United States, 1945* 9:177–178 and *Foreign Relations of the United States, 1949*, 2:424–427.

6. Quotes and commentary from Welles's columns are from Naremore, *Magic World*, 114–115.

7. Darlene S. Rivas suggests that more study of this characterization of U.S. postwar policy toward Latin America be explored. See her chapter "United States–Latin American Relations, 1942–1960" in *A Companion to American Foreign Relations*, edited by Robert D. Schulzinger.

8. For a detailed discussion of the context and consequences of the art exhibit, consult Ninkovich, "Currents."

9. Ibid., 227. A more recent study of the exhibit is Littleton and Sykes's *Advancing American Art*.

10. "Advancing American Art: Exhibition Records, 1946-1977," *Archives, Manuscripts, Photographs Catalog*, Smithsonian Institution Research Information System. At http://siris-archives.si.edu/ipac20/ipac.jsp?uri=full=3100001˜!209243!0#focus. See also Grovier, 9.

11. John Simkin, "William Benton," *Spartacus Educational*. At http://www.spartacus .schoolnet.co.uk/USAbentonW.htm.

Bibliography

Adams, Dale. "*Saludos Amigos*: Hollywood and FDR's Good Neighbor Policy." *Quarterly Review of Film and Video* 24 (2007): 289–295.

Agee, James. *Agee on Film*. Vol. 1. New York: McDowell, Obolensky, 1958.

Andrade, Mário de. "Brazil Builds." In *Depoimento de uma geração: Arquitetura moderna brasileira*, ed. Alberto Xavier, 177–181. Rev. ed. São Paulo: Cosac and Naify, 2003.

Arndt, Richard T. *The First Resort of Kings: American Diplomacy in the Twentieth Century*. Washington, DC: Potomac Books, 2005.

Barajas, Frank P. "The Defense Committees of Sleepy Lagoon: A Convergent Struggle against Fascism, 1942–1944." *Aztlán: A Journal of Chicano Studies* 31, no. 1 (2006): 33–62.

Barry, Iris. "Latin America." *Bulletin of the Museum of Modern Art* 8, no. 5 (June–July 1941): 13.

Benamou, Catherine L. *It's All True: Orson Welles's Pan-American Odyssey*. Los Angeles: University of California Press, 2007.

———. Review of the video *Brazilian Images: The 1940s Photographs of Genevieve Naylor*. *H-LatAm*. July 1996. http://www.h-net.org/reviews/showrev.php?id=14851.

Bender, Pennee. "'Flash From Brazil'—1940s' Newsreels Present Latin America." In *American Visual Cultures*, ed. David Holloway and John Beck, 116–124. London: Continuum International, 2005.

Brewer, Susan A. *To Win the Peace: British Propaganda in the U.S. during World War II*. New York: Cornell University Press, 1997.

Brown, John. "The Purposes and Cross-Purposes of American Public Diplomacy." *American Diplomacy* (August 15, 2002): n.p. At http://www.unc.edu/depts/diplomat/archives_roll/2002_07-09/brown_pubdipl/brown_pubdipl.html.

Buñuel, Luis. *My Last Sigh: The Autobiography of Luis Buñuel*. Trans. Abigail Israel. New York: Vintage Books, 1984.

Burton-Carvajal, Julianne. "Surprise Package: Looking Southward with Disney." In *Disney Discourse*, ed. Eric Smoodin, 131–147. New York: Routledge, 1994.

Calder, Robert. *Beware the Serpent: The Role of Writers in British Propaganda in the United States*. Ithaca, NY: Mc-Gill-Queens University Press, 2004.

Callow, Simon. *Orson Welles: Hello Americans*. London: Jonathan Cape, 2006.

Cartwright, Lisa, and Brian Goldfarb. "Cultural Contagion: On Disney's Health Education Films for Latin America." In *Disney Discourse*, ed. Eric Smoodin, 169–180.

Chase, Gilbert. "Radio Broadcasting and the Music Library." *Music Library Association Notes* 2, no. 2 (March 1945): 91–94.

Creel, George. *How We Advertised America: The First Telling of the Amazing Story of the Committee on Public Information that Carried the Gospel of Americanism to Every Corner of the Globe*. New York: Harper and Brothers, 1920.

Cull, Nicolas J. *The Cold War and the United States Information Agency: American Propaganda and Public Diplomacy, 1945–1989*. Cambridge: Cambridge University Press, 2008.

——. *Public Diplomacy: Lessons from the Past*. Los Angeles: Figueroa Press, 2009.

——. *Selling War: The British Propaganda Campaign against American "Neutrality" in World War II*. New York: Oxford University Press, 1995.

Dain, Phyllis. "Harry M. Lydenberg and American Library Sources: A Study in Modern Library Leadership." *Library Quarterly* 47, no. 4 (October 1977): 451–469.

Deckker, Zilah Quezado. *Brazil Built: The Architecture of the Modern Movement in Brazil*. London: Spon Press, 2001.

Denning, Michael. *The Cultural Front: The Laboring of American Culture in the Twentieth Century*. London: Verso, 1996.

Donaldson, Scott. *Archibald MacLeish: An American Life*. Boston: Houghton Mifflin, 1992.

Doob, Leonard W. *Propaganda: Its Psychology and Technique*. New York: Henry Holt, 1935.

——. *Public Opinion and Propaganda*. New York: Henry Holt, 1948.

Dozer, Donald Marquand. *Latin America: An Interpretive History*. Tempe: Center for Latin American Studies, Arizona State University, 1979.

Erb, Claude C. "Prelude to Point Four: The Institute of Inter-American Affairs." *Diplomatic History* 9, no. 3 (1985): 249–269.

Espinosa, Manuel. *Inter-American Beginnings of United States Cultural Diplomacy, 1936–1948*. Washington, D.C.: Department of State, 1976.

Federal Records of World War II. Vol. 1: *Civilian Agencies*. Washington, D.C.: National Archives and Record Service, 1950.

Fein, Seth. "Hollywood-U.S.-Mexican Relations, and the Devolution of the 'Golden Age' of Mexican Cinema." *Film-Historia* 4, no. 2 (1994): 103–135. At http://www.publicacions.ub.es/bibliotecadigital/cinema/filmhistoria/Art.Fein.pdf.

Fejes, Fred. *Imperialism, Media and the Good Neighbor: New Deal Foreign Policy and United States Shortwave Broadcasting to Latin America*. Norwood, NJ: Ablex, 1986.

Félix-Didier, Paula, and André Levinson. "The Building of a Nation: *La guerra gaucha* as Historical Melodrama." In *Latin American Melodrama: Passion, Pathos and Entertainment*, ed. Darlene J. Sadlier, 50–63. Chicago: University of Illinois Press, 2009.

Ferreira, Argemiro. "Fiction, Nostalgia, and Reality in the Good Neighbor Policy." In *Studies in Honor of Heitor Martins*, ed. Darlene J. Sadlier, 159–170. Luso-Brazilian

Literary Series, vol. 3. Bloomington: Department of Spanish and Portuguese, Indiana University, 2006.

Finn, Helena K. "The Case for Cultural Diplomacy: Engaging Foreign Audiences." *Foreign Affairs* 82, no. 6 (November–December 2003): 15–20.

Fitzpatrick, Kathy A. *U.S. Public Diplomacy's Neglected Domestic Mandate*. Los Angeles: Figueroa Press, 2010.

Friedman, Max Paul. "There Goes the Neighborhood: Blacklisting Germans in Latin America and the Evanescence of the Good Neighbor Policy." *Diplomatic History* 27, no. 4 (August 2003): 569–597.

Frye, Alton. *Nazi Germany and the American Hemisphere, 1933–1941*. New Haven: Yale University Press, 1967.

Gabler, Neal. *Walt Disney: The Triumph of the American Imagination*. New York: Alfred A. Knopf, 2006.

Girona, Ramon, and Jordi Xifra. "The Office of Facts and Information: Archibald MacLeish and the 'Strategy of Truth.'" *Public Relations Review* 35, no. 3 (September 2009): 287–290.

Good Neighbor Tour: An Imaginary Visit to the Republics of Latin America. 10 vols. Washington, DC: Pan American Union, 1943.

Goodwin, Philip L., and G. E. Kidder-Smith. *Brazil Builds: Architecture Old and New, 1652–1942*. New York: Museum of Modern Art, 1943.

Grovier, Kelly. "Gum and Gothic." *Times Literary Supplement*, November 5, 2010, 9.

Haines, Gerald K. "Under the Eagle's Wing: The Franklin Roosevelt Administration Forges an American Hemisphere." *Diplomatic History* 1, no. 4 (1977): 373–388.

Hanke, Lewis. "The Development of Latin-American Studies in the United States, 1939–1945." *The Americas: A Quarterly Review of Inter-American Cultural History* 4 (July 1947–April 1948): 32–64.

Hastings, Salina. *The Secret Lives of Somerset Maugham*. London: John Murray, 2009.

Haussen, Doris Fagundes. "Radio and Populism in Brazil." *Television and New Media* 6, no. 3 (August 2003): 251–261.

Hellmer, Joseph R. "Radio and the Americas." *The Inter-American* (October 1943): 38–39.

Hershfield, Joanne. "Dolores Del Río, Uncomfortably Real: The Economics of Race in Hollywood's Latin American Musicals." In *Classic Hollywood, Classic Whiteness*, ed. Daniel Bernardi, 193–156. Minneapolis: University of Minnesota Press, 2001.

Horkheimer, Max, and Theodor W. Adorno. *Dialectic of Enlightenment: Philosophical Fragments*. Ed. Gunzelin Schmid Noerr. Trans. Edmund Jephcott. Stanford, CA: Stanford University Press, 2002.

Humphreys, R. A. *Latin America and the Second World War*. Vol. 2: *1942–1945*. London: Athlone Press, 1982.

Jameson, Fredric. *Postmodernism, or, The Cultural Logic of Late Capitalism*. Durham, NC: Duke University Press, 1991.

Johnson, Melissa A. "Five Decades of Mexican Public Relations in the United States: From Propaganda to Strategic Counsel." *Public Relations Review* 31, no. 1 (2005):

11–20. At http://www4.ncsu.edu/~mjohnson/pdfs/fivedecadesofmexicanpublicrel .pdf.

Knopf, Blanche. "The Literary Roundup: An American Publisher Tours South America." *Saturday Review of Literature* (April 10, 1943): 7–10, 34.

Kracauer, Siegfried. *Propaganda and the Nazi War Film*. Originally published 1942. Supplement in *From Hitler to Caligari: A Psychological History of the German Film*, 271–331. Princeton, NJ: Princeton University Press, l974.

Kraske, Gary A. *Missionaries of the Book: The American Library Profession and the Origins of United States Cultural Diplomacy*. Westport, CT: Greenwood Press, 1985.

Laves, Walter H. C., and Francis O. Wilcox, "The State Department Continues Its Reorganization." *Political Science Review* 39, no. 2 (April 1945): 309–317.

Lee, Muna. *American Story: Historical Broadcast Series of the NBC Inter-American University of the Air by Archibald MacLeish*. Handbook 1. New York: Columbia University Press, 1944.

Leonard, Kevin A. *The Battle for Los Angeles: Racial Ideology and World War II*. Albuquerque: University of New Mexico Press, 2006.

Lessa, Orígenes. *O.K. América: Cartas de Nova York*. Rio de Janeiro: Leitura, 1945.

Levine, Robert M. *The Brazilian Photographs of Genevieve Naylor, 1940–1942*. Durham, NC: Duke University Press, 1998.

Littleton, Taylor D., and Maltby Sykes. *Advancing American Art: Painting, Politics and Cultural Confrontation at Mid-Century*. Tuscaloosa: University of Alabama Press, 1989.

Lotz, Rainer E., and Horst J. P. Bergmeier. *Hitler's Airwaves: The Inside Story of Nazi Radio Broadcasting and Propaganda Swing*. New Haven, CT: Yale University Press, 1977.

Loy, Jane M. "The Present as Past: Assessing the Value of Julien Bryan's Films as Historical Evidence." *Latin American Research Review* 12, no. 3 (1977): 103–128.

MacLeish, Archibald. "The Art of the Good Neighbor." *The Nation*, February 10, 1940, 170–172.

Mauad, Ana Maria. "Genevieve Naylor, fotógrafa: Impressões de viagem (Brasil 1941–1942)." *Revista Brasileira de História* 25, no. 49 (January/June 2005). At http://www .scielo.br/scielo.php?script=sci_arttext&pid=S0102-01882005000100004&lng=en& nrm=iso.

Maxwell, Allen Brewster. "Evoking Latin American Collaboration in the Second World War: A Study of the Office of the Coordinator of Inter-American Affairs (1940–1946)." PhD diss., Fletcher School of Law and Diplomacy, Tufts University, 1971.

Maymí-Sugrañes, Héctor J. "The American Library Association in Latin America: American Librarianship as a 'Modern' Model during the Good Neighbor Policy Era." *Libraries and Culture* 37, no. 4 (Fall 2002): 307–338.

McCann, Bryan. *Hello, Hello Brazil*. Durham, NC: Duke University Press, 2004.

McCann, Frank D. *The Brazilian-American Alliance: 1937–1945*. Princeton, NJ: Princeton University Press, 1973.

McCarthy, Todd. *Howard Hawks: The Grey Fox of Hollywood*. New York: Grove Press, 1997.

McMurry, Ruth Emily, and Muna Lee. *The Cultural Approach: Another Way in International Relations*. Chapel Hill: University of North Carolina Press, 1947.

Merryman, John Henry, Albert E. Elsen, and Stephen Urice. *Law, Ethics and the Visual Arts*. 5th ed. Netherlands: Klewer Law International, 2007.

Miller, Jean A., and Chancey O. Rowe. "Films Reinforce Hemispheric Ties." *Foreign Commerce Weekly* (June 2, 1945): 6–11.

Moreno, Julio E. "J. Walter Thompson, the Good Neighbor Policy and Lessons in Mexican Business Culture, 1920–1950." *Enterprise and Society* 5, no. 2 (2004): 254–280.

Moura, Gersão. *Tio Sam chega ao Brasil: A penetração cultural americana*. São Paulo: Brasiliense, 1984.

Naremore, James. *The Magic World of Orson Welles*. Rev. ed. Dallas: Southern Methodist University, 1989.

———. *More than Night: Film Noir in Its Contexts*. Berkeley: University of California Press, 1998.

———. "The Trial: Orson Welles vs. the FBI." *Film Comment* (January–February 1991): 22–27.

Ninkovich, Frank A. "The Currents of Cultural Diplomacy: Art and the State Department, 1938–1947. *Diplomatic History* 1, no. 3 (July 1977): 215–237.

———. *The Diplomacy of Ideas: U.S. Foreign Policy and Cultural Relations, 1938–1950*. Cambridge: Cambridge University Press, 1981.

Nye, Joseph S. "The Decline of America's Soft Power," *Foreign Affairs* 83, no. 3 (May–June 2004): 16–20.

———. *Soft Power: The Means to Success in World Politics*. New York: Public Affairs, 2004.

Ogilvie, John W. G. "The Potentialities of Inter-American Radio." *Public Opinion Quarterly* 9, no. 1 (Spring 1945): 19–28.

O'Neill, Brian. "The Demands of Authenticity: Addison Durland and Hollywood's Latin Images during World War II." In *Classic Hollywood, Classic Whiteness*, ed. Daniel Bernside, 359–385. Minneapolis: University of Minneapolis Press, 2001.

Ortiz Garza, José Luis. *La guerra de las ondas: un libro que desmiente la historia "oficial" de la radio mexicana*. Mexico City: Editorial Planeta Mexicana, 1992.

Pagán, Eduardo Obregón. *Murder at the Sleepy Lagoon*. Chapel Hill: University of North Carolina Press, 2003.

Paulmier, Hilah, and Robert Haven Schauffler, eds. *Pan-American Day: An Anthology of the Best Prose and Verse on Pan Americanism and the Good Neighbor Policy*. New York: Dodd, Mead, 1943.

Piedra, José. "Pato Donald's Gender Duckling." In *Disney Discourse*, ed. Eric Smoodin, 148–168.

Pierson, Donald. *Negroes in Brazil: A Study of Race Contact at Bahia*. Chicago: University of Chicago Press, 1942.

The Proclaimed List of Certain Blocked Nationals: Promulgated Pursuant to the Proclamation of July 17, 1941. Administrative Order. Washington, D.C., 1941. Available at http://www.archive.org/stream/ProclaimedListOfCertainBlockedNationals/ s0012#page/n1/mode/2up.

Prutsch, Ursula. *Creating Good Neighbors? Die Kulture und Wirtschaftspolitik der USA in Lateinamerika, 1940–1946.* Stuttgart, Germany: Franz Steiner Verlag, 2008.

Quintaneiro, Tania. "Cinema e guerra: Objetivos e estratégias da política estadunidense no Brasil." Centro Brasileiro de Estudos da América Latina (CEBELA), n.d. http://www.cebela.org.br/imagens/Materia/041-069%20tania%20quintaneiro.pdf.

Rabe, Stephen G. "The Elusive Conference: United States Economic Relations with Latin America, 1945–1952." *Diplomatic History* 2, no. 3 (July 1978): 279–294.

Rankin, Monica A. *¡México, la Patria!* Lincoln: University of Nebraska Press, 2009.

Reich, Cary. *The Life of Nelson A. Rockefeller: Worlds to Conquer, 1908–1958.* New York: Doubleday, 1996.

Richard, Alfred Charles Jr. *Censorship and Hollywood's Hispanic Image: An Interpretative Filmography, 1936–1955.* Bibliographies and Indexes in the Performing Arts, no. 14. Westport, CT: Greenwood Press, 1993.

Rivas, Darlene S. *Missionary Capitalist: Nelson Rockefeller in Venezuela.* Chapel Hill: University of North Carolina Press, 2002.

———. "United States–Latin American Relations, 1942–1960." In *A Companion to American Foreign Relations,* ed. Robert D. Schulzinger, 230–254. London: Blackwell, 2003.

Rivera, Rodolfo O. *Preliminary List of Libraries in the Other American Republics.* Series of the ALA Committee on Library Cooperation with Latin America, no. 5. Washington, D.C., 1942.

Roberts, Beth Alene. "United States Propaganda Warfare in Latin America, 1938–1942." PhD diss., University of Southern California, 1942.

Rohde, Alfred W. Jr. "German Propaganda Movies in Two Wars." *American Cinematographer* (January 1943): 10–11, 28.

Rostagno, Irene. *Searching for Recognition: The Promotion of Latin American Literature in the United States.* Westport, CT: Greenwood Press, 1997.

Rowland, Donald. *History of the Office of the Coordinator of Inter-American Affairs.* Washington, DC: U.S. Government Printing Office, 1947.

Sadlier, Darlene J. *Brazil Imagined: 1500 to the Present.* University of Texas Press, 2008.

Saragoza, Alex. "The Selling of Mexico: Tourism and the State, 1929–1952." In *Fragments of a Golden Age: The Politics of Culture in Mexico since 1940,* ed. Gilbert Joseph, Anne Rubenstein, and Eric Zolov, 91–115. Durham, NC: Duke University Press, 2001.

Sarantakes, Nicholas Evan. "The Politics and Poetry of Advice and Consent: Congress Confronts the Roosevelt Administration during the State Department Confirmation Incident of 1944." *Presidential Studies Quarterly* 28, no. 1 (Winter 1988): 153–168.

Schale, Richard. *Donald Duck Joins Up: The Walt Disney Studio During World War II.* Ann Arbor, MI: UMI Research Press, 1982.

Selected List of Books in English by U.S. Authors. Chicago: American Library Association, 1942.

Smith, Robert C. *Murals by Cândido Portinari in the Hispanic Foundation of the Library of Congress*. Washington, DC: U.S. Government Print Office, 1943.

Smoodin, Eric. *Animating Culture: Hollywood Cartoons from the Sound Era*. New York: Routledge, 1993.

———, ed. *Disney Discourse: Producing the Magic Kingdom*. New York: Routledge, 1994.

Spiller, James. *"This Is War!* Network Radio and World War II Propaganda in America." *Journal of Radio and Audio Media* 11, no. 1 (May 2004): 55–72.

Steele, Richard W. *Propaganda in an Open Society: The Roosevelt Administration and the Media, 1933–1941*. Westport, CT: Greenwood Press, 1985.

Telotte, J. P. "Crossing Borders and Opening Boxes: Disney and Hybrid Animation." *Quarterly Review of Film and Video* 24 (2007): 107–116.

Tomlinson, John. *Cultural Imperialism: A Critical Introduction*. Baltimore: John Hopkins University Press, 1991.

Tota, Antônio Pedro. *O imperialismo sedutor: A americanização do Brasil na época da segunda guerra*. São Paulo: Companhia das Letras, 2000.

Trask, Roger R. "George F. Kennan's Report on Latin America (1950)." *Diplomatic History* 3, no. 2 (July 1978): 307–312.

———. "The Impact of the Cold War on United States-Latin American Relations, 1945–1949." *Diplomatic History* 1 (Summer 1977): 271–284.

Tuchman, Barbara. *The Proud Tower*. New York: Bantam, 1967.

Van Dyke, Willard. "Reminiscences of Willard Van Dyke." New York: Columbia University Oral History Research Office, 1981.

Welles, Orson. Foreword to *The Sleepy Lagoon Case*. Prepared by the Citizens' Committee for the Defense of Mexican-American Youth, Los Angeles, CA, 1942. Hollywood: Mercury, June 1943. LL, 6-1301.

Welles, Sumner. "The Roosevelt Administration and Its Dealings with the Republics of the Western Hemisphere." Washington, DC: U.S. Government Printing Office, 1935.

White, John W. *Our Good Neighbor Hurdle*. Milwaukee: Bruce, 1943.

Williams, Daryle. *Culture Wars in Brazil: The First Vargas Regime, 1930–1945*. Durham, NC: Duke University Press, 2001.

Williams, Raymond. *Culture*. London: Fontana, 1981.

———. *Keywords: A Vocabulary of Culture and Society*. London: Fontana, 1976.

Woll, Allen L. *The Latin Image in American Film*. Los Angeles: UCLA Latin American Center Publications, 1977.

Index

9 780292 756854